D1758430

The Journey Home

Emerging out of the Shadow of the Past

**Edited by David Clark and
Teresa von Sommaruga Howard**

Peter Lang

Oxford · Bern · Berlin · Bruxelles · New York · Wien

Bibliographic information published by Die Deutsche Nationalbibliothek.
Die Deutsche Nationalbibliothek lists this publication in the Deutsche Nationalbibliografie;
detailed bibliographic data is available on the Internet at http://dnb.d-nb.de.

A catalogue record for this book is available from the British Library.

Library of Congress Cataloging-in-Publication Data

Names: Clark, David, 1946 April 8- editor. | Howard, Teresa von Sommaruga,
    editor.
Title: The journey home : emerging out of the shadow of the past / David
    Clark, Teresa von Sommaruga Howard.
Description: Oxford ; New York : Peter Lang, [2022] | Includes
    bibliographical references and index.
Identifiers: LCCN 2021038388 (print) | LCCN 2021038389 (ebook) | ISBN
    9781800795808 (paperback) | ISBN 9781800795815 (ebook) | ISBN
    9781800795822 (epub)
Subjects: LCSH: Children of Holocaust survivors--Biography. | Holocaust,
    Jewish (1939-1945)--Psychological aspects. | Holocaust survivors--Homes
    and haunts. | Dwellings--Psychological aspects. | Holocaust memorials. |
    Collective memory. | Pilgrims and pilgrimages.
Classification: LCC D804.195 .J68 2022 (print) | LCC D804.195 (ebook) |
    DDC 940.53/180922--dc23
LC record available at https://lccn.loc.gov/2021038388
LC ebook record available at https://lccn.loc.gov/2021038389

Cover images: Street in Vienna (Photo by Teresa von Sommaruga Howard); Yellow Star
(Shutterstock_1252864699 by Barbara Ash); Candle (Shutterstock_582678 by Lotus studio);
Berlin table and Shabbat candles (Photo from Teresa's family collection); Couple on steps
of apartment building, Berlin (Photo from Teresa's family collection); Photo of Diti Ronen's
great-grandmother's house in Oradea (Postcard from the early twentieth century); *Levetzowstraße Mahnmal* (Photo by Ceci Epstein). All images are reproduced with permission.
Cover design by Brian Melville for Peter Lang.

ISBN 978-1-80079-580-8 (print)
ISBN 978-1-80079-581-5 (ePDF)
ISBN 978-1-80079-582-2 (ePUB)

© Peter Lang Group AG 2022

Published by Peter Lang Ltd, International Academic Publishers,
52 St Giles, Oxford, OX1 3LU, United Kingdom
oxford@peterlang.com, www.peterlang.com

David Clark and Teresa von Sommaruga Howard have asserted their right under the Copyright,
Designs and Patents Act, 1988, to be identified as Editors of this Work.

This publication has been peer reviewed.

For all our parents and grandparents.
Whether we knew them or not, they shaped our lives.

Contents

Figures

Foreword: Home is where the heart is

One of the more popular songs of my youth was a ballad by American singer and songwriter, John Denver, entitled *Take Me Home, Country Roads*, that spoke about the yearning to return "to the place I belong". Reading *The Journey Home* brings me back to those days and the special memories I had of that song. Denver's sentiments may have been directed towards West Virginia and not Western Galicia where my survivor father had been born, but the feeling was similar. A desire to see one's home, a yearning to belong, a longing for a sense of roots. The home may have never been mine, the belonging was to people and families long destroyed and the roots were deeply set in soil I had never stepped on. But the longing was there, nonetheless.

"Never get attached to any object or place in case it keeps you from escaping on time", was my mother's credo, and it took its place of honour in my psyche as a member of the second generation. In my case, it was strengthened by being raised on stories of Jews who were swallowed up by the Nazi maw as they had been emotionally unable to tear themselves away from their homes\marriage beds\familiar streets on time, in order to run. Cut your geographical and material ties so you can get out faster. Don't make them in the first place so that they won't slow you down. Those were the messages that we were given so that we would have a head start, "the next time around".

Whether voiced openly, as it had been in my childhood home, or just alluded to by suggestion, members of the second generation brought up with those sentiments often found it difficult to become attached to any of the places where they lived, always remembering stories – heard or imagined – of how their parents were torn from their homes, whether by fleeing on their own or being dragged away by the Nazis and their accomplices. As a result, many felt a sense of rootlessness, or a deep-seated feeling of not really belonging, a common thread heard among members of the second generation when evaluating their lives. Echoes of that feeling appear

throughout this volume where members of that generation describe what
for many became a (lifelong) journey back to their parents' former homes
in order to find what they were missing.

How is the desire to see one's parents' home connected to a sense of
roots? After all, decades had passed. Did these second-generation members not have roots of their own by now, deeply fixed in their own country
of birth? Some obviously did, but others still felt themselves in need of a
geographical anchor, hoping to close a circle by being able to stand on the
same soil where their parents had been born, studied, prayed or played,
creating a personal paraphrase of Genesis 3:19, "For you are dust and to
dust you shall return".

One group of second-generation members made the trip together with
their survivor or former refugee parents. Others went after their parents'
death. Those with elderly parents, unable to travel, went without them but
often communicated to them how they had retraced their family history.
Some undertook the journey to help them come to terms with the burden
of the past. Others saw it as part of the grieving process for a lost world
and family that they would never know.

I undertook such a journey over a third of a century ago, in the days
when Poland was still semi-communist, the Berlin wall had not yet fallen
and luxury items such as good vodka or imported oranges could only be
bought in the State-run Pewex stores with foreign currency, preferably dollars. I had asked my father, an Auschwitz and Buchenwald survivor who was
then an active and healthy man in his mid-80s, whether he wanted to join
me, but he refused to even consider the possibility. He did, however, give
me the address of his former home in Bochnia, where he had been born
and lived throughout his childhood, right near the area of the Bochnia
Ghetto where his father, sister and first wife had either been shot or from
where they were sent on their final journey.

In early 1988 I found myself standing in front of that house in the dead
of night, having convinced the Polish bus driver of the group I was leading
to make a detour off the main road to Krakow in order to search for a particular house on a particular street, "off to the top left of the *Rynek* (town
square)" as my father had directed. It was more than a decade before the first
mobile phone with a camera would become available and the word "selfie"

would become part of our lexicon, and so a member of the group gladly offered to take a picture of me in front of the long one-storey building as a memento of that midnight visit. The street was deserted, the house locked. My only real memory was looking at the side of the house and seeing the apple tree that my father had described being outside his bedroom window. When I returned home my father showed definite interest in the picture, but little connection to the town. He had put it far behind him, living very much in the present and not in his distant the past.

Six months later I was back there again, leading another group, this time in the daylight. Again, I took a picture of the building but did not make any effort to enter. It was only in 2007 when I came to Poland on a belated honeymoon and took my husband to see where his late father-in-law had been born and raised, that our private guide knocked at the door and asked the tenants if they would allow us to look around. Despite the decades that had passed since the war, the house looked much like my father had described it with the big surprise being the enormous garden on a large plot of land behind the house. For the first time I could picture my family as it had been while living there, a well-to-do strictly Orthodox Jewish family. Visiting the local archive, I found the original deed to the house and listings of my father's birth, his parents' marriage and that of his grandparents as well. Continuing further up the winding street I came to the area of the former ghetto and newly dedicated memorial for the town's Jews murdered during the Holocaust.

This was indeed the journey of a member of the second generation in search of her roots. A journey to close a circle and get a glimpse of my origins. None of the locals whom I came across on that visit had any connection to my family, but I wondered whether their parents or grandparents had ever come across mine and if so, when and in what capacity. Some things are better not thought about.

A number of second-generation members journey to their parents' former homes to participate in a memorial ceremony, affix a plaque or a memorial stone to a building or a sidewalk. I did none of the kind, but at my visit to the Bochnia Holocaust Memorial, I laid a small stone next to the marker in the same fashion that Jews leave a rock on a tombstone to show that someone has been there, that someone remembers.

And maybe, in addition to closing circles and looking for roots, journeys of second-generation members to their parents' former homes are a way of figuratively laying that stone, showing that someone still cares and remembers. "To be unremembered is to die a second death", writes Rabbi Theodore Friedman in an essay entitled *Do you Remember*? And so, these visits are actually an affirmation of life, having transmitted the onus of remembrance to a new generation.

Judith Tydor Baumel-Schwartz
Ramat Gan, June 2021

Preface

This book owes a huge debt to the large number of accounts of journeys undertaken by the second generation, children of Holocaust survivors or refugees, to places connected with their family history. I first became aware of these stories through articles in *Second Generation Voices*, the magazine published by Second Generation Network in the UK. Such accounts resonated deeply with my own life story and experiences, being constantly uprooted as a child, so that travel became as much part of my identity as being Jewish. Later, my academic career involved either research on migrants or in teaching tourism studies.

Through my involvement with Second Generation Network, I also became more proactive in dialogue on German soil with Jews and gentiles of descendant generations growing up under the shadow of the Holocaust. In 2005, I attended my first workshop organized by Teresa von Sommaruga Howard, *Breaking the Silence: Mending the Broken Connections*, with three Jewish, four German, one Irish and one English participant. I gained a new sense of hope and compassion as a result of being able to share the pain and terror we all felt in varying degrees and ways. All this was led by our two facilitators with a gentle touch and a great deal of sensitivity. In 2011, I attended a conference organized by the Evangelische Akademie Arnoldshain, near Frankfurt, on *Coming to terms with the burdens of history*, where I led a workshop on the transformative experience of undertaking journeys to where parents or grandparents had come from. The presentation was based on accounts of such journeys in *Second Generation Voices*. In the same year I also attended a second workshop in Germany organized by Teresa on the theme of *Breaking the Silence*.

In 2019, I presented a paper on the emotional impact of undertaking journeys to places connected with family history at a Holocaust conference in Uzhhorod, Ukraine. Following the conference, I was sufficiently encouraged to embark on a book project and gathered a small group of people together to take the venture forward. The result was twenty people each committed to writing a chapter for this anthology. It comes at a particular junction in time, with the waning of the first generation, on the one hand and the extraordinary flourishing of creative talent on the part of the second generation, on the other. There is now a wealth of fiction and non-fiction books, documentary films, visual arts and theatre, exploring issues of second and third generation descendants of the Holocaust.

Even more extraordinary, has been the process of bringing this book to fruition, writing my own story, while also seeking to nurture and engage with my fellow contributors to the book. Such an experience has been as transformative as any of the journeys I had previously undertaken, giving me a new perspective on my own life story.

David Clark
London, June 2021

I first met David Clark in 2002 after I gave a presentation at the local reform synagogue about being the daughter of a Jewish refugee from Berlin a month after the then rabbi had also given one about himself being a refugee from Berlin. David and his then wife, Anne, approached me as complete strangers and asked me to join them for *Pesach Seder* [Passover meal]. I jumped at the invitation. Even though I had dreamt about the possibility, as a patrilineal Jew, it was a barrier I never thought I would cross. Even though my father had often described Jewish festivals, usually at just the right time of year, I had celebrated almost none.

I always felt my Jewish heritage. It had been a powerful part of my identity for as long as I could remember. Since that Pesach celebration, I have learnt to read Hebrew, joined the community and reclaimed a rich and creative history that had been lost. Now, when I hear the music, it tingles my soul.

I first visited Germany in 1996 to attend a group analytic symposium in Heidelberg. It began a slow realization that I wanted to break an internal prohibition to go and see where my ancestors had lived, so I finally took a train journey through Europe to Vienna, where my grandfather had come from and to Berlin, my father's home. In Vienna I also took part in another conference, *The Presence of the Absence*, where it became clear to me that second generation from all backgrounds needed a place just to talk to each other and so a series of workshops, *Breaking the Silence: Mending the Broken Connections* was born. These continued in Germany for thirteen years and hosted people from all over the world. David attended two of these workshops over the years.

When David invited me to co-edit this anthology, I again jumped at the opportunity. I had recently published an article based on these workshops *Sociopolitical Trauma: Forgetting, Remembering, and Group Analysis.* I had also written a paper for the European Federation of Psychoanalytic Psychotherapy (EFPP) conference in Belgrade in 2018, *Finding my Song: Trauma, Discontinuity and the Large Group*, which makes connections to Muslim second generation experience.

Being second generation, with mixed parentage led to a mixed career. Initially I qualified as an architect and worked in social housing providing and repairing houses, often for refugees who had sought refuge in southeast London and later, as a group analyst working with larger groups where the emphasis, through encouraging dialogue, is on seeking to understand the unconscious social forces that lead to political extremism. I have several articles published in the Journal of Group Analysis on this work. These two perspectives on the world, both inherited from my parents, led me to co-writing *Design through Dialogue: A Guide for Clients and Architects*, with Karen Franck.

The opportunity to co-edit this book has enabled me to make use of all these rich experiences and to broadcast that being second generation need not be the life sentence it is often felt to be but can become a source of enormous live-giving creativity. Second generation are a group of people, who once they are given time, space and understanding, are able to give up the search for the 'normal' and know from their own life experience that the unimaginable can and does happen – this is a gift and a warning to the world.

Teresa von Sommaruga Howard

Bibliography

von Sommaruga Howard, T. (2019). Sociopolitical Trauma: Forgetting, Remembering, and Group Analysis. *Transactional Analysis Journal*, 49 (4) 233–247. DOI: 10.1080/03621537.2019.1649846.

von Sommaruga Howard, T. (2022). 'Finding my Song: Trauma, Discontinuity and the Large Group'. In *A Psychoanalytic Exploration of Social Trauma: The Inner Worlds of Outer Realities*. London: Routledge.

von Sommaruga Howard, T., and Franck, K. (2010). *Design through Dialogue: A Guide for Clients and Architects*. London and New York: Wiley.

Acknowledgements

Much of my life I had to constantly re-orient myself in new surroundings, language, norms and expectations. This required a great deal of perseverance and courage on my part. Yet, I only realized later in life that whatever I had accomplished over the years, I owed in large measure also to the help and support I received from countless others along the way.

In my formative years, I received much love and attention from my parents, sometimes intermittently; my sister Deirdre was my most constant companion in those early years and a tower of strength for me in adulthood. I was blessed to meet all four of my grandparents and formed a close relationship with two of my great aunts Liese Rosenthal and Hilde Braunthal. I found trusted and loyal friends wherever I went. François Moisy in Vienna, Francis Landy in London, Don Savage and Luciano Martinengo in Montreal, Josef Gugler in Kampala and Connecticut, Ismael Khalfan in Nairobi, Christine Wardle at Brandeis University, Massachusetts. Back in London, I found a warm welcome in Wimbledon Reform Synagogue, receiving much support from my Rabbis Danni Smith, Sybil Sheridan and Sylvia Rothschild, as well as from the Ask Sunday Group. In my neighbourhood of Colliers Wood, I am much indebted to Keith Spears, who founded 'Making Colliers Wood Happy' and to Christopher Killerby, our choirmaster at 'Colliers Wood Chorus'; they made me feel 'at home'. I also owe much to my friendship with Elaine Sinclair, Christeen George and Lyn Greaves at what was then Thames Valley University, to my PhD supervisors Tom Selwyn and Jonathan Webber, as well as Yochanan Altman at London Metropolitan University and more recently Professor Natalya Kubiniy at Uzhhorod National University, Ukraine.

I would also like to thank my family. My first wife, Anne, who encouraged me to reclaim my Judaism, my twin sons, Michael and Malcolm, who taught me that each day is an opportunity for wonderful new discoveries. Nina Kosiedowska to whom I'm now married, who taught me how much our cultures have in common, as well as to appreciate our differences.

Finally, in terms of compiling this particular volume, I would not have been able to complete the task without the invaluable and unfailing support of my co-editor, Teresa von Sommaruga Howard.

David Clark

I have learnt that this journey is never over. It takes a lifetime to face what could not be faced by previous generations. In this work, I would like to acknowledge my Granny Betty and my Gramps, who in my early years gave me a glimpse of what could be possible in life, my grandmother Renate, who taught me that survival with dignity is possible, my Grandfather Franz, whom I never knew but gave me my big-story family name, my son Jerome whose birth initially opened the door to my feelings and later brought me in touch with what I had already lost and survived several times before he was born. To my nieces Sara and Emilie who keep my hope up when it is flagging, and my three younger sisters, Dwariko, Judith and Astrid who always challenged my perspective in life and kept me thinking and most significantly, to my mother and father who bequeathed me an extremely rich and diverse heritage that continues to provide precious material to draw from.

History always has a habit of repeating itself and in my case, just as my grandmother had to go on living without her adolescent son when he was forced to seek refuge in England alone, I too had to go on living after my son was taken to New Zealand by his father. Many people accompanied me as I lived with and made meaning from what was a devastating experience. I would like to profoundly acknowledge them here. The first was Gill Parker, my first analytic psychotherapist who gently mothered me through a long period of growing up and opened many doors for me. Pat de Maré who helped me to understand the implications of socio-political events through my work in the larger group and trusted me to take on one of his long-standing groups, Ben Renshaw and Diana Roberts who taught me the power of touch through rebirthing, Peter Heinl who guided me back to my roots in Berlin and Vienna, Dick Blackwell who has been a wise and encouraging counsel in my work and Melanie Hart, who helped me to consolidate so much of what had gone before and finally to Kate Heath whose patient attention is connecting me to the sound of music in my family.

And of course, David from whom I have learnt so much about the importance of dogged determination in this process.

Teresa von Sommaruga Howard

We both wish to acknowledge eighteen authors who contributed chapters to this book. Each one was specially commissioned and despite the difficulties many encountered when asked to focus on their own experiences as second generation instead of those of their forebears', they persevered with the writing process. Without their courage, skill and perseverance this book would not have been possible. We have gained and learnt so much from all of you in the process. Many have included material previously published elsewhere and we gratefully acknowledge the use of such material.

Rosemary Schonfeld and Diana Wichtel previously published full-length books describing their search for lost family. Schonfeld, R. (2018). *Finding Relly, My Family, the Holocaust and Me*. Elstree, UK and Chicago: Vallentine Mitchell, and Wichtel, D. (2017). *Driving to Treblinka, A Long Search for a Lost Father*. Wellington, NZ: Awa Press.

David Clark wrote a chapter linking his second-generation background to his career choices, in Baumel-Schwartz, J., and Rafael-Vivante, S. (eds), (2021). *Researchers Remember: Research as an Arena of Memory for Offspring of Holocaust Survivors*. Bern: Peter Lang.

Naomi Levy also wrote a chapter for Baumel-Schwartz, J., and Rafael-Vivante, S. (eds), (2021). 'On Being Second Generation and My Major Life Choices'. In *Researchers Remember: Research as an Arena of Memory for Offspring of Holocaust Survivors*. Bern: Peter Lang. She also has an article in the *Child Survivors Association Newsletter* of January 2019 entitled, 'Three days in Krakow', covering similar ground.

Gina Burgess Winning wrote about her journey to lay down *Stolpersteine* in Germany in *Second Generation Voices*, 2011, 47.

Barbara Dresner wrote about her Journey to Poland in *Second Generation Voices*, 2001, 18.

Peter Bohm wrote about his journeys involving commemorative events in the *AJR Journal*, [Association of Jewish Refugees Journal], 2018, 18.

Teresa von Sommaruga Howard has written two papers that link to this book: (2019), 'Sociopolitical Trauma: Forgetting, Remembering, and Group Analysis', *Transactional Analysis Journal*, 49 (4) 233–247 and (2022), 'Finding my Song: Trauma, Discontinuity and the Large Group'. In *A Psychoanalytic Exploration of Social Trauma: The Inner Worlds of Outer Realities*. London: Routledge.

Abbreviations

AJR	Association of Jewish Refugees.
BDM	*Bund Deutscher Mädel* [The young women's equivalent of the Hitler Youth for boys and young men].
COD	Cash on Delivery.
Covid-19	Coronavirus disease, first identified in December 2019.
DNA	Deoxyribonucleic Acid [Carrier of genetic information].
EFPP	European Federation of Psychoanalytic Psychotherapy.
EP	European Parliament.
EU	European Union.
FPÖ	*Freiheitlichen Partei Österreichs* [Freedom Party of Austria, a far-right populist party].
G2G	Generation 2 Generation.
GP	General Practitioner.
IWM	Imperial War Museum.
KaDeWe	*Kaufhaus des Westens* [A Berlin department store]
KPD	*Kommunistische Partei Deutschlands.* [German Communist Party]
KPO	*Kommunistische Partei-Opposition* [German Communist Party Opposition – a splinter group of the main German Communist Party, KPD].
MBE	Member of the British Empire.
MEP	Member of the European Parliament.

NATO   North Atlantic Treaty Organization.

Nazi   Originally *Nationalsozialistische Deutsche Arbeiterpartei*,
              NSDAP, or National Socialist German Workers' Party,
              later referred to as *Nationalsozialismus*, the ideology and
              practices associated with Adolf Hitler and the Nazi Party.

NGO   Non-Governmental Organization.

ODMS   One Day's Military Spending towards 'peace-making'.

OE   Overseas Experience

ORPO   *Ordnungspolizei* [Law Enforcement Police in Nazi
              Germany].

ORT   Organization for Rehabilitation through Training [A
              Jewish agricultural and craft training school].

PTSD   Post-Traumatic Stress Disorder.

RAF   Royal Airforce.

Red Army   The Workers' and Peasants' Red Army initially and later
              armed forces of the Union of Soviet Socialist Republics.

RP   Received Pronunciation.

SA   *Sturmabteilung* [The Nazi Party's original paramilitary
              wing, also known as the Brownshirts].

SD   *Sicherheitsdienst* [Security and Intelligence agency of the
              Nazi Party].

SS   *Schutzstaffel* [Paramilitary organization of the Nazi party].

U-Bahn   *Untergrundbahn* [Underground railway].

UK   United Kingdom.

UNESCO   United Nations Educational, Scientific and Cultural
              Organization.

UNHCR   United Nations High Commissioner for Refugees.

USA, US	United States of America.
USSR	Union of Soviet Socialist Republics.
VOs	Visiting Orders.
VVN	*Vereinigung der Verfolgten des Naziregimes* [Union of Victims of Nazism].
Waffen-SS	Armed SS-the military branch of Nazi SS.
	Wehrmacht [The armed forces of the Third Reich, during the Nazi era].
WIZO	Women's International Zionist Organization.
ZIM	Zim Integrated Shipping Services Ltd [A publicly held Israeli international cargo shipping company].

A note on the text

The spelling of place names

Readers will notice that place names in what is now Poland, the Czech Republic and Slovakia, are not consistently spelt in English, apart from Prague, Warsaw and Lodz. All others appear in either Polish, Czech or Slovak as there are no easy English equivalents.

We have also used the German double 's' or ß for German street names as they appear like this on street signs in Germany.

Some of the contributors learnt to 'know' and to pronounce the names of these places through the descriptions they heard in their families. The names themselves are evocative and assume symbolic importance, particularly as they connect their ancestors' history to the scenery of these specific places. Learning how the place names are spelt is all part of the journey of discovery, both for the authors and the readers.

The use of the words Holocaust and Shoah

Many writers in this collection use the word Holocaust rather than Shoah. We would prefer to use the word Shoah but recognizing that it is not a word understood outside of the Jewish community, the word Holocaust is mostly used throughout.

The word Holocaust is derived from the Greek *holokauston*, a translation of the Hebrew word *olah*, meaning a burnt sacrifice offered whole to God. The word was chosen and gained wide usage, in the immediate post-Second World War period, to describe the ultimate manifestation of the Nazi killing program, the extermination camps, where the bodies of the victims were consumed whole in crematoria or open fires.

In Israel and France, Shoah, a biblical Hebrew word meaning 'catastrophe', became the preferred term for the event, largely in response to Claude Lanzmann's influential 1985 documentary, *Shoah*. This word is also preferred by Hebrew speakers and those wishing to focus on the Jewish experience or who are uncomfortable with the religious connotations of the word Holocaust. Shoah emphasizes the annihilation of the Jews and not the totality of Nazi victims, which also included the Germans deemed intellectually, physically, or emotionally unfit who were murdered through the T4 'Euthanasia' Programme, as well as the Roma and Sinti, pejoratively known as Gypsies, homosexuals and Jehovah's Witnesses.[1]

---

[1]   <https://www.britannica.com/story/what-is-the-origin-of-the-term-holocaust>.

DAVID CLARK AND TERESA VON SOMMARUGA HOWARD

Introduction

Journeys towards the past

This book focuses on the experiences of second-generation descendants
of survivors or refugees from Nazi persecution, returning to the original
places connected to their families.

As they get older, making these journeys towards their parents' former
'home' becomes increasingly important in the lives of many second generation born of Jewish refugee and survivor parents. As Werner Bohleber
(2010: 121) explains,

> It is beyond an individual's capacities to integrate such traumatic experiences into
> a narrative context that is purely personal; a social discourse is also required con-
> cerning the historical truth of the traumatic events, as well as their denial and de-
> fensive repudiation.

As we now know this was the post-war context, a time when defensive
silence about the past predominated in society that left traumatized survivors alone with their experiences, unable to either fully acknowledge
them or consciously pass them on (Bohleber, 2010: 121).

This is the atmosphere within which many of the second generation
grew up. They were often left with the difficult, even impossible, task of
making sense of a situation that made no sense. As a result, many learn
they are not quite right, their parents are not quite right, feel ashamed of
who they are and often work hard to deny the obvious differences between
themselves and mainstream society around them (Beaglehole, 1990: 11).

Family history is often buried and lost as remembering what happened
then and there is accompanied by unbearable pain and unwanted memories
that cannot be shared. Many second generation grow up learning to face

their parents' violent reactions to what seem like inconsequential events, that made no sense and then blame themselves for triggering them. It can make for an unstable and frightening upbringing. With almost no access to their history there are usually two reactions: to follow their parent's model and continue to ignore the past or to try to discover what happened and to make some sense of it. It is a confusing and disturbing legacy.

One route to unravelling something of the reality of this lost and traumatic history is the search for a home, or *Heimat*, that often becomes a lifelong obsession. Some return to their parent's country or town of origin in search of lost narratives, piecing together what they can of what was there before the destruction meted out during the Nazitime.

As Helen Epstein (2001: 5–8) writes,

> A person whose family has survived genocide finds a hole in the place of a history … I was doing what many members of second generation are doing through genealogical research or by undertaking pilgrimages to the places where our families lived … I began to build a bridge over that abyss that divides before the war and after the war.

Triggers for these journeys

It is interesting to think about why it is that certain individuals decide to embark on such journeys.

Dina Wardi (1992: 27–31), an Israeli group psychotherapist who worked with second generation, explains that many children born immediately after the *Shoah* [Hebrew word for Holocaust] were often unconsciously and symbolically designated 'memorial candles', as living reminders of everything their parents had lost.[1]

The journey home is one way of making sense of this emotional burden and breaking free from it. For many it becomes an obsession that is usually

---

1   A more detailed explanation of the use of these two words, Shoah and Holocaust, can be found following the list of abbreviations and the notes on spellings.

triggered by a life crisis or a growing awareness that the past can no longer be ignored.

Bernard Marin (2002: 239), the son of a Polish refugee to Australia, developed 'ferocious headaches' almost immediately after his father died. They persisted for six years gradually becoming more severe despite pain-killers. Desperate he finally sought help from a therapist, who suggested the headaches may have something to do with grieving for his father, the father he never really knew. At first, he dismissed this but eventually settled into a long search into the past, back to Poland, to a family and friends he never knew existed. In the process, his headaches disappeared. They had served to call him to discover his father's heart ache – his father's silence about his past.

Other crises such as a death of a loved one or significant events such as illness often open up the prevailing emptiness into a chasm leading to an urge to finally face what previously felt impossibly out of reach. Many second generation discover their Jewish roots after their parents have died and go on a long quest to find out more – often involving going back 'home'.

Journeys back home

Frost and Selwyn (2018: 2), both noted anthropologists working in the tourism field, state that the idea of home encompasses attachment to spaces and places, while also making it clear that 'home' is a place situated simultaneously in both a material and an imagined world. Symbols and connotations associated with the home and the homeland then become very important. It is not unusual for survivor refugee families to have no symbolic reminders of their lost home.

Finding long-lost objects are all the more important for our travellers. When Gina Burgess Winning is handed back a cooking pot that belonged to her grandmother or Peter Bohm is given a single crystal glass belonging to a relative, these are poignant moments.

In most cases not only was the house and its contents lost forever but also the whole cultural context that defined a way of life. The street, the shops, the community activities, that were outside the home, part of everyday life, were left behind, never to be seen again. The entire social fabric that existed before the Shoah had not just been disrupted, but completely broken, leaving many adrift of any kind of support.

The return to the physical 'home' by descendent generations is a way of populating what was lost. In this way it ceases to remain an empty emotional space in the mind. It is by walking the streets, touching the walls, sitting in cafés and taking *Kaffee und Kuchen*, as our parents may have done, that the reality of a culture lost is given life.

These themes are illustrated in this book, which is divided into three parts: journeys undertaken with a first-generation parent, those undertaken without a parent and journeys undertaken as part of a commemorative event.

Journeys undertaken with a first-generation parent

Journeys with a first-generation parent often take on added poignancy, as well as added responsibilities. Many times, such a parent is already elderly and requires a certain amount of extra care.

Sometimes this brings about a closer relationship with the parent as in the case of Diti Ronen and Naomi Levy, or a more nuanced relationship as Janet Eisenstein and Teresa von Sommaruga Howard found, or to a form of re-orientation that emerged for Tina Kennedy.

What is also noticeable is the degree of ambivalence felt by the first generation about returning back to their birth country. For many, there was a great deal of reluctance even to contemplate a return journey, wishing to leave it all behind, never to return.

Many were persuaded at a later stage, with grown-up children, to go back to their hometown, either through an official invitation from their respective cities such as Teresa's father received from Berlin or an organized trip by a Jewish organization that enabled Janet to visit Berlin with her mother. Even here, the ambivalence felt by the first generation is palpable. Janet's mother became all excited at seeing some of the sites connected with visiting places that held dear memories of visiting the Tiergarten and the zoo, shopping on Kurfürstendamm or picnicking on the shores of the Wannsee. Yet being at a Shoah site or memorial felt too painful for her. Although present physically, she absented herself emotionally. This was especially true when they visited the villa at Wannsee, notorious for its close association with plans for the Final Solution.

Elaine Sinclair's father, faced with the reality of being in his grandparents' apartment in 2003, sixty-four years after last seeing them, still with much of the old furniture, carpets and crockery being used by the occupiers who had taken over the apartment on his grandparents' deportation to their deaths, fled from the scene in horror. It was too much to bear.

For the second generation accompanying a parent to their hometown, a new sense of the past, of the place where their parent had grown up, emerged. Until then, the pre-war period had only been recounted in fragments and had taken on the quality of a fairy tale, a myth or a horror story. Seeing these places through the lenses of their parents' reactions and recollections on the spot brought the reality of that past into a previously missing immediacy, allowing a new reality to surface and a new meaning to be constructed.

At the same time as observing their parents' conflicted feelings in the present, the grown-up children were seeing for themselves, both the pain and the joy of their parents' previous life, perhaps for the first time.

Independent journeys without a first-generation parent

For some, the first journey to a parent's 'homeland' might have been almost accidental. Vivian Hassan-Lambert tagged on to a summer holiday between school and university inter-railing in Europe or when Rosemary Schonfeld attended a 40th birthday celebration. For most, a great deal of forethought and planning went into the first journey and even more so for subsequent journeys.

What soon becomes evident is that the compulsion to visit certain places or to seek out certain people becomes stronger as time goes by.

Rosemary went to great lengths to rediscover a lost aunt and in the process revisits her family's birthplaces in the Czech Republic.

Yet, as time goes by, first-generation parents are less able to make the journey themselves, while the loss of such a parent provides yet another impetus to undertake the journey. For some, it is still possible to communicate with the absent parent even though they were unable to be with them. Vivian writes home, very movingly to her mother and, decades later, she rediscovers that letter, which is at the core of her chapter in this book. Marian Liebmann on returning from visiting Berlin for the first time and seeing the apartment block where her mother had lived before the war reports it all back to her mother on her return.

Zuzana Crouch retraces her mother's steps to the forced labour camp and stands on the same steps where her mother stood upon liberation and received a letter from her beloved husband stating that he too had survived. Absent parents are ever-present for their descendants on such journeys.

Few people dared to undertake such journeys on their own. It is possibly only in the first flush of youth that they might venture out into the past. Vivian took a six-month tour of Europe and Israel that ended by going to Bratislava to meet a woman who had enabled her mother and grandmother to survive in hiding during the Holocaust. Oliver Hoffmann travelled to Berlin from New Zealand, while in his early 20s. Many seek the company of other family members, or failing that, seek companions, with similar interests in retracing their family history to join them, as did Barbara Dresner.

It is not a journey to be undertaken lightly and as time marches on the grieving and mourning process accompanies them virtually every step of the way. The lighting of candles, reciting Kaddish, the mourners' prayer at gravesides, visiting monuments and death camps, are significant and transformative rituals as Barbara, Zuzana and Diana Wichtel discovered. Occasionally, the grieving and mourning takes centre stage, as Rosemary found when she took her father's ashes to be scattered in the river running by his hometown in the Czech Republic.

Until recently travel within what used to be known as Western Europe was relatively easy compared with the complexities of travel in former communist countries, especially before the Iron Curtain came down. Both Diti Ronen and Elaine Sinclair found themselves having to negotiate different maps to those their parents had used in their youth and so journeys to former communist countries rely to a great extent on careful pre-planning and prior research. Both Barbara and Rosemary discovered that it also helps to encounter kind people along the way who are willing to assist with further guidance, directions and even documentation relating to family history.

Journeys for commemorative events

Journeys undertaken specifically in connection with commemorative events take on quite a distinctive character. Some of them have an official presence, complete with speeches and an invited audience.

Yet, while descendants were sometimes able to actually go inside their former 'family homes', much of the action often takes place immediately outside, in the courtyard or on the pavement, in the in-between or liminal spaces.

In his seminal chapter on liminality, Turner (1969), uses the metaphor of the threshold to describe an experience involving both physical and socio-emotional space, that generates new insights enabling the possibility of returning to a former social world with a newly acquired status or knowledge.

Some of these ceremonies and events also have elements of 'communitas'. Turner (1969: 360) explains:

> What is interesting about liminal phenomena ... is the blend they offer of lowliness, homogeneity and comradeship we are presented in such rites, with a 'moment' in and 'out of time' and in and out of secular social structure.

The *Stolpersteine* project

The *Stolpersteine* project is one example that facilitates such ceremonies. German artist Gunter Demnig began his *Stolpersteine* project in the

Figure 0.1. *Stolpersteine* in Berlin (Photo taken by Teresa von Sommaruga Howard).

mid-1990s. *Stolpersteine* [stumbling stones] are 10-centimetre square brass plates laid in pavements, bearing the names and relevant dates of victims of the Shoah, in front of their former homes.

There are now over 75,000 stumbling stones located in twenty-four countries. Their installation is organized through a combination of individual, state-sponsored and grass-roots efforts. Several of our authors were involved in arranging for *Stolpersteine* to be laid near former homes.

A granddaughter's initiative

Gina, whose mother came to Britain in 1939 as an unaccompanied child on the Kindertransport, decided to have *Stolpersteine* placed outside the former home of her grandparents in Germany in a small village near Marburg, north of Frankfurt.

On the day of the ceremony, the pastor opened the proceedings, a cousin read the Jewish memorial service and Gina (Burgess Winning, 2011: 7–8) read out her tribute to her murdered relatives. She writes,

> The hall was full. Taking several deep breaths, I made it through the four pages of German. Returning to my seat I noticed that many people in the audience were crying, the mayor and the *Ortsvorsteher*, [head of Village Council] made speeches. The pastor closed with a prayer. I had a strong sense of communal warmth and sorrow uniting all those present.

Clearly, many people in attendance were deeply affected by this ceremony, including Burgess Winning. There was a sense of comradeship, of grieving and mourning together. But it was not quite the unstructured homogeneity envisaged by Turner when he described 'communitas'. Something else was taking place. Social structure was still visibly maintained; the pastor, the head of the local historical society, the mayor and the *Ortsvorsteher*, all had their assigned customary roles.

Such ceremonies link both the personal and the public past, affirming family history, while placing it squarely within the setting of recorded public history. Unusually, this particular event took place in a village, involving a religious ceremony for the laying of *Stolpersteine*. In cities, they tend to be fairly secular affairs, though usually involving the recitation of the mourners' prayer, the Kaddish, as a symbolic reminder of the Jewish heritage of the victims (Mandel and Lehr, 2020).

Non-Jewish initiatives

Peter Bohm writes about several visits in connection with commemorative events. On a visit to Berlin in 2014 with his wife, they discovered that *Stolpersteine* had recently been placed in the pavement outside the former home of his wife's grandparents, thanks to a local high-school project.

The following year, Peter contacted an organization in Vienna, known as *Steine der Erinnerung* [Stones of Memory] to find out whether something could be placed outside his own grandparents' former home. He discovered that a resident in the same block of flats was arranging a commemorative plaque in memory of residents murdered in the Shoah; Peter was able to add his grandparents' names to the list and in the following year attended a ceremony to unveil the plaque.

Denk Mal am Ort, Germany

Another form of commemoration occurs without erecting stones, plaques or monuments. Just as Demnig's *Stolpersteine* were conceived as 'counter-monuments' to be trodden upon, noticed and reflected upon, performative events that leave no material traces can also be viewed as counter-monuments.

The *Denk Mal am Ort* [Commemoration on Site] initiative had a similar set up to the Dutch Open Jewish Homes project, with local neighbourhood groups involved in arranging such an event, with speeches and testimonies. Here is what Merilyn Moos writes about the event to which she was invited in 2018, to talk about her mother's family:

> There were about thirty people listening in the courtyard, many, though not all, who lived in one of the apartments around the courtyard. Afterwards, there was a queue to speak to me. They wanted to tell me the stories of their parents under Nazism, of the relatives, some who had stood up to the Nazis and been killed, some who had fought and been killed and how they now felt about the losses and contradictions of it all. It was as if I was healing their historic wounds. But what they did not know was that they were healing mine. It is almost the only time I have felt 'at home'.

Postmemorial work

Stephen Frosh (2019: ix) a clinical psychologist and professor at Birkbeck College, London, interested in the application of psychoanalytic thinking to social issues, describes the notion of postmemory as a field of study concerned with the transgenerational impact of personal and social trauma. Several writers have drawn attention to the idea that for the individual to make sense of their traumatic experiences, society should pay attention and make reparation. Aleida Assmann (2016: 4) a German professor of literary studies whose work focuses on how societies remember inquires

> into the way such events are remembered individually, how they are passed on or silenced as collective experience, how they are publicly recognized, and in what forms of media and ritualized commemorations they are being continually reconstructed.

Such a process requires not only recognition and acknowledgement of past injustices and suffering but also engagement in what Marianne Hirsch (2012), a professor of comparative literature and gender studies at Columbia University, terms postmemorial work. She makes it clear that postmemory is an imaginative process, involving an act of identification with past trauma, while seeking to go on living in a way that gives the past its due weight and recognition.

The very active participation of non-Jews in organizing commemorative events, plaques and *Stolpersteine* and undertaking considerable research about the victims who used to live in these localities is not only remarkable, but it also facilitates some healing and assuages some guilt. One wonders where did such non-Jewish organizers, researchers, volunteers and organizations actually spring from and how did they attract willing people and even local dignitaries to attend such events?

It is our contention that facilitating the giving and receiving of Shoah testimony is generally provided by a combination of individual and communal activism at the local level and, at the same time, a significant degree of institutional and political support also needs to come from state institutions at the local, national and international level. For example, the manner in which political action such as the German government paying reparation was instituted also publicly acknowledges that something terrible happened. When such effort is put into offering a form of repair, it also helps to validate the giving of testimony, even to this day.

Shoah memory as public agenda

An important feature of these commemorative events is the way they link across boundaries. There are *Stolpersteine* in at least twenty-four countries. In Vienna, the *Steine der Erinnerung* project takes its inspiration from the *Stolpersteine* project. Similarly, the *Denk Mal Am Ort* project takes its inspiration from the Dutch *Open Jewish Homes* project.

A second important feature is that crucially such events both combine family memory and collective memory. Yet, these events would not be taking place without the sanction of a whole raft of other agencies and institutions at the local, as well as at the city, regional, national and international, level.

In Germany, from the 1960s onwards, there was a concerted effort to research local history in the Nazi era (Wiedmer, 1999). Many towns and cities began inviting former residents who had fled into exile to come back on official visits; Munich came first in 1961, Hamburg in 1965, Berlin in 1969 and many others soon followed (Schenderlein, 2020). Many towns also began to hold annual interfaith ceremonies for victims of the Shoah.

With the unification of Germany, teaching about the Holocaust became compulsory in secondary schools all over Germany in 1992 (Vitale and Clothey, 2019). As a result, many high-school projects focused on researching the fate of Jews in their locality during the Nazi era, producing booklets on the topic and, in some cases, arranging for *Stolpersteine*.

In 2000, the International Holocaust Remembrance Alliance was set up and currently includes thirty-four member countries. Many European countries have adopted Holocaust Memorial Day, just to indicate the extent to which the Shoah is very much part of the international public discourse.

Despite this increase in Holocaust remembrance, there has been a sharp increase in overt anti-Semitism as well as a growth in Holocaust denial in many countries. Yet all these initiatives, whether at the local, national or international level, are providing a supportive forum for testimonial voices to be heard and for 'engaged' people to hear such voices, enabling some repair both for survivors and their families.

Detachment and attachment to ancestral homes

As Marianne Hirsch (2012) suggests, postmemory is an imaginative process. For those of the second and third generation travelling back to parental or grandparental homes, viewing the physical buildings, or the places where they once stood, is not simply to gaze on a place, but to superimpose on to the site something that is unseen, requiring descendants to link fragments of what has been passed down through family stories, photographs and research on to the scene in front of them.

Mary Douglas (1991) a British anthropologist, known for her writings on human culture and symbolism, points out that although the home can be seen as a physical space, it is the inhabitants who provide its structured domesticity, allocate the resources and give care and attention within those spaces. The notions of 'home' go beyond the mere materiality of the physical space and include the people and their relationships and even beyond that, the immediate physical and social environment in which the home is located.

Merilyn Moos' first encounter, with her mother's childhood home in Berlin, or so she thought, was almost a joyous one, in which she tried to re-imagine her mother and her aunts living there as children. What is involved here is the materiality of the apartment connecting in Moos' imagination with the fragments she had pieced together from what her mother had told her about her childhood, as well as fragments she had been able to glean from researching her family history. All these things came together in her imagination, so she was able to see the physical reality of the apartment in its present state and, at the same time, the recreated picture in her mind of what it would have been like when her mother was growing up. The linden trees she could still see from the balcony evoked a memory of what her mother had recounted to her. She could imagine her mother, as a child, hiding under the kitchen table. Even the present mess in the apartment is something she felt that her grandparents would not have tolerated. All these family stories, memories and cultural knowledge helped Merilyn to conjure up a picture in her mind, while viewing the apartment in the present.

Returning 'home': Learning from indigenous cultures

Pacific Islanders living elsewhere in the world provide some insight into the importance of having a 'homeland' that lives on with them in the mind. It is a rich resource that also includes cultural memory and origin stories entwined with family landmarks, surrounding landscapes and cityscapes. In Māori culture, when a person first meets someone new, they greet each other with a '*mihi*': a ritual for telling the story of their family history that also links them to important local landscape features such as a mountain or river and often the canoe that originally brought their ancestors to Aotearoa New Zealand.

For Melanesians, according to McGavin (2017), the concept of homeland is anchored in '*Peles*', or strong cultural attachment to a home and place, that locates a person's family origins in an indigenous space, whether village or town and includes the surrounding seascape, starscape and spiritscape. A Melanesian inherits this affiliation through birth irrespective of where they are born and ties them to a specific locality. Such bonds to place are a crucial component of Pacific Island identity; yet there is also a performative aspect to this identity over time. As McGavin puts it, the genealogical attachment to place is part of the 'being' aspect to identity. There is also an expectation of embodiment and enactment, the 'doing' part of identity. Such 'doing' is closely scrutinized by those remaining back home. When there are 'return' visits, these are perceived as opportunities for diasporic islanders to 'remember' or re-learn their cultural knowledge and to display appropriate attitudes and behaviours (McGavin, 2017: 126–127). These journeys 'home' then become a necessary part of identity maintenance, further reinforcing them as Pacific Islanders.

It is the performative element that our authors found to be crucial. As an illustrative example, Hooper-Greenhill (2000) refers to Māori ritual ceremonies that express tangible and intangible Māori artistic and cultural traditions (*taonga*). She explains that they entail elaborate traditions of encounter, challenge, welcome and responsive calling, moments of silence for the dead, speeches, blessing services and greetings (Hooper-Greenhill, 2000: 51). These performative acts weave together collective history, place history and genealogy, to keep the memory of ancestors alive and rooted in specific places, thereby reinforcing Māori identity by providing vital links between the past and the present.

Something similar is being created and re-enacted by our twenty contributing authors. The social and geographic context for pilgrimages to ancestral homes or to places where relatives were murdered or buried may seem a far cry from the Pacific Islands or New Zealand. Yet, the journeys described in this book provided each narrator with opportunities for performative actions, which helped them to connect to those who had gone before them, at least in spirit. A bond or connection, between the living and the dead, that until then had felt to be hanging by the thinnest of threads could be strengthened.

Each of our contributing authors describe how the past was brought into the present through a perfomative act that linked genealogy with place. Most of our authors did not come prepared with any ready-made or clearly laid-out scripts in advance. They just set off in search of a past that seemed nebulous and out of reach and yet, along the way they discovered that they were able to strengthen their connection to relatives whom they had never known or only remembered fleetingly. Whether it was through laying a *Stolperstein*, lighting a memorial candle, or reciting the *Kaddish* [the mourners' prayer], they found it drew them much closer to their 'lost family'. But so did walking through the main door of apartment blocks where parents or grandparents had once lived, climbing the same staircases, walking on the same pavements and sitting by the same courtyard fountain where a parent had played as a child. Throughout these journeys, there are countless instances of performative actions that helped to weave together a sense of place that was closely connected to those relatives who had lived or died there.

Some of our contributors found they were quite adept at creating their own rituals to help them solidify that sense of connection between important places, ancestors and themselves. Diti Ronen, in her chapter, describes how it became possible to physically embody the connection with her great-grandmother and the family home in Oradea:

> In spite of the past
> You are here. I

Walk your way
From the shop to your home
From your home to your shop
Counting one hundred
From edge to edge
Paving the memory
By my steps.

The house still stands in its glamour.
The big two Stars of David in its gates.

History disorients, too

Visiting ancestral homes can bring joy but also pain. A sense of delight and comfort can emerge as an imaginative reconnection with a past, that had previously seemed lost and beyond grasp, becomes possible. It can also be a disheartening experience that only serves to heighten the immense sense of loss, grieving and deep injustice that can never be fully addressed. This is especially the case where the place itself, the house, the apartment block, is no longer standing, long since demolished.

There is also a form of deep disorientation to cope with when visiting former homes in parts of Europe, especially in Central and Eastern Europe, as they have repeatedly had their boundaries changed over the last few centuries. The country or town of their ancestors' memories no longer exist as they were. Poland, for example, with its origins in the mid-tenth century has been through huge political and turbulent shifts throughout its history. In the year 1000, recently Christianized, it received official recognition from the Holy Roman Emperor Otto III. This was followed by the Congress of Gniezno that formally established the See of Gniezno and its subordinate dioceses. Then in 1386, the young queen of Poland, Jagwiga, married the Lithuanian prince Jagiello, forming the Jagiellonian dynasty and eventually, in 1569, the union of the Polish and Lithuanian Commonwealth. In 1772, foreign powers partitioned large parts of Poland. Russia took over territory in the East, Prussia in the West and Austria in the South. Following the Congress of Vienna in 1815, there were further partitions and uprisings, leading to new divisions of Polish territory. After further uprisings, the vestigial powers of the Polish kingdom were completely abolished. It was not till the end of the First World War that Poland regained its independence and some of its territories.

It was at this time that the European map was redrawn to form newly independent countries. The German, Austro-Hungarian, Russian and Ottoman empires were broken up as the victorious allies embraced the notion of self-determination and new nation states were created or re-established. Austria, Hungary, Czechoslovakia and Yugoslavia were carved out of the former Austro-Hungarian empire; Finland, Estonia, Latvia and Lithuania were from previously Russian-held lands, while Poland and Romania were fashioned from lands previously held by Russia and the Austro-Hungarian empire.

Names of countries, towns and villages changed then and again after the Second World War as boundaries were redrawn and the iron curtain established. Maps were redrawn again after the fall of Communism in many of these countries. In Yugoslavia the end of this era released brutal conflict, while the creation of the Czech and Slovak Republics and the reunification of Germany were achieved more peacefully.

Himka and Michlic (2013) have edited a very informative book on this recent history in these countries and how it affected the Jewish populations.

Journeys home: Reconnecting the dots

The journeys described in this book, although focusing on very different aspects of the physical journey 'home', illustrate how often growing up in the shadow of the Shoah is confusing and identity sapping. Without the actual physical external reality to mirror a long-felt internal experience of 'homelessness', seeing the place for the first time brings a new sense of relief and confidence, often being able to trust one's own experience for the first time.

What impels descendant generations to undertake such journeys is the sense of loss and detachment from a place of origin and the search for reconnection or at least for a new connection.

We suspect that all descendent generations growing up after massive socio-political trauma suffer similar preoccupations, which may throw light on why those born in an adopted country sometimes turn against it. These stories are not only inspiring but also revealing, as each author pulls back the curtains of apparent adaptative integration so often expected and proclaimed by host cultures.

Bibliography

Assmann, A. (2016). *Shadows of Trauma: Memory and the Politics of Postwar Identity*. S. Clift, (trans.). New York: Fordham University Press.

Beaglehole, A. (1990). *Facing the Past: Looking Back at a Refugee Childhood in New Zealand 1940s–1960s*. Wellington, NZ: Allen and Unwin.

Bohleber, W. (2010). *Destructiveness, Intersubjectivity and Trauma: The Identity Crisis of Modern Psychoanalysis*. London: Karnac.

Burgess Winning, G. (2011). '*Stolpersteine Verlegung* [stone-laying] in Laisa', *Second Generation Voices*, 47, 6–8.

Douglas, M. (1991). 'The Idea of Home: A Kind of Space', *Social Research*, 58 (1), 287–307.

Epstein, H. (2001). 'Looking Back and Looking Forward', *Second Generation Voices*, 18, 5–8.

Frosh, S. (2019). *Those Who Come After: Postmemory, Acknowledgement and Forgiveness*. London: Palgrave Macmillan.

Frost, N., and Selwyn, T. (eds) (2018). *Travelling towards Home, Mobilities and Homemaking*. Oxford: Berghahn.

Himka, J., and Michlic, J. B. (2013). *Bringing the Dark Past to Light, the Reception of the Holocaust in Postcommunist Europe*. Lincoln: University of Nebraska Press.

Hirsch, M. (2012). *The Generation of Postmemory: Writing and Visual Culture after the Holocaust*. New York: Columbia University Press.

Hooper-Greenhill, E. (2000). *Museums and the Interpretation of Visual Culture*. London: Routledge.

Mandel, R., and Lehr, R. (2020). 'Failing to Remember: Afterlives and *Stolpersteine* in the Nordic Region', *Journal of Jewish Studies*, 71 (2), 365–396.

Marin, B. (2002). *My Father, My Father*. Carlton North, Victoria, Australia: Scribe Publications.

McGavin, K. (2017). 'Be (longings): Diasporic Pacific Islanders and the Meaning of Home'. In J. Taylor, and H. Lee (eds), *Mobilities of Return, Pacific Perspectives*. Canberra: Australian National University, 123–146.

Schenderlein, A. C. (2020). 'German Jewish Travel to Germany and West German Municipal Visitor Programs'. In A. C. Schenderlein (ed.), *Germany on Their Minds, German Jewish Refugees in the United States and Their Relationship with Germany*. Oxford: Berghahn Books.

Turner, V. (1969). *Ritual Process, Structure and Antistructure*. London: Penguin.

Vitale, M., and Clothey, R. (2019). 'Holocaust Education in Germany: Ensuring Relevance and Meaning in an Increasingly Diverse Community', *FIRE: Forum for International Research in Education*, 5 (1), 41–62.

von Sommaruga Howard, T. (2019). 'Sociopolitical Trauma: Forgetting, Remembering, and Group Analysis', *Transactional Analysis Journal*, 49 (4), 233–247.

Wardi, D. (1992). *Memorial Candles: Children of the Holocaust*. Routledge: London.

Wiedmer, C. (1999). *The Claims of Memory, Representations of the Holocaust in Contemporary Germany and France*. Ithaca: Cornell University Press.

Websites

<www.denkmalamort.de/what does-denk-mal-am-ort-mean/>
<www.openjoodsehuizen.nl/en/page/506/what-is-open-jewish-homes>

PART I

Journeys with a survivor or refugee parent

1 'Heimish' at last

> Janet, I know how interested you are in the past. I've never wanted to talk about it, but I think when we are in Berlin, and we see the sights, then things will come back to me – really I wanted to go and see a new place, or go to Spain, because I love the country. But on the other hand, I felt this is something I ought to do for you. There was a time when I did not want to go to Berlin at all, but my sister – you remember Auntie Lilli – said don't be silly, you must go, you must see it. After all you were born there.
>
> – Eva Evans, May 2006

My mother, Eva, was having misgivings about going back to Berlin before we had even boarded the flight. Her body language reflected her words. She was listless and dragged her feet while my father and I rushed on ahead with the baggage. At the time, I commented, "She's never been one to talk about the past, so this trip is putting her in a position where she needs to talk … and I think she finds that very difficult."

It was the main reason why I brought my video camera along on the AJR (Association of Jewish Refugees) organized visit to Berlin. I reasoned, if I played the role of 'interviewer', she would be less inhibited and more readily open up to me about her feelings. Besides, it would give me the chance to film my own private video diary, in the quiet of my hotel room, to reflect on how the trip was affecting both of us. I had never been to my mother's birthplace before and I was keen to record our shared trip to Berlin for posterity.

Within one hour of our arrival the tables had turned. Even on the coach to the hotel she was excited. In my video diary I noted, "She was quite like a child. She jumped up and said I know that street." I remember my father pointing to a signpost to the zoo. She bounced up again, looking thrilled, telling us she had loved visiting the zoo when she was young. When she saw directions to Halensee, her eyes lit up, remembering how she had

Figure 1.1. Eva as a child, with her father (From family collection).

swum in the lake. Until now, any happy recollections of her childhood in Berlin had been locked away in the back of her mind. As these memories returned to her, a childish delight pervaded her whole being.

In my mind's eye, it seemed my mother had become the young Berliner again, – no longer dragging her feet but sprinting ahead of us, wearing her prized running shoes, the ones she had received in March 1936 to celebrate her 12th birthday, the trainers with the special 'spikes', she had so often described to me. 1936, the year when swastika banners hung from buildings, monuments and lined the main boulevard of Unter den Linden, heralding the start of the Olympic games.

On our first evening in Berlin, we attended an 'orientation evening' where our tour guide introduced herself. She was born in Berlin and had tragically lost both her parents in the Holocaust. Afterwards, she emigrated to South America and then returned to Germany as a 16-year-old but with mixed feelings. Once she found her metier; working as an 'heritage' tour guide, she became more settled.

I found the 'orientation evening' stimulating and interesting but my mother was bored and told me she disliked the discussion on anti-Semitism. This had stemmed from a particular incident that occurred at the airport in Berlin. Our tour guide had displayed a plaque with the words AJR (Association of Jewish Refugees) in the coach window but then she grew concerned that it was a security issue. The coach driver responded, "Why is everyone frightened, why have they got to be so frightened? ... Well, I don't understand (why) with the Jews there's always an issue."

The tour guide explained his comment showed a lack of education, but my mother reacted unexpectedly.

> My own opinion is that anti-Semitism is a fact of life, it's something you have to live with, and you're very lucky if you don't come across it, which in my profession I don't. We're not talking now about extermination camps or concentration camps. We are talking about ordinary life, what happens to you, and a bit of anti-Semitism here and there, I think you have to take that as a sort of sport. Because that it is what it is to some people and if you're going to take it so seriously, I think that's no good at all.

I found her statement bewildering. It trivialized a serious matter and ignored the fact she was a victim of persecution herself. Here we were in her hometown, the place from where she had been forced to flee because of anti-Semitism.

As I review the video footage today, I notice this mismatch between my mother's reaction to events on the trip and my own. In-between her occasional infectious outbursts of enthusiasm, she is calm like a still pond whereas I am a pebble 'splashing' in, forcing ripples that end up touching me not her. I think this has always been the nature of our relationship. I provoke a reaction in her which she does her best to reject and I end up getting upset. She wants to please me, but it is clear and it has always been so, she would rather be left alone and who can blame her? Why should she have to hark back on the unpleasant past she would sooner forget? Perhaps, I should explain a bit about her background.

Eva grew up in Berlin as if she were an only child. Her siblings were a decade older. At the time, she resented her parent's overprotective nature even though it was understandable; the Nazis were gaining power and Hitler was turning his wrath on the Jews, eroding their civil rights and liberties. Her father (my grandfather), Dr Felix Klopstock, a successful

GP (General Practitioner), was forced to give up his job and make way for an Aryan doctor who would replace him. Later, on the notorious orchestrated 1938 pogrom of *Kristallnacht*, he was arrested and imprisoned in Sachsenhausen concentration camp. There he suffered the hardships of gruelling manual labour, near starvation and cruelty at the hands of Nazi guards, witnessing many of his friends and relatives dying as a consequence. Eva's mother (my grandmother) Annie Klopstock, fought for his release, lambasting a Gestapo officer on a daily basis, until he was finally released.

In January 1939, having been granted a six-month-visa, they escaped to England, but more upheaval followed with the start of the Second World War. Eva and her parents were evacuated from London. During this time, Eva was forced to move to countless different schools and her father was interned which was another massive blow to him, after his imprisonment in 'Sachsenhausen'. Even though the conditions of his internment were nowhere as bad as concentration camp, it came as a shock to him. When he was finally released, he was reinstated as a GP in Barrow-in-Furness but perhaps because of all the hardship he had endured, his health rapidly deteriorated and he died there.

Despite all the instability, Eva succeeded in passing 'O and A levels' and graduating from University College London with a degree in languages. Some years later, Eva met her Viennese husband Robert, a refugee like herself, at a local tennis club in Belsize Park. Two refugees, she would say, drawn together by shared accents, and a feeling of familiarity as if they had been part of each other's lives forever. In 1957 they got married and went on to have three children – two girls and a boy – I am the youngest.

Our AJR trip was not the first trip my mother had made back to Berlin. She and my father were invited by the mayor of Berlin on a visit two years before. The trip made little impression on her although she was pleased to be reunited with a long-lost cousin she had not seen since leaving Berlin. More than a decade before, we had also joined my father on a private trip back to Vienna. Afterwards, she said simply and proudly, "I think daddy regained his 'birth right.'" I am convinced she did not think the same would ever happen to her. Her childhood memories were more complicated and tinged with sadness whereas my father had happier memories of life in Vienna. I always wondered if this was why my father had no qualms about us spending our summer holidays in Austria, although we never visited Vienna and only ever stayed in the Austrian Alps. In these picturesque alpine villages, my father would fish for trout and we would climb the mountains. An idealized recreation of the vacations my parents spent as children but inoculated from any bad memories.

And yet – and yet – that was not quite the case. In truth, our journeys were fraught with anxiety. We would travel to Austria by train. In the sleeper couchettes, crossing through France and Germany to Austria, there would invariably be an argument and my father would lose his temper. Perhaps, it was the officious looking uniforms worn by the train guards that triggered my father, but on one unforgettable journey, I remember a German train guard threatened to lock us in our compartment and call the police when we reached the next station. It was as if we were being transported into a different time – Jewish refugees on the verge of being captured by SS guards. It was all so unexpected particularly because my father was normally the gentlest man.

On these holidays, my parents told me I was never to tell anyone why I spoke German so fluently. It was my first lesson in subterfuge. I had to say that I had learnt German in school. The painful feeling of having something shameful to hide, but not knowing why, remained with me until I returned to Berlin many years later on my own.

For my mother, the German language resurrected ghosts from the past. She hated it when English people tried to speak German to her in public and was quick to respond in English. Yet in the comfort of our home, she spoke German freely to my father. I know now it was partly in response to refugees being advised by the government at the time to refrain from speaking 'the enemy language' but I also think it was because she was deeply conflicted about her 'mother tongue'. This was expressed during the course of our trip when I asked her what she missed most about Berlin.

Well, I can't really remember missing anything, it's just this feeling of being in new surroundings and not being in control of the language … when I was in school in Germany, I was a good student. I was very good at writing essays. I had these dreams of becoming a journalist but when I came to England, I suddenly realized this was not to be and I think this cast a shadow over all my life then. Although, I learned very good English, I've always felt that I couldn't really be perfect and not being able to express my feelings just the way I would have done if the German language was still mine.

My parents 'managed' pretty well or rather coped after arriving in England. They grew resilient as so often happens with refugees. Both were successful in business and work – my mother got an MBE (Member of the British Empire) for services to the European Community. She proudly wore it on the lapel of her jacket throughout our trip. My father ran a popular and busy restaurant in Belsize Park, memorable for the striking old red fire engine displayed on the forecourt. We had a settled and comfortable family life but almost never spoke about the past. If they had any feelings of profound 'loss' you would have never known it. Both had lost close family members who were deported and murdered. But they had also lost their *Heimat* – belongings, books, toys, schools, past identity, language skills, culture and feelings of familiarity.

In later years, I wondered how they coped so well. They had been uprooted in the tender years of puberty (at least in my mother's case) and from everything they held dear. Of course, they viewed themselves as the 'lucky ones' and it is true, they were not 'concentration camp' survivors. Maybe, they felt they did not deserve to feel sad, or perhaps they felt guilty for surviving. It is more than possible such feelings of loss were pushed out of sight and mind – 'the buried trauma' – as it is so often described by psychologists when talking about their generation.

After viewing the American 'Holocaust' mini-series broadcast in 1978, my mother spoke to us for the first time about her experiences. This fictional drama depicting a family not unlike her own with a doctor as head of the family, opened the floodgates. But just to qualify … the floodgates to the facts – lacking all embellishment, devoid of emotion. She simply explained her history and why they had been forced to leave Germany. I never asked any more questions about the past, nor did they volunteer information. Only after I had left home and saw them from afar did I grow more curious. And especially so when we embarked on our trip to Berlin and I saw my chance to elicit unspoken feelings that had been too painful to touch.

During our trip, my mother was still restrained when it came to expressing her feelings, but I felt she was more reflective. For example, when I asked her why she felt she had no attachment to Berlin, she explained her feelings about it for the first time in a candid way.

> It may be because I really only lived through unhappy times ... I think I was always under pressure, unhappy, because of my parents. I could observe how much they suffered, and although they shielded me from it, the whole atmosphere was so sad. I don't want to think about it. And when my friends talk about Berlin ... I don't even want to hear the word Berlin.

So here we were in a Berlin she did not want to hear about, visiting Jewish memorial sites she did not really want to know about. Before long it became clear, we were on entirely different journeys. When we visited Villa Wannsee, in southwest Berlin on the second day of our trip, I remember listening to the museum curator talk about the infamous meeting chaired by Reinhard Heydrich where the plan for the Final Solution was discussed. From the corner of my eye, I was aware my mother had her focus elsewhere. She was now standing by one of the tall windows, staring out at the Wannsee, drinking in memories with her eyes. Later I asked her what was on her mind then.

> Suddenly I remembered, although, I must say this in German, there were certain picnic places there and signs which said, *Hier können Familien Kaffee kochen*. And that became a sort of a proverb in our house, and if you don't understand it means 'Here people can boil coffee' or 'make coffee' and you can have your picnic. Well, we didn't actually ever make coffee, we just brought the thermos flask. But the big thing was our sandwiches.

It hit me then how different our perspectives were. Her need was to pick out a few 'rosy memories' in among an entanglement of thorns whereas I was dwelling on the potent history of the place.

I often wondered why my mother's history affected me so strongly. At the Jewish Museum in Berlin, I realized I was not the only one to feel this. My visit there threw into sharp relief how feelings of anxiety and displacement can be passed down through the generations. I found the Holocaust Tower – the silent, cold empty space with its unreachable ladder – emotionally

overpowering and the Gardens of Exile with its uneven surfaces disturbing.
By the time I returned inside the museum, I felt utterly disoriented and
uneasy. Afterwards, I spoke to the museum curator hoping my mother
would not overhear me. I was sure she would never understand. "Stop being
hysterical", she would say. I told the curator, "Even though I'm second generation, I still feel this feeling of unsteadiness, like I don't really belong."
She responded, saying, "I'm third generation and I still feel that now." It
felt reassuring to know I was not alone.

That evening we were welcomed into the home of a work colleague
of my mother, a professor and his family. My mother was excited. His
home reminded my mother so much of her own home in Berlin with
its sweeping high ceilings and maze of interconnecting rooms. The
professor, who was not Jewish, knew nothing about my mother's background despite knowing her reasonably well. Once they deduced the
purpose of our visit, they refrained from asking us too many questions.
Perhaps, they were afraid to tread on sensibilities and thought it best
not to pry.

The following day we visited the famous 'Holocaust Memorial' of
stones in the Cora-Berlinerstraße. Underneath the memorial was a subter-
ranean information centre and some exhibition rooms. Inside one of the
darkened rooms, you could see letters on display which had been written
by Holocaust victims – many of them young children. Tragically, in some
cases they were bidding their families farewell knowing they were being
sent to death. My mother refused to look at any exhibits and stared only
at the lit up 'exit sign', determined as she was to leave the room as quickly
as possible. Later I commented, "My mother … just wanted to escape.
She didn't want to stay down below, she said I've seen it all before and she
wanted to go outside. But my father was very strict, and said she has to stay
here because otherwise we'll lose her."

At the time, I was very upset she wanted to leave us. It is only now
I understand why. She was not running away from us; she was running
from her history. No more than a child herself when she left Germany;
these letters might well have been written by German school children of
her own age whom she might have known.

Figure 1.2. Janet's mother, Eva, at the Berlin Holocaust Memorial
(Photo taken by Janet Eisenstein).

After our visit to the Holocaust Memorial, we were invited to a reception at Berlin's town hall to meet the mayor. In fact, it turned out to be the assistant mayor, André Schmitz. For some reason, this upset our German tour guide and an argument ensued. By the time we filed into the very grand reception room with heavy chandeliers and a huge mahogany table where wine glasses and carbonated bottles of water had been laid out, everyone was feeling tense. André Schmitz gave a speech about Berlin's past and after he finished speaking, it was time for questions. Nobody said anything. Silence descended. For some reason, this bothered me. It had happened earlier in the day after a talk given by the President of the Bundesrat, Wolfgang Thierse. Later in my video diary, I reflected on this, "I can't, we can't sit here passively, we have to say something, we have to make a noise, whatever it is – I don't want them to think we don't have anything to say for ourselves." In the end, I broke the silence both times. On the second occasion, I introduced my mother to the assistant mayor. I had my doubts about her having the courage to speak out, especially in such an intimidating situation, but they were misplaced. She turned out to be surprisingly articulate. She gave him a potted history of her life in Berlin. I had never heard her speak so openly before and especially not in front of such a large crowd. I was really glad about this and yet afterwards when it came to joining the mayor in a toast, I could not bring myself to take a sip of wine, yet my mother emptied her glass.

That evening, I sat in the quiet of my room, contemplating why I had not joined in on the toast. Throughout our visit – superbly organized by Susie Kaufman and Carol Rossen – we had witnessed evidence at every juncture of the horrific crimes of the Third Reich. It was clear that Germany was doing its best to remember and reconcile itself to the past, but I wondered if we were ready to forgive and forget. Could we or they ever understand the pain, and would an acknowledgement ever be enough? For me, the toast had represented a symbolic acquiesce of some sort, however ludicrous that sounds, and the silence an acceptance of Germany's terrible past.

We saved our visit to my mother's home and school for the last day. I remember how my mother's face turned ashen when she looked up at the building that used to be her home. The original block of flats where she lived had been bombed and was now a modern, anonymous looking block which bore no resemblance to the home she remembered. Perhaps, she was hoping to mourn something there or retrieve lost memories but there was nothing for her to hang them on for even the foundations of the building had vanished. Later that year in an interview with the AJR, she said, "We haven't got a *Heimat* … it's in Berlin but in a house that isn't there anymore."

On the same day, we visited her secondary school called the *Cecilien Schule* [Cecelian School]. It was now a primary school. Even though the exterior of the school was unchanged (unlike her home), she refused to explore the inside of the school and wanted to leave immediately. Later, in one of my interviews with her, she admitted to having been unhappy at school. It turned out she was one of the last remaining Jewish girls at *Cecilien Schule*. From 1933 a statute was passed to keep Jewish children out of mainstream schools and universities.[1] In my mother's case, an exception was made due to her father having been awarded an Iron Cross First Class in the First World War, but she felt alone and ostracized in the school. One incident stuck out in her mind:

> I was invited to a birthday party by a little girl in my class and her father made an appearance in a Nazi uniform – a brown shirt. He seemed a very pleasant man and I think he realized that I was Jewish. Perhaps, my friend told him. Well, he was quite friendly, but on the other hand you felt that he was terribly surprised that a Jewish girl had been invited to this birthday party. Although nothing was said, I was very conscious then, and said to myself I would never go to that house again.

We spent the final afternoon shopping in 'KaDeWe', one of Berlin's big department stores, searching for an elusive *Keilkissen* [a reading pillow] that she remembered having as a child. We never found it. To this day, I do not know if it was a relic from Berlin's long forgotten past, but I found myself staring at my mother's back as she sped energetically up the escalator in search of it. Old and new Berlin had collided. Her Berlin was frozen in time. This new Berlin was different. Her Berlin had been ravaged and bombed beyond recognition and coiled up inside herself into a ball of grief. Yet strangely … after everything, she told she was convinced her character had been formed here.

> And people who come from Berlin have got this reputation of being very energetic, and outspoken, and that I think this is me all over. I recently wrote a letter to a friend, she asked me, "Do you know Berlin?" and I replied, "Do I know Berlin? I was born there! I'm a typical product of Berlin." And in fact, I told a little anecdote that when I took a group visit to Brussels there was a strike, I had to rebook twenty people to different places and different planes, and I was told by one of the German members of our party that only someone from Berlin could have done that.

1   The Nazi law 'Against Overcrowding in Schools' instigated on 25 April 1933, established a quota so that no more than 1.5 per cent of the total enrolment in German public schools and universities should be taken up by non-Aryan children. This was based on the spurious perception that Jews were vastly over-represented in the professions but correspondingly under-represented in manual trades (Heyman, 1938; Kaplan, 1997). Exceptions were made on a discretionary basis for children of men who had fought in the German army during the First World War.

It was an interesting observation. At the beginning of the trip, she described how disconnected she was to Berlin and now she was showing pride at being labelled a 'Berliner'.

Later, in our final hours, we unwound in a café on Kurfürstendamm. We pondered a little over the trip. She did not regret coming. She told me she actually enjoyed being in Berlin with me, showing me the sights. We talked about Berlin's climate. She had always loved it – never too hot in summer and never too cold in winter. As if to reaffirm her words, the sun smiled down on us as we sipped *Kaffee* both feeling a bit lighter, closer … a little more at peace.

More than a decade passed before I made a second trip to Berlin but this time alone. I had written and produced a short fictional film called, *Kinder* [Children], which was being screened at the old Babylon cinema, in Mitte, Berlin as part of the 'Welcome Refugee' festival. Many of the themes explored in my film germinated from my trip to Berlin with my mother – ideas about identity, returning in later life to revisit the past – a buried past literally hidden under the floorboards. It was fortuitous that *Kinder* was the ticket that brought me back to Berlin and to a 'refugee festival' of all things.

After the film screening, I gave a 'Question and Answer' about the film. I was inundated with questions. I remembered the silence I had been so afraid of in Berlin the last time I had been here. This time the silence was embedded in the film, but the story provoked the audience to speak. I also made a friend in the audience who was a primary school teacher called Steffi. She took me on a tour of old East Berlin where she lived. As we walked through the winding streets, she introduced me to countless acquaintances and told them about my mother's background and later as I will describe, she invited my mother to speak at her school. It seemed to me that this time around, people were more receptive to hearing about my mother's history or maybe, without her, I found it easier to respond more freely. I realized I needed to make this journey alone; to see Berlin through the lens of my own eyes. A new Berlin greeted me. The people I met were friendly and open and the atmosphere upbeat compared to the heaviness I had left behind in 'Brexit Britain'. I also took a train to Sachsenhausen, the concentration camp just to the north of the city, a journey my mother would never have made. I saw the block where my grandfather had been taken on the fateful *Kristallnacht*. I witnessed how dreadful the conditions were. When I told my mother, she was flabbergasted, "I cannot understand why you went." I told her, "I went because I needed to find out about my family's history."

In retrospect, my perception of my mother being a still pond is perhaps wrong. I believe there were waves underneath the surface – huge crashing waves. The surface had to be calm if only to contain them. My constant prodding and pushing – the stone splashing in – was a way for me to release them. Only after Berlin I learnt, it was the next generation, my generation and my children's generation's job to express the inexpressible. Already my daughter had written a paper at university entitled, *A Narrative of Mourning: Post Memory* and my son a dissertation about 'Enemy Aliens'. They had the right distance to delve into those indigestible memories in order to preserve them.

Except then, only recently, my mother took me by surprise. As a result of my friendship with Steffi – she was invited to speak about her background via Zoom to Steffi's class at the *Grundschule am Teutoburger Platz* [Primary School on Teutoburger Platz]. The children posed many questions even asking her if she had a *haustier*, [pet] in Berlin. She delighted the children with her candid responses in fluent German. Later she received a 'thank you' from the German President himself; Frank-Walter Steinmeier who had heard about her talks. In the last paragraph of his letter, he wrote, "I have learned that your father, Dr Felix, Klopstock was deported to Sachsenhausen. I plan to visit the memorial there this year. When I do your father and the humiliation that he and so many others were subjected to will be on my mind." This heartfelt letter from the German President meant so much to her. I was moved by her willingness to finally share her history – age 97.

In the wake of Brexit, I applied for German citizenship. It was hard decision to make as my mother did not approve. For my part it was never as simple as wanting a European passport. It was something else. Perhaps, it was the culmination of both my trips to Berlin. While in 'Sachsenhausen' I had phoned a relative whom I had never met before. He had grown up behind the iron curtain. I was invited to his flat to meet his family. They shared their *Abendessen* [evening meal] with me – a cold supper of *Butter, Brot und Käse* [butter, bread and cheese] and all the food was entirely familiar – *heimish* [homely]. I had never lived in Berlin, but I felt at home. I was not ashamed to say it.

Bibliography

Heyman, C. L. (1938). 'German Laws against the Jews', *Current History*, 48 (3), 38–43.
Kaplan, M. (1997). 'The School Lives of Children and Youth in the Third Reich', *Jewish History*, 1 (2), 41–52.

2 Kraków: A visit with my mother to her hometown

My journey to remembrance has been slow with many interruptions. This changed when on a long holiday to Australia, where I chanced upon an exhibition about the Dunera Boys in the Melbourne Jewish Museum. My father, Dennis Goodman, had been one of them and the memorabilia there had made it evident that the diary he had kept during his internment in Australia was of historical value. When home, I decided to transcribe his diary and study the history of the time. This opened up many questions about my family that I was unable to resist, and a new project emerged that has become all consuming.

I had grown up with a sense of my parents' histories and had the impression that I knew all that there was to know. On closer examination, beginning with my father's story, I realized that this was not so. Sadly, my father was no longer with us. He had passed away in 2007. I was aware that since his retirement he had been pursuing lines of enquiry about his ancestors in Germany going back to the eighteenth century. While working on his diary, I found a large plastic box in a cupboard at my parents' home containing unknown photographs that went back to the early twentieth century. Over many weeks, my mother Lea and I went through these photographs working out who the people were and the likely year when they had been taken. The photographs were of the family on both sides taken before the War, during the War and immediately after the War. This was a difficult task for my mother, and we could only work through them an hour at a time because she would develop what she called 'a tension headache'.

As we went through the photographs connected to my mother and her story and that of her my maternal grandmother, Baba, I would ask questions and she would respond. It became evident as we progressed that we had embarked on a new journey together.

It was through the experiences of going through the photographs and transcribing and researching my father's diary that I also developed a strong desire to know more about my parents' lives before the War. I suggested to my mother that we visit Kraków, her hometown, together, for a few days and walk around and be in the different places she would go to as a little girl in the hope that detailed memories would come back to her. My mother agreed readily.

I had been to Kraków twice before and on both occasions, I had only touched the surface of my mother's history and that of her family; there was so much more to learn. The first time I was in Kraków was in 1996, with my husband Albert and a Polish business acquaintance who had kindly arranged everything for us; the hotel, a guide and where we would go. I was curious back then to see where my mother was born though alongside was apprehensive about how it would be. It turned out to be an emotionally intense experience; when there, I was constantly thinking about my Polish family and of those who had perished in the War.

At the hotel, that had plainly been a large family home, we were greeted by a receptionist who, having made the necessary registrations, then asked if we would like to visit Auschwitz, something she could arrange for us. I was dumbfounded. I had grown up knowing that my maternal grandfather, Mendel Apelzon, had been murdered in Auschwitz-Birkenau at the young age of 32, so to me, the place represented one of profound horror. How could she suggest such a thing? The offer felt distasteful and unfeeling.

From the hotel we took a tram to the city centre. Looking around the tram and the scenes of the city outside, I was astonished to see that nothing appeared to have changed since the War. The tram was old, and it felt eerily haunted by Baba. She had died in a car accident in 1981, having survived the War and I missed her. I was very aware that she had steadfastly refused to return to Poland after the War, and I then understood why. For some reason I had thought that Kraków had been destroyed and looking back, maybe because in our family there was the sense of destruction; lives destroyed, a way of life destroyed.

We were in Kraków for a short time and the guide took us round. Walking the streets was overwhelming; I struggled to be in the moment with my mind in the past seeking to fathom the enormity of what had been lost. My most vivid memory was of standing in a square in Kazimierz and looking at a synagogue, hearing the sound of prayers, and imagining my family attending the service.

I had gone armed with one address that my mother had given me, ostensibly that of her maternal grandparents' flat. Inexplicably, I had not asked for the address of her own home. We found what I thought then was the right building and that brought out a feeling of tenderness, imaging my mother playing in the backyard that we were able to see. But, when in Kraków with my mother, it was plain that we had been to the wrong place.

Walking around the city, it became quickly evident to me that Kraków was a sophisticated city and was much the same as it had been in the 1930s. This put paid to the notion that my mother was "a Polish peasant", a phrase that my father would love to say every now and then and that in my naivety growing up, I had taken literally. It had simply been a reflection of Frankfurt snobbishness and encapsulated my sense that if it had not been for the War and my parents' resulting displacements, they would never have met. I was beginning to understand the societies to which they had each belonged.

By societies, I am thinking as well of people's physicality. This was brought to mind when seeing a group of young school children at the Wawel Castle. I was drawn to one little boy in the group with light blond hair and almond shaped eyes and was struck by the resemblance to my youngest son of about the same age then who has the same features. It was my maternal grandfather, Mendel, who had brought the light blond hair into the family that some of us have inherited. And because it was not all of us, that has made the feature all the more impactful.

The second time I was in Kraków was in the Summer of 2003. We had gone as a family on the occasion of my father's 80th birthday; he had had a long-held wish to retrace my mother's and Baba's escape route from Kraków, over the Tatra mountains to Kežmarok in Slovakia.

For me, it was a different experience from previously since my children were with us and their company drew me away emotionally from the past. Now that they are independent adults, I have found that I have both the emotional space and time to fully explore family history.

So, when my mother and I went to Kraków in June 2018, it was the third time I was there and the experience on that occasion was transformative.

Having thought I knew about my Polish family's experiences during the War, the plan had been to focus on my mother's pre-war childhood. It was not to be; we came to explore as well the terrible years of the German occupation.

My mother has difficulties walking and I was not sure how we would manage. In the event we went from bench to bench as we made progress down the many streets and alleyways of Kraków. While on each bench, I would ask her questions and would type up each response on my iPad there and then as she spoke while occasionally reading back what I had typed to make sure I had heard correctly.

The first places we decided to find were my mother's home and her maternal grandparents' home and these were across the old city from where we were staying. While we strolled, my mother would point out, fondly, places of interest. When we reached the Planty Gertrudy, one of the parks built in the early nineteenth century to encircle Kraków's Old Town, my mother began to reminisce about her young childhood.

We sat on a bench, and she talked about one of her first memories of being in a pushchair and wearing only one shoe. She talked about playing where we were and making designs in the beaten earth with a stick with other children around. She mentioned having been to a kindergarten she thought was a Jewish one and that she had liked a boy called Karolek. She remembered being taken by Baba to visit customers of Mendel's wholesale business and that they had made a fuss of her. I sat there cherishing every detail.

We soon found my mother's street, Ulica Jozefa Sarego, just off the Planty Gertrudy, as she had recalled. I took pleasure in seeing my mother's delight in being back in the street. I could join her in admiring it and the imposing buildings around us. She had been uncertain of the number of her building but found it nevertheless by simply looking around. It was number eleven and we stood in front of her window on the ground floor, taking it all in. We tried the buzzer belonging to apartment 1, having decided that was where she had lived but there was no response. Soon after someone opened the front door to the building, and we went in. Her home had been on the ground floor on the right. I looked at the stone steps in front of the entrance and I appreciated the fact that these had existed when my mother and her parents had lived there. My mother described what the apartment was like inside and their living arrangements, giving me a sense of how it had been.

We then made our way to her maternal grandparents' home in nearby Ulica Bozego Ciała, stopping briefly for a rest and a drink. This was where Baba had lived with her sisters Mania, Esther and Bronja and half-brother Jacob. My mother remembered visiting the apartment as a little girl and salty dried broad beans and dried peas being on the table to nibble. Whenever she used to go there, a big fuss would be made of her; the thinking was she was a wonderful child. My mother explained that her maternal grandfather, Henoch, had bought hats that were seconds, would put them right and sell them on. He had worked from home making enough money to feed the family.

My mother also thought that her parents had met for the first time at the apartment, Mendel having come to visit from Lodz, where he lived at the time. He had been given an introduction to Grandfather Henoch maybe just for someone to visit, maybe for business in Kraków. She did not know.

Working from a street map, I found Ulica Bozego Ciała. On this occasion I was leading; my mother could not precisely remember its location, a contrast to finding her old home. I felt excited walking the streets, discovering. Ulica Bozego Ciała had a different feel; there were shops and people milling around. The apartment was on the first floor above both a shop selling herring and a café, with the entrance between the two premises. As we contemplated how to get in, a tall young man entered the building and we casually followed him. The ground floor area led to a backyard that was both familiar to my mother and unfamiliar, the surrounding balconies having been modernized. My mother pointed to her grandparents' balcony that wrapped round the entire first floor and spoke of how she had played there and, in the backyard as well. Having seen photographs of her as a little girl I felt that I was with her picturing how it had been for her.

While chatting, we saw the same young man from earlier on her grandparents' balcony. He looked down at us quizzically. We explained our presence and he asked us if we would like to see the apartment. We readily agreed and went back into the building and up the beautiful old staircase and he welcomed us in. It turned out that the original apartment, which belonged to friends of his, had been divided into two and both sections were being let out. We were standing in one part and he was there to ready everything for a new let.

My mother sat herself down at the dining table and began a conversation with the young man, finding out all about him while I looked around. Plainly the apartment had been modernized but the beautiful parquet floor was unchanged though possibly restored. As with the stone steps leading to my mother's old home, I reminisced about the fact that my family had walked around on the very same floor not so long ago. It was also a fun thought that I could come and stay in the apartment should I wish to. Following that enriching experience we visited Kazimierz where we had lunch.

Food became an important part of the visit. We saw *pierogi* [a delicious sweet or savoury filled dumpling] on many menus and my mother was keen to have some. I wondered why and her response was to say they are *kreplach* [The Jewish version of filled dumpling]. It had not occurred to me they were essentially the same; I had grown up with Baba's delicious kreplach so was keen to try pierogi as well and that is what we had for lunch but with a cheese rather than a meat filling. It was a disappointment for me because of the filling but for my mother it was different, evoking memories of the past.

Something of that flavour happened a second time when we were in the main square of Kazimierz. We were thinking of having a rest and a drink when my mother heard a tune to which she responded bodily in an instant. I was taken by her reaction and turned to see a female singer standing in front of two musicians at a café close by. I followed my mother and we sat beside the musical group for some tea. Her face was transformed as she soaked in the sound, and she told me that she had not heard such music in years. The group classified their music as klezmer and yet it was unfamiliar to me and nothing like the klezmer music I had heard before.

Following tea, we visited the Jewish Community Centre which was opposite a synagogue. I was struck by the presence of a policeman and policewoman standing by its gate and that brought to mind the fact that we had seen a police van patrolling the streets nearby. Did Kazimierz need protecting I wondered with unease; for me there were echoes of the traumatic past that the area had been through.

It was while sitting together outside a café later that afternoon that I began studying closely the tragic history of the Jewish community of Kraków during the German occupation as written up in *A Guide to Jewish Cracow* that my mother had brought along. I was incredulous realizing that my mother had been in hiding on the Aryan side of Kraków from October 1942, Baba later joining her in the following December, through to March 1944 during which time the ghetto was liquidated. The reality of their everyday lives had simply not occurred to me until then nor how they had been able to remain in Kraków initially until well into 1941. So many questions came to mind, leading to detailed research on the German occupation of Kraków on my return home, both from a general perspective and that of Mendel and Baba.

Sometimes, during the trip to Kraków, my mother and I would ponder about the experience of being there together. On one such occasion my mother told me that not until then had she spent as long as three days just focusing on her story and that that had enabled her to remember so much more. For me, the trip became a coming together with her, leading, paradoxically, to greater individuality and a finding of and listening to our own separate voices.

My mother and I parted ways at Kraków Railway Station. She took the train to Warsaw, and I took the train to Kraków airport. I enjoy travelling by train, contemplating life and the countryside. Sad to be parting from my mother and at the same time looking forward to the train journey, I settled in a comfortable seat by the window. The carriage was peaceful and fairly empty of people. It was a beautiful early afternoon with a clear blue sky, and I sat back looking out at the blond fields of wheat. As I did so, it dawned on me that Mendel's ashes were there, scattered among the wheat gently swaying in the breeze. It was an overwhelming thought which felt just right.

On my return home, with the stay in Kraków still fresh in my mind, I wrote a piece incorporating all that my mother had told me during the stay and included the photos I had taken. Before finalizing it, I asked my mother to let me have her amendments that I later incorporated.

After finishing a book for the family about my father's diary that I had already started, I resolved to create another book, this time about the trip with my mother to Kraków. While doing so, I realized that it needed a section on the general history of the German occupation of Kraków detailing the measures that were imposed in rapid succession on the Jewish community of the city. This led to many fruitful hours of reading in the British Library and Yad Vashem. Studying these measures was painful, shocking and sad but it felt necessary to better understand the family's situation and to have a more detailed picture of Mendel as a person.

Having completed that section, I focused on researching as many websites as possible for archival documentation on my mother's family. This turned up Mendel's 1941 application for a *Kennkarte* [basic identity document].[1] That was an exciting experience because the application had a photo of him that I had not seen before and nor had my mother. I have since obtained from the Kraków Archives a very good scan of it that we treasure. Seeing the photo for the first time brought tears to my eyes – knowing and understanding so much more about him, he had ceased to be a remote figure from the past.

Presently, I am nearing completion of another section based on the piece I had put together on my return from Kraków, that now encompasses the entire wartime period as well as the period following the liberation of Kežmarok in 1945, up to 1948. It has been a complicated endeavour and I have worked closely with my mother to ensure that it is as truthful as possible.

Working with her on that section has been enjoyable and fascinating because it touches on rescue organizations that I had not known existed during the War. It has felt like a joint enterprise in that my mother had done some research into her story many years ago before the advent of the internet and the ongoing digitization of archives. This has meant that between the two of us we have been able to reconstruct not only her escape

---

1   Kennkarte were introduced in July 1938, in use inside Germany during the Reich, including occupied incorporated territories, which every adult German citizen, men only, and every Jewish citizen, both men and women, was issued and was expected to produce when confronted by officials.

route across the Tatra mountains but also work out the rescue organizations behind the employment of the guide who had helped her, and Baba make their way from the Polish/Slovak border to Kežmarok.

This enterprise continues with research into 'the children's train' that she was on with Baba in April 1946 from Prague to Aix-les-Bains, France. The children who were with them, that Baba came to look after in homes in Aix-les-Bains until 1948, were Holocaust survivors from Poland. This is turning out to be another fascinating area of study.

The feedback from the family has been greatly encouraging. For me, the most important readership is the next generation and I have been incentivized by their genuine interest in all that I have been doing. Alongside, is my relationship with my mother that has blossomed during this project that constitutes not only a record but a memorial to the many members of the family who perished in the Holocaust.

Bibliography

Duda, E. (1990). *A Guide to Jewish Cracow*. Warsaw: The Jewish Information and Tourist Bureau.

3 Lost in transportation

I worshipped my father. When he broke his promises, I worshipped him. When he walked out on us, I worshipped him. When the bailiffs came, I worshipped him. When my mother disintegrated in front of my eyes and started abusing me, I worshipped him. When, as a young child, I travelled all day to visit him in far-flung prisons, I worshipped him. When he was released from prison on remand and jumped bail with some young woman to the 'Costa del Crime', I worshipped him. When he consorted with vicious East End gangsters such as Ronnie Knight and Freddie Foreman, I worshipped him.

After all, surely anyone who had gone through what he'd had to endure as a young boy and suffered such unthinkable losses could be forgiven anything?

So ran the narrative of my relationship with my father until a family trip to Vienna to revisit the places and ghosts of his childhood, when I began to see my relationship with Henry Kennedy, born Heinz Kuhe, in a completely different light.

While I can't remember ever having had a specific conversation with my father about being wrenched from his home in Vienna as a 13-year-old boy, waving goodbye to his mother as she put him on the Kindertransport, never to see her again, I somehow knew this about him. I knew that at Dovercourt, a Butlin's holiday camp on the Essex coast used over the winter months to house the refugee children, he wasn't one of those selected for 'adoption' by the English families who came to visit on Sundays. I knew he was to remain in the camp during one of the coldest winters of the century, when the hot-water bottles froze to the sheets overnight. I knew, too, that at this time he still expected to be reunited with his family. This seemingly innate knowledge coloured my perception of him throughout his life. The dead were not mentioned, but their absence was always present. It flavoured everything despite his immutable smile that would warm a room and draw everyone to him. He was a hero to me, a hypnotic, saint-like figure who could do no wrong.

When I was in my teens and learnt of Buddhism, my father morphed into a Buddha figure: thoroughly equanimous in the face of suffering, his own and that of others. He accepted it with a smile and a shrug while trying his utmost to alleviate the situation of those he professed to love. And my father loved everyone equally, showering anyone he met not just with praise but with lavish gifts going way beyond his modest means. On the face of it, he was an easy man to love. Ironically, his frequent absences at 'Her Majesty's Pleasure' (in prison) probably made it easier to worship him, as he was seldom around and thus more able to keep this breezy facade in place. Furthermore, with my mother, also a Jewish refugee from Vienna, dissolving in shame and unable to cope alone with the financial wreckage my father left in his wake, being with him was like being lifted into heaven from the quagmire that my everyday life had become.

One of my favourite childhood memories is of him handing me some coins and me making my way through some tables to the far side of a smoke-filled room. There, I ask in my politest 4-year-old voice for a Bounty Bar, before skipping back gleefully to my father with our – well – bounty. With great concentration I unwrap it. As anyone who is familiar with Bounty Bars will know, it comes in two separate pieces. One I hand over to my dad, the other I eat with painstaking deliberation. I know that its completion will mark not only the end of my month's quota of chocolate but also signal the end of visiting time. Looking back, my heart breaks that these snatched moments in prisons around the country were such highlights for this little girl.

Over the years we received our twice-monthly quota of VOs (Visiting Orders), but school and studies meant I was lucky if I got to see my father once a month. Even this precious time was frequently taken up by my mother needing to speak to my father privately and talk serious grown-up stuff, while my elder sister and I sat quietly as ordered. They spoke of things such as how she'd keep the roof over our heads after my father had been convicted of criminal bankruptcy with the house deeds half in his name. Of course, I understood nothing of this at the time and would simply be embarrassed, no mortified, when my mother ended up shouting at my father, screaming and thumping the table, before crying uninhibitedly. My father would watch on mute, occasionally glancing at me and braving a wink to reassure me that all this was some kind of elaborate game that would soon be over. For him it would be, as he was led back to his cell, but for us, who had to face Mum's uncontrollable rage and violence for days afterwards, it was anything but over. For some reason, I interpreted this wink and calmness as an act of bravery rather than the awkward embarrassment it really was. My dad was the hero and my mum the villain – roles I would unfairly attribute to both for most of my life. Dad would flash one last smile before lining up with the other men to be searched as they filed out of the room.

But hang on, this isn't how the story's meant to unfold. Holocaust survivors make good. They become upright citizens of their adoptive countries. They endeavour to make the ghosts of their murdered parents proud and somehow justify their own survival. How did this story turn sour? How did the boy who'd just 'celebrated' his 13th birthday three days before setting off from Vienna on the Kindertransport come to lead such a thoroughly unconventional life? How too could someone who claimed 'family is everything' come to desert his own so easily and so often? These were questions I was unable to contemplate until fairly recently, triggered by a family trip to his old home in Vienna and again by his death two years ago.

I can't remember how we all ended up in Vienna in the winter of 2001. The details of getting Dad to agree to it, buying tickets, booking hotels and him not reneging at the last minute are all a blur. But there we all were: Dad and his latest girlfriend; me, my husband and our 9-month-old son; and my sister and her boyfriend. OK, so we'd arrived on different flights and were staying in different hotels, but still, nominally, this was a family trip and a remarkable event given our family dynamics, or lack of them. Three cold, wet days stretched before us to visit the remnants of his childhood. In some ways, the places we visited and the stories he recounted over those following days had little meaning for me. They were largely the familiar 'safe' tales, and most of the buildings had disappeared or changed over the years. It felt a little like my father was a tour guide delivering the Heinz Kuhe Vienna Tour: it was impossible to see the connection – particularly an emotional one – between the man and the boy. Only on one occasion did I see his face light up as he described how he'd save his Groschen to buy *Bratwurst* [seasoned sausage] each weekend from his favourite stall at the Karmelitermarkt, just around the corner from his home in Ferdinandstraße. It was a rare moment of unguarded reminiscence. Aside from this, what was extraordinary was the simple fact of spending three days with my father – the longest time by far we'd spent together in decades – and observing close up the dynamics of his relationship with his girlfriend, with us, and his interactions with those around us, all of which threw an uncomfortable light on my fantasy of him.

He insisted on staying in the best hotel in Vienna to impress and placate his girlfriend, despite living in council-run sheltered accommodation while paying off debts through a court order of £1 per week. It was as if he were back on the Costa del Sol with his gangster friends and their fast cars and yachts, playing the Big Shot by keeping one step ahead of the debt collectors. The rest of us stayed in budget hotels nearby. His legendary generosity was ill-judged and indiscriminate, a desperate attempt to please and impress the person in front of him. He said one thing to one of us and the complete opposite to another five minutes later, pandering to each of us to avoid any form of conflict and smooth his path through this difficult reunion. Our time together was rationed, as he had to take his girlfriend designer-brand shopping in the fashionable Goldenes Quartier. My sister, who'd flown over from Israel for these few precious days, was particularly upset, leading to an angry confrontation in the hotel restaurant on our last day together. She shouted, cried and smashed crockery. My father attempted to pacify her; winked as if to reassure the waiters; tried simultaneously to placate his girlfriend; and floundered in the impossible task of pleasing them both while retaining his good-guy image. Looking on, it was as if the decades had been seamlessly swallowed up, the drab grey prison walls replaced by more opulent surroundings, my mother by my sister, but other than these incidentals nothing had changed. At that moment it dawned on me that nothing about our family dynamics ever would or could change.

However, what the trip did do was change my internal narrative and expectations. While Vienna hadn't brought me and my father any closer, it had clearly exposed this small, vulnerable 13-year-old boy trying desperately to say the right thing, to hide his terrifying insecurity, to fill the silences with noise and to succeed in what he saw as his role in keeping everything together. It had revealed a man who, for all his frequent insistence on the power of love, especially that for his children, was clearly incapable of understanding the true meaning of the emotion and the responsibilities that come with it. His calmness and equanimity stemmed from a complete absence rather than from wisdom and compassion. He was not selfless but self-less. His long absences in prison had helped keep him at arm's length; and its walls had, brick by brick, propped up the illusion of a lovingly devoted and heroic father unjustly locked behind them.

The trip blew apart the fantasy and revealed to me that this storyline was no longer supporting me in adulthood, even if I'd needed it in childhood. Finally, I could see the reality and end the pretence that my father was worth idolizing. I realized that the burden of history was simply too great for him to be a father in any normal sense of the word. He was a shadow who'd emerged from the darkness of Nazi persecution – a fictional character with a fictional name. The Heinz Kuhe/Henry Kennedy timeline had been snapped in two somewhere between Vienna and Harwich in 1938 and was now two completely separate entities.

The impact of the trip continued to reverberate in the months and years following. I saw how I'd always played a bit part in my father's life and how this pattern had become the blueprint for most of my relationships. I'd left the literal and metaphorical wreckage of my home and my mother as soon as I could. Aged 15, I applied for and secured a scholarship to Mill Hill School as a boarder. Unfortunately, I didn't take to institutional life as well as my father had, not helped by being one of only a handful of sixth-form girls in a boys' boarding school and having come from the local comprehensive system under the assisted place scheme. I didn't understand the public-school etiquette, nor was I ready emotionally for relationships with boys. I was a fish out of water and very unhappy. Following an incident during my return home for the Christmas holidays that resulted in me receiving a black eye, the Headmaster of Mill Hill and his family took me in for protection. I was to live with them for the remainder of my school years. It was an act of kindness for which I will be forever grateful. I didn't return home again or see my mother for many years.

After school, I moved on to Bristol University, where I continued the fish-out-of-water theme, unable to find my 'tribe'. Like my father, I fitted in everywhere and nowhere at the same time. My sister, living alone in London, suffered from depression and a string of illnesses – no doubt fallout from our childhood experiences – so I spent as many weekends and holidays as I could hitching up to London to care for her. Meanwhile, in Marbella, my father was picking up his latest girlfriend, with whom he had a child at the age of 65. I seldom saw him, and for all his words, he showed little actual interest in my sister or me.

His legacy haunted me in the workplace too. His get-rich-quick and only-mugs-work-in-offices-all-their-lives sermons meant I left jobs at the drop of a hat. If the sun was shining, I simply didn't turn up for work. In retrospect, I can see how the notion of planning ahead became anathema to my father when his world disappeared overnight, but it was anachronistic advice to pass on to me. Unfortunately, I took this advice to heart, and it was further reinforced by my own experience of him vanishing overnight for years at a time and my world crashing down in a few brief moments. We both lived by the creed of eat-dessert-first.

My life rolled on, I met my husband, we lived together for a while, got married and had a son. I don't mean to diminish any of these momentous life experiences. I remain to this day happily married, and our son Felix is a wonderful, intelligent, sensitive young man. But, with hindsight, I'd say I didn't thrive in any of these circumstances – more survived them.

A period when I do feel I thrived was when for several years I taught refugees English for Westminster City Council. I immediately felt a bond with my students, who were rootless and far from home. I felt a strong sense of belonging among them. Another time I felt part of something bigger than myself was when, living in North London, I discovered the second-generation community. The commonality of conditions and experiences was striking, and some of my seemingly obscure and illogical feelings and fears suddenly made some sense. To be among people with a shared under-standing was a huge relief. I discovered that none of us took anything for granted, and that while underlying fear was our persistent shadow emotion, even this fear had to remain unacknowledged and unvoiced in the face of our parents' far greater and 'legitimate' suffering. However successful we were by society's norms, we tended to judge ourselves harshly, living with the constant dread of failure and the fear of not being good enough. At the end of each academic year, I would be newly astounded when my students, instead of failing their exams, passed with flying colours and I was not sacked on the spot but lived on to teach another year. Discovering that this was a shared sentiment even for the most highly qualified in the group was a normalizing yet sad reminder that it wasn't just me, with my own specific legacy of sudden truncation and trauma, who felt disoriented and provisional.

Something else we had in common was a fear of groups and, perhaps unsurprisingly, a fear of authority figures and a distrust of people in general. One of my father's rare reminiscences from his childhood described how the very same neighbours who'd regularly taken him in while his mother worked late in her shop formed part of the jeering mob as she was made to scrub the street in front of their block of flats. After such knowledge, it's hard to regard others with the same open trust or belief in humankind's essential goodness. Add to this my mother's violence and instability and you have a perfect storm for fear, shame and hypervigilance – a toxic cocktail of emotions from which I'm still attempting to heal. To give myself the illusion of safety, I live largely by excessive control and manipulation; by constant busyness and distraction, or, alternatively, by chronic procrastination bordering on paralysis. Any person or situation that might trigger unwelcome feelings I simply avoid or, failing that, I repress my feelings by persuading myself that things aren't so bad. This habit started in early childhood when I found and cut out a harrowing image from a newspaper and stuck it to my bedroom wall. Whenever my feelings threatened to overwhelm me, I'd kneel before the photo of The Girl running from the napalm bomb, or Kim Phuc as I now know she's called. I'd no idea back then that the photo was famous or that this graphic depiction had helped to bring about the end of the Vietnam War. All that mattered to me then was that her suffering was worse than mine, so I skilfully used her to shield me from my own reality, which paled into insignificance by comparison. I still had the skin on my back, so I should quit complaining or crying. And so, day by day, year by year, I learnt to minimize and deny my feelings until I became a stranger to myself.

Even today, I still struggle to have a relationship with myself, particularly a caring and loving one. I've tried therapy, mindfulness and various self-compassion and loving-kindness practices. I've trained as a yoga teacher and moved to Devon to be closer to Gaia House, a meditation centre in the Buddhist tradition. All have been useful tools for which I'm incredibly grateful and from which, to a degree, I've benefitted. However, with hindsight, I recognize that for many years I was largely using meditation as yet another way to bypass the whole tricky arena of my emotions, my 'self' and my pretty much non-existent relationship to it. I brought to my practice the ingrained patterns of self-criticism and the not-good-enough self, and further reinforced them. This wasn't the fault of Buddhism, but the way I approached it, with unresolved trauma and insufficient guidance.

Slowly, however, with the benefit of time and some skilled Buddhist teachers, this dissociation is beginning to heal. I no longer use meditation and other practices as defences against the self, but as a coming home to wholeness. I used to need films or books or the plight of others to access my emotions. Now I'm learning to feel directly and to converse with the frightened young child who resides within me. I would have loved my father to have had this same opportunity to converse with his younger self, instead of always needing to live one step removed from himself. But I've also come to respect that healing comes in its own time and at its own pace. That my father succeeded in creating a life for himself, however unconventional, I am happy and grateful.

Since my father's death in 2018, I've been able to more fully immerse myself in the painstaking journey of reclaiming my personhood. Finally, for example, I feel able to call my father's mother my grandmother. Prior to this, such a naming would have felt like a gross misappropriation of his suffering. Stating that my grandmother was murdered in Auschwitz feels vastly different from the previously distanced 'my father lost his mother'. Coming slowly back to life, to my life, there has been pain and sorrow, as well as joy and a host of questions. One I've still not resolved is the question regarding how much my father's early trauma from the Holocaust explains the decisions he made throughout his life, but thankfully it's mostly lost its compulsion. Now, in my 50s, I've come to appreciate my father as both villain and victim, saint and sinner, and plenty more besides. And to love

Figure 3.1. Tina with her father (Photo taken by Tina's husband Richard Dennison).

him as the flawed individual he truly was instead of the character he tried to be and in whom I'd believed. He wasn't worthy of my worship, but he was deserving of my love. I've also come to acknowledge that, even with a generation's breathing space, I have many of the same character traits my father displayed, even if they haven't landed me in the same deep water. Perhaps I'm more of my father's daughter than I realize ... and maybe she's not such a bad person to be after all.

4 Faraway country, faraway time?

We arrived in Bratislava exactly eleven years to the day before my mother was to die. Its opening moments did not bode well for a trip she had been so reluctantly persuaded to take. She had hardly stepped back on Slovak soil after forty-eight years away when I turned aside for one minute and she tripped over an unseen black step and fell, as if in slow motion, but I was too far away to catch her. Blood. On her head, down her cheek, over her yellow jumper (yellow!). All my anxieties about shepherding her safely through a dangerous journey, and her anxieties about returning 'home', were made manifest in that moment.

The hospital was deserted and straight out of film noir: gloomy corridors, crumbling patient trolleys, poor lighting. The doctor who finally took an x-ray told her sadly: it wasn't like this forty or fifty years ago. Fortunately, the blow to the head was nothing serious, but the visit to the hospital, where she had started training as a doctor in 1946, may have caused her to reflect on how the loss of her Slovak medical career had perhaps been no bad thing.

My mother, then called Eva Rottensteinova, had left Slovakia for good in 1949, not because of the Nazis but because of the communists. They had furnished the final blow to her ambition of becoming a doctor like her father, who had escaped, alone, to England in 1938 on the back of a visa scheme offered by Britain to 200 Czechoslovak Jewish medics. After nearly two years on the course at Comenius University, in Bratislava, she was kicked out. In the eyes of the new communist regime, her father was bourgeois and a traitor to the country. This was the final insult after her experience of the Shoah, which she had narrowly survived in hiding in Hungary with her mother from 1942 to 1945. Others, like her aunt, grandparents and many members of the extended family, did not make it through.

Her aunt, Margaret Kreisler, known also as Margit or Mansi, was amongst the first batch to be rounded up in Slovakia, one of a thousand unmarried women who were deported to Auschwitz in Spring 1942 and of whom only a couple of hundred survived. On the way there Margit took a small but decisive act of heroism that probably saved my mother's life, and therefore ultimately mine too. A smoker, she wrote "Don't Follow" on her cigarette packet, added her parents' address and flung it out of the window. Quite extraordinarily, and thanks to an unknown helper who picked up and posted the packet, this warning did arrive home. Margit herself though could not be saved, and she was killed in Auschwitz a few weeks later, aged 38.

In 1949 my mother and grandmother moved to London. Eva was unable to resume her medical studies and took work far below her intellectual abilities. After meeting and marrying my father, himself a Jewish Slovak refugee (though from before the War), they had me, their only child, and moved from Bayswater to South London. Despite this unusual trajectory, which took so many Jewish survivors to Swiss Cottage, Hampstead, Golders Green, they managed to find their tribe in a neighbourhood less popular with Continental Jews.

In my childhood, everyone around my family seemed to be an émigré from Germany, Austria, Czechoslovakia, or Hungary. A heavy central European accent in the elderly was the norm. This went unquestioned by me: it was just how things were. Multiple languages were spoken in phone calls or over coffee and cake, though none of them directly to me. Despite the central European atmosphere my parents wanted me to be an English girl, a fresh start – but from what?

Until my late 20s I hadn't given much thought to why my family felt different to those of my school friends in suburban Wimbledon. From my mother's kitchen sprang Rigó Jancsi, Dobos Torte, Pozsonyi Kifli. She was an excellent pâtissière. She and my grandmother, wearing headscarves to protect their shampoo-and-sets from the steam, laboured for a long day each Autumn to produce yeast pastries for breaking the Yom Kippur fast. Battenburg cake or Jammy Dodgers were things unknown.

In 1988 I went to the Ruach Conference in Leeds, billed as 'The First Gathering of the Alternative Jewish Network'. One of the alternative subgroups that got together there was for the second generation; that was the first time I had come across that term. I think all of us at that session experienced something of a revelation. "You mean I'm not the only person whose parents lower their voices when saying 'Jewish'? Who need to be telephoned daily?" From this, and the ensuing affinity group, my 'Holocaust journey' took me to Gaby Glassman's twelve-week course for children of survivors, second generation conferences and lots of reading.

I did not share much of this second-generation journey with my mother. As always, I was afraid of upsetting her, by implying that I was burdened by the legacy she had laid on me. The mythology of my childhood was that it had been untroubled. Unlike her, I had not lived through life-threatening anti-Semitism, I had not lost my education to Hitler – what problems could I possibly have had?

I joined the Second Generation Network. Its journal, *Second Generation Voices*, often featured an article by a 'child' who had undertaken a 'roots tour' back to the old country. Until then I had never thought of going back, and not only because travel in Slovakia was impenetrably difficult pre-1993 when 'Czecho' split from Slovakia. For me it had been unimaginable that I could actually go back there; it was locked faraway in time and in space. But now the possibility arose. A WIZO (Women's International Zionist Organization) group was travelling to Poland in May 1997. It was to be headed by the founder and then Director of the Beth Shalom Holocaust Centre in Nottinghamshire, Dr Stephen Smith, and co-led by survivor Arek Hersh. I suggested it to my mother. Auschwitz had been the final destination of not only Margit but my mother's grandparents, my paternal aunt and others. It was time to visit. And we could then piggyback onto this a visit to her hometown, Brezno, to my father's hometown, Zlaté Moravce, and of course to Bratislava, where she was born and had briefly been a medical student. My mother herself was not initially keen on going on the 'roots' part of the trip though she felt an obligation to see Auschwitz.

I don't think I would have undertaken such a trip on my own. What would be the point? The point was to go together, to pull that unreachable past into the present. My hope was that coming right up against the scenes of her youth would trigger memories in my mother and that the experience would create a new bond between us. I would finally be able to winkle those stories out of her, to make it impossible for her to wriggle out of telling me about it all, properly. No more "Oh, you know that story", "Oh, I've told you that so many times already." Even if she had, the defensive emotional blocking so many of us of the second generation recognize, meant that I had always found it hard to focus on or to retain that information. Perhaps now the drops of family history that had come my way over the years would finally coalesce into a puddle.

Back in 1997 the Internet wasn't yet 'a thing'. This partly explains why I was not going armed with the names of local contacts to meet, addresses of family properties, locations of gravestones etc. My goals were vague – just visits to the towns associated with my parents' pre-war lives. Perhaps I was yet again the rabbit in the Holocaust headlights, unable to look that glare in the face.

On the trip I kept a journal.

Bratislava does not seem to have been upgraded or even, in some cases, cleaned since the war. Everything is shabby, behind Western Europe, its people unfriendly. The hotel is a faded simulacrum of Western luxury – the Swedish-style black leather armchairs in the lobby are cracked, with worn-away arms, the whole place is slightly 'off'. A classic piece of seventies architecture and interior design, down to the orange flip-top bin and orange patterned curtains. Even velvet padded walls in the lift. Lots of glass and bronze and decaying tubular statuary in the car park.

I'm totally dependent on her for the language. I'm pleased and proud of her being multilingual though feel infantilized and stupid for my muteness. Do people wonder why she speaks Slovak, and I don't? There's something of a parallel here with her time in hiding in Hungary dependent on her mother for communication. Even though there was no Nazi threat this time, I have been wearing my *Magen David* [Star of David] inside my shirt from Vienna onwards. My mood varies between childish pleasure and thrill, anxiety, fear, deadness.

"I wouldn't have come back here for anyone except you", she said on the border.

We wanted to go to the Bratislava Jewish Museum to buy a copy of the Shoah autobiography written by my paternal aunt, Klara Chlámtáčová, who not only experienced a long imprisonment in Theresienstadt but gave birth there. Her daughter survived, extremely against the odds, and she herself died in Israel only in September 2020, at the age of 99.

Having failed to find the synagogue we attempt to go by taxi to the Jewish Museum. Our taxi driver has to consult with two others as to its whereabouts. Eventually he does take us to Zidovská Ulice (Jewish Street), now *Judenrein* [Free of Jews] and suspended above a new, fast road since the days any actual Jews lived there. The museum is unpleasantly close to what Hitler intended – a record of a vanished race – vanished locally, at any rate. Immediately on arrival we buy my aunt's Holocaust autobiography, on display right there on the ticket desk, though the man isn't overawed by being told the purchaser is Klara's sister-in-law. The museum includes the documents of March 1942 ordering the deportation of Slovakia's Jews. That's one month before my mother and her mother left.

We left Bratislava in our hired car, with me doing all the driving on mercifully empty roads. First stop on the road tour was Zlaté Moravce. This was the town in which my father grew up, and strangely, coincidentally where my mother spent many summers staying with favourite cousins. Her future husband's family were well-known in the town, and she knew of them, but never knowingly met him then. Seeing the road sign was a surreal but exciting moment. And particularly poignant because I couldn't share it with my father anymore. He had died seventeen years earlier.

Driving into the village from the main road feels promising. It looks like the 1930s. Small old low-key homes behind metal chain-link fencing, even two men scything the grass! Once in the pretty yet somehow unremarkable town centre, I press my mother to accost old ladies. After a few missed opportunities she suddenly addresses an old woman whom I hadn't seen hove into view. She was wearing black from head to toe (there must be a shop that stocks these items specifically). After drawing blanks on the names Csato (my grandfather) and trying Weisz (my grandmother), she remembers. Yes, the Weisz store, it sold general goods. Her mother used to shop there; she was just a small girl. My mother tells her that I am their granddaughter. No evident reaction. As she leaves, she says, "They were Jews."

We set off in search of the location of this store. We are walking down the road past the river and I'm taking a shot of the apartment block we guess is the spot when two women point out an old woman calling to us – it's our informant again. "No, not that place – past the main road." So on to the next swathe of crumbling Stalinist tower blocks. I take more meaningless pictures of yellow towers and collect a stone (rather than leaving one). People look at me strangely, not for the first or last time. My mother isn't interested in coming all the way: she waits on a bench till I've finished, saying, "I'm really surprised at you."

Finally, we arrived in Brezno. This was my mother's hometown aged 5–15, at which point in 1942 she and her mother escaped cross-country to Hungary, reluctantly leaving the grandparents to their fate. It felt quite extraordinary just to be able to drive right up to it and realize it had been here all along, all those years, and not vanished into a puff of smoke the moment she left it. It was for real! It did not just live in stories reluctantly handed over in incomplete fragments. And yet this strange place also had nothing to do with her, me, or our lives today. We whisked through the town square and on to the very distant-seeming Hotel Partizán up in the hills. As so often in Slovakia, a spectacular view of mountains and fir trees spooled out, the air sweet and forest-scented. Suitcases dumped, we dashed back down to catch one hour in Brezno and the past before the darkness chased us back to the safety of our hotel in the 'now'. Amazingly, my mother found her street, Kuzmanyho Ulica, immediately, leading off from the town square, and their building was still there – their stationery shop on the ground floor, their apartment above it. I've since seen this building featured in a coffee-table photo book about Brezno (yes, there is such a thing). I imagine it didn't face a lot of competition for inclusion. My mother, though, was disappointed with that yellow and brown building. It felt smaller and less imposing than she remembered.

She refused to pose for more than one shot with the building behind her. And it never occurred to me to ask her to take a photo of me in front of it, either. Was it not my family history, too? This was the time for memories to be triggered and questions asked. But communication did not flow. It was disablingly difficult for me to ask her questions about anything, although the odd new family story slipped out under the pressure of this emotionally intense encounter. She would not have been willing to be interviewed on tape about her responses, so I tried doing this surreptitiously and took notes later. She remembered going to the 'Neolog' synagogue, a non-Orthodox, modernist form of Judaism initiated in Hungary, only a block or so away, carrying her grandpa's tallit. Moving over there from the house, we found that it still existed as a structure despite its Jews having gone. Visiting hours were over but we peeked in through a side window – now it was just a hall with a skeletal balcony, no furniture at all but the basic remains of the Ark, where the Torah scrolls had been kept. We followed this up with a walk round some of the square, past what had once been all Jewish-run shops and the statue of Slovak politician Milan Stefanik under which the class used to picnic every 4 May. It was all grass then, she said. Leaving town, we drove past what I guessed might have been her primary school, as the road was *Školská* [School Street] but the building had no name and my mother didn't recognize it. Anyway, by this time she'd had enough. Her willingness to engage was running out.

A day later we drove across the border into Poland to rendezvous with the WIZO group in Kraków, and then on with them to Auschwitz.

Again, I was struck by the discordance of the present banging up against the past. Arriving by coach, we crossed streams of Poles cycling, driving or walking to church past the gate. The houses just down the road nonchalantly sported flowerbeds and allotments. Auschwitz-Birkenau itself was deserted. Around the barracks and railway lines, and the infamous entry gate, it was all grass and wildflowers and birds. The presence of Arek, who himself had been a prisoner in Auschwitz, brought the reality of what had happened into that moment. It was an honour to be there with him and Stephen. Each of those two had their differing but exceptional insights into that tragedy, and each were people of absolute integrity. Our group stopped to say Kaddish at the Ash Pond, into which were dumped the ashes of many of the many thousands incinerated at *Krematorium IV*. For us two it was finally a graveside Kaddish for my mother's aunt, grandparents and sister-in-law, a chance to leave a stone for each of them to show them we had been. It felt like a completion and a necessity.

Poland seemed like a graveyard. It left a bad taste in my mouth. Our visit had, sadly, preceded the renewal of life and energy in the Polish Jewish community that is so much more evident today.

Days later, descending through the clouds into London, I felt some sense of relief at our both being still alive and back in England. Soon after I returned to my flat, I called my mother. She said that having gone 'home', that chapter was now over. Despite her initial reluctance, she was pleased to have gone – and pleased to have returned. As was I. Four months later she was to have a stroke that disabled her body but fortunately not her mind, put her in a wheelchair for the last eleven years of her life, and that would have made such a trip virtually impossible. Unwittingly I had taken her there in the nick of time.

There were a few other anecdotes that she told me in the couple of weeks that followed, memories that had been triggered by the visit. She reiterated that it was a good thing to have done. The matter had been put to bed, so to speak, and it stayed there, in effect, for ever. Her stroke felled all else around it and occupied all her and my energies, putting a final stop to almost anything apart from dealing with the here and now. I too went into Holocaust dormancy.

Four years before our trip, my mother had been interviewed for a Holocaust testimony project run by Yale University and the British Library. I had been enormously relieved that a stranger had been able to get some of the stories down on tape and secured for the future in a way I would not have been able to do. The three videotapes containing nearly two and a half hours of interview sat around in a drawer, first hers and then mine, uselessly. Twenty years later I happened to meet Helen Stone who had turned the Spielberg testimony tapes of her mother, who came to Britain on a domestic visa, into an educational audio-visual package. She had recently co-founded Generation 2 Generation, a charity to support members of the second and third generation who hold some form of testimony from a survivor relative to turn these into professional, high-quality, educational tools. Through many iterations, my three tapes became a forty-five-minute presentation that I have now delivered to a range of audiences, all of whom seem to find it moving and meaningful.

What would my mother make of this? Sometimes I feel guilty to be putting her on display like this without her permission, in a context she has no control over. But I have to assume that, by doing the recording in the first place, she has implicitly given permission for it to be used in the wider world. I even hope that she would be pleased, impressed and moved that I have taken the trouble to do this. She may have lost her hoped-for profession as a doctor, but I like to think that she might be a bit chuffed to be having a posthumous career as a Holocaust educator.

5 Living with humiliation: Reflections on a trip to Berlin with my father

In 2001, the city of Berlin invited my father as a former citizen for an official visit. The invitation didn't come out of the blue as I had organized it through some German colleagues to celebrate his 80th birthday. He was delighted, if a little nervous and could hardly believe that the city would really pay for his fare and accommodation.

My father had been a Jewish refugee from Berlin in 1936. He was 15 years old and had been given a place at an English boys' boarding school on the Isle of Wight. From the photo you can see how young he was, too young to travel completely alone into a strange country speaking little of the language.

Growing up, this was just something I knew but there was never any intimation about the detail of that journey or the emotional cost. Not long after I had made my first visit to Berlin in 1999, I had a dream. I was alone without money in Ostend and panicky about how to make the crossing over the channel. As I had never been to Ostend, it slowly dawned on me that I had dreamt my father's refugee experience of leaving Germany, so I wrote to him to check it out. He replied,

> Yes, I was quite alone travelling by train from Berlin via Cologne and Ostend in Belgium. I only remember snippets, such as getting a glimpse of the famous *Kölner Dom* [Cologne Cathedral] and actually speaking French to some Belgians in the same compartment and regretting that I knew so much less English. I can't remember anything much about how I got to Bembridge, but I think I was picked up in London and sent to Portsmouth by train, then by ferry steamer to Cowes on the Isle of Wight, then by the little local train to Bembridge. On my arrival, the only thing I remember are the words of welcome spoken by the headmaster who for some odd reason called himself 'the warden': "I hope you will be happy here."

Figure 5.1. Teresa's father, Lorenz von Sommaruga, as a 15-year-old before leaving Berlin in 1936 (From family collection).

Before making that first visit, my father had written me a list of 'must-sees' and afterwards, just to be sure that I had appreciated it, he wrote to check my reactions.

> The only impressions I had of East Berlin were first gained during my first visit in 1957 when there was no wall and later during visits to the *Museuminsel* and in particular the *Pergamonmuseum* which, I hope, you did not miss. I grew up very much in the west in Charlottenburg and Wilmersdorf. Friedrichstraße was about the farthest east I ever got, though I had visited the theatres and the *Staatsoper* nearby.

> Did you take a bit of time to visit the Berlin surroundings, Grunewald, Wannsee, the Havel River with its many lakes and islands easily explored by passenger boats? I hope you did, because it is there where Berliners get their *Erholung* [recovery or recreation] on weekends and this, in my opinion, makes Berlin one of the most pleasant cities to live. I can think of no other city where such landscapes are so easily available for

its citizens. All one needs is a short trip by U-Bahn or S-Bahn or even by bus and there you are *im jrünen* [in green nature] as Berliners put it in their own dialect.

So, two years later, I joined my father in Berlin for an action-packed fortnight. The first week was hosted by the city who organized various receptions and visits. The second week we stayed on so Dad could show me 'His Berlin' – the beloved city of his childhood. I took what I thought was this last opportunity to take in everything I could of my father's early life.

We stayed at the Kempinski Hotel just off Kurfürstendamm, the same venue that his mother had taken him for a special tea to celebrate passing his exams. It was still a very sumptuous hotel and although an exceptional treat gave some sense of the pressure his mother put on him to achieve at school.

Although not obvious at the time, the whole trip was to prove transformative for both of us.

Even though my father had visited Berlin many times before, mainly on business, he had not been back since the wall had come down and so he had never come across any of the new Shoah memorials built since then. Being with him in Berlin, enabled me to witness who he was in his own context, to encounter these memorials together and to disentangle his trauma and its impact on me. For the first time it was possible to see what I had not been able to see previously despite the fact that it had been staring me in the face all my life. The trip gave me a perspective that would not have been possible in any other place or time.

The first organized event was a reception at the *Berliner Rathaus* [Town Hall]. There, after the formal welcome from the mayor of Berlin we were treated to a group of school children singing German folksongs. My father started to cry as he remembered the words and quietly joined in. For some reason I had not expected that. I had never seen him sing before and never German folk songs.

The next day we were taken to the Jewish Cemetery at Weissensee. My father was quite sure the graves would have been wrecked by the Nazis, but despite being convinced there would be nothing worth seeing, we got on the bus along with everybody else. When we arrived, he was amazed to discover that the cemetery was still there just as he had remembered it. As we walked through the trees towards the grave, he muttered, "Even

with so much shit in the world there is still some decency!" We did find
my great-grandparents' grave. Even though the black granite headstone
was lying flat on the ground, it was fully intact. Afterwards my father had
the stone reinstated and I could really begin to believe that I had roots in
Berlin. Prior to that I had never seen any concrete evidence that related
me to this city. It was as though the grave had given me something solid
to stand on. The shame I had always felt about my multi-faceted heritage
started to lift. I could now see some of the generous legacy I had been given.
Perhaps I could embrace and celebrate it.

The next stop on our itinerary was the place of execution at Plötzensee.
This visit reminded me of memories, from my childhood, that my father
was very in touch with the various forms of ubiquitous terror that lurked
everywhere during the Nazi time and this place of horror brought it out of
the shadows. I knew that he was gratuitously beaten up on his walk to and
from school. I also knew that in 1935, after having heard so much singing
of anti-Semitic songs in Nazi-style morning assemblies, one day he joined
two other boys by walking out of the school assembly. By "putting himself outside of the community" in this way, he was forced to leave school.
This is the second verse of 'Volk ans Gewehr', [People to Arms] as he still
remembered it many years later. This is his translation.

> Many years have passed,
> The people were betrayed and lost,
> While traitors and Jews had won
> By demanding millions of victims.
> But then the people were given a leader
> Adolf Hitler who gave us back our freedom;
> People to arms. People to arms.

Eighteen months after being expelled from public school, my father was
to leave Germany. With no memories of Europe, none of this made any
sense to me growing up on the other side of the world in Aotearoa New
Zealand but I knew he was different to other fathers. His world seemed
to have a more intense hue. Nothing could be taken at face value. And
then, when you least expected it there were powerful reactions to what
seemed to me as a little girl, quite innocuous questions. "No, you cannot

join the Girl Guides!" In a strange reversal of history, I was removed from morning assemblies, after I came home from school saying, "Did you know Jesus was killed by the Jews!" Hearing a brass band or a mention of the Volkswagen brought similar volcanic eruptions.

Violence always hovered in the air, just as it must have done throughout my father's childhood. In a letter he wrote,

> The word *Schutzhaft* [protective detention] was a typical Goebbels euphemism, at that time applied to all those whom the Nazis imprisoned without any kind of trial. It was a cynical misuse of the law on protective custody which applied in cases where anyone was threatened by violence, usually from some vengeful criminal. The implied fiction was that the incarcerated person had to be protected from the 'wrath of the populace'.
>
> The Nazis had lots of code expressions like that. For instance, Goebbels labelled tales of Nazi atrocities which people would only tell with bated breath to very trusted friends and relations *Greuelmärchen* [atrocity fairy tales]. In the very early days from about April 1933 the terror started and the first concentration camps were created. If you were called on to be taken away it was usually about five in the morning and it could be the *Gestapo* or just some SA or some other trumped up "authority". You could then either rot there forever, or you could be released, or your family could receive a parcel COD (Cash on Delivery), with your ashes in it. The idea was that while it was a criminal offence to tell *Greuelmärchen*, they made darned sure that the population knew perfectly well what went on, so that they should have every opportunity to fear it. This is how terror works!

It is not an understatement to say that Plötzensee was gruesome. It was not a surprise although neither of us had known of its existence before. Here, various forms of brutal executions were employed by the Nazis that started in 1933 immediately after Hitler came to power. Initially they used an axe to decapitate prisoners. This was until 1936. Then from 1937, they used the guillotine and then the most horrific of all, on Hitler's orders from December 1942, an iron frame with eight iron hooks was installed to carry out a particularly dishonourable death by hanging. My Dad's reaction to the place was a strange mixture of revulsion and curious recognition. He knew this was what the Nazis were capable of. I could barely take it in but watching my father slowly realize what he had managed to escape was strangely comforting. No longer did I have to wonder alone about the kind of atmosphere he had grown up in. Now I could share this knowledge with him.

Rosenstraße was our next stop. This was where 2,000 Jewish men, married to non-Jewish women, had been subjected to an early-morning round-up by the *Gestapo*, [Secret State Police] and the *Waffen-SS*, [the military branch of the Nazi Party's SS organization] and the police in February 1943. After being rounded up the men were imprisoned in Rosenstraße for two weeks while their non-Jewish wives and relatives gathered in front of the building, brought food and demanded their release. Each day the police drove the women away, but each day they reassembled with increased numbers. Eventually the men were released and put to work in Jewish institutions.

I watched my father stand in front of the memorial at Rosenstraße and read the German text. Then I noticed that he had started to translate it into English on sight for those who were unable to read German. In this moment, I see my father looking completely at home. It is the first time I have ever seen him not looking like a fish out of water. I reflect, "Of course, Germany had been his home. German was his mother tongue!" He even added ironic asides, which led me to remember his whimsical love of the language. He always had a ready supply of limericks, Jewish jokes and quotes from the nonsense poems of Christian Morgenstern, which he thought were completely untranslatable into English, but he nevertheless persisted in reciting them 'at the drop of a hat' and translating them into English all the while explaining all the unique and amusing Morgenstern-made-up words.

The first of two transformative moments that week was at the Mahnmal in Levetzowstraße, the Memorial to the Transports to Auschwitz from Berlin. To explain the word, *Mahnmal*. It is used here in contrast to *Denkmal* as it is an evocative word in German, saved for monuments of tragic events that should never happen again. Standing together looking up at the huge steel sheet with cut-out dates and numbers, my father suddenly and quietly said, "I have just realized something, if I had not left when I did, I would not be here now. Neither would you. It's quite a thought isn't it!" He had recovered an unthought known (Bollas, 2018). A new consciousness of a terrible thought he had always unconsciously known about had

Figure 5.2. Levetzowstraße Mahnmal [Memorial to transports leaving for Auschwitz from Berlin] (Photo taken by Ceci Epstein).

dawned. Not only was he no longer living in the city where he had grown up, but before this moment, he had not been able to allow himself to imagine what might have happened to him if he had not left Berlin when he did. By moving to the other side of the world he had ensured that his life would provide few reminders. The idea that he might have been murdered in Auschwitz had apparently not occurred to him before.

He had avoided that fate by escaping to England but refuge there was not to last long. After four years studying and trying to work, my father was classified as an Enemy Alien by the British government. In June 1940 at the age of 19, he had the infamous experience of being interned on the Dunera to Australia. This was one experience he could never talk about. It took me many years to understand why.

In early 2000, I was in Melbourne and bought a copy of Bartrop and Eisen's book, *The Dunera Affair: A Documentary Resource Book*. On the dust jacket it says,

> These victims of Hitler's pre-war persecution (most of whom were Jews), were re-victimized through internment during Britain's invasion scare of 1940, then shipped out of the country in appallingly crowded and unsanitary conditions, as well as in the care of brutal military guards who pilfered and destroyed their precious personal belongings. On arrival in Australia, the majority were sent to Hay, into extreme heat and to an alien treeless landscape. Later – doctors, lawyers, businessmen and academics included – were enlisted to pick fruit or work on the waterfront.

I was very pleased to have found this book as it documented the experience and I naïvely took it to my father to read. His response was not as welcoming as I had hoped. "At my age I have decided that I don't have to do anything that I don't want to." I agreed. With the pressure off, he suggested I leave the book with him while he thought about it. Three weeks later, he held it out in a small carrier bag barely touching the handles, as though it would contaminate him, saying, "I don't want to read it. You know we were not so well behaved either!" and with that, he pushed me out the door. I stumbled out overwhelmed with sadness. As I sat in my car and burst into tears at first not understanding what had just happened, the light dawned. This experience was my first conscious recognition of transgenerational transmission of trauma. As the unwitting bearer of the unbearable I was pushed out of sight in the same way as the unbearable had always been pushed out of my father's consciousness. In this flash of a moment this unbearable pain was transmitted to me. I have no doubt that this kind of transmission happened many times while growing up but then I had no idea where all the feelings that often flooded me came from.

The whole experience of internment by a government that he thought had offered him safe refuge had shocked him more than I realized. After his death, I discovered copious notes, diaries and letters he had written documenting the experience and the injustice of it all. I was so excited to have what turned out to be a beautifully written gift and in it discovering his concern for justice. Transcribing his pencil notes has enabled me to learn about his sensitivity and to continue mourning his loss.

It was his internment in Australia that led to our eventual emigration to Aotearoa New Zealand. On his way back, he had seen 'the land of the long white cloud' from the sea. It was love at first sight. After the war and to get as far away as possible from Europe, we emigrated to 'God's Own' as a family. There he found safe refuge at last! He wanted to forget and start afresh though, in the background, there was always a haunting shadow I could not really fathom.

The second transformative moment in Berlin occurred on the last day when we were invited to the *Deutsches Bundestag* [German Government Building] for a formal meeting. There I heard him ask a question. He stood up as soon as the opportunity presented itself. With his voice trembling, he said,

> I have a question about the Common Agricultural Policy. Do you think there is any chance that the Common Agricultural Policy will be more attuned to the general tendency throughout the world towards free trade? See, I come from New Zealand, which is a country which is completely free trade. We have an agriculture which is in no way subsidized and has to stand on its own feet. We see that here in Europe, people and sometimes large firms who call themselves peasants get very heavily subsidized not just to grow food for their own needs but to grow large quantities of excess food, which they then sell at very low prices in the world market, which disturbs our trade and that of Australia, for instance Canada and other countries. Is there any chance that one of these days that these terrible borders around the EU will fall?

There was a ripple of applause. Noticing his nervousness, I pondered what this apparently simple question meant and why it was important to ask it in this context. What was the subtext?

After the question and almost overnight my dad became agitated and lost his pleasure. Suddenly his gratitude turned to frustrated anger! "Why do they have no air conditioning, horrible food, allow smoking in restaurants, crowds, bicycles and trams everywhere, narrow streets, dark rooms in this country?"

At the airport as he was leaving, he didn't turn around to wave goodbye. He just disappeared looking straight ahead. As I stood there watching him go, I felt distressed and alone, feeling I must have done something terribly wrong. "But what?" I wondered. Since then, I have gradually untangled what my father was coping with and what he had coped with for most of his life.

My father died in 2016. After this return to Berlin and until his death he constantly pondered his mixed feelings about Germany. He often talked with me about them. Why he wondered was he still wanting to read in German and about German history? Why his continuing love of rye bread with caraway seeds, salami and rollmops and yet ... he knew he could never go back there again, "It gives me the creeps!"

Before he died, ruminating yet again about his feelings, he told me two important things that he had never told me before. He said that as he was walking along Kurfürstendamm a cyclist shouted, "Get out of the way!" but what he heard was only, "Get out!". Over breakfast on another occasion, he told me, "I know it doesn't make sense, but I feel shame for not having been able to stop what happened."

These were two clues that, although they gave me some relief at the time, also gave me cause for puzzlement. I did not really understand what he was telling me. Many years later, I realized that Europe's Common Agricultural Policy resonated with his lingering feelings of being shut out, or as he would say, "chucked out" not only from the country of his birth but also the country of first refuge. Deep down, he could not expel the feeling that Europe did not want him. The visit had resurrected the powerful distress he felt about his expulsion from his beloved home, customs, language and food. The buried past had revealed itself in the present. Even going to the other side of the world, marrying a non-Jew, bringing up a new family and the passage of time had not fully insulated him from the pain now breaking through into his consciousness. But why did he feel shame? He knew it didn't make sense.

He had felt enormous gratitude at being invited to return to his city of birth, but the trip had collapsed the distance he had carefully placed between the new present he had constructed for himself in New Zealand and the past in Europe, putting him in touch with the long-buried pain of losing his home not once but twice. These feelings had never been given a name or even directly talked about. Now he tells me he feels shame. Was it shame or something much deeper that he had no words for? Perhaps it was humiliation, a feeling that is often misunderstood to mean something like embarrassment or even shame. It is much more than that. In both situations, he was subjected to an overwhelming and inexorable power that he could do nothing about. As Phil Leask (2013: 130), writer and researcher, based

at University College London, who writes on German history and literature, as well as on the meaning and significance of humiliation, suggests,

> humiliation is a demonstrative exercise of power against one or more persons, which
> consistently involves a number of elements: stripping of status; rejection or exclu-
> sion; unpredictability or arbitrariness; and a personal sense of injustice matched by
> the lack of any remedy for the injustice suffered. It is something actively done by one
> person to another, even if through institutions or directed in principle at groups. It
> is a demonstration of the capacity to use power with apparent impunity.

Leask further clarifies that as humiliation leads to a strong sense of having
been wronged by others, it should be distinguished from shame as that
involves the person alone having done wrong and diminishing to themselves. Feeling humiliated is so unbearable that it is often redefined as
shame, to "serve as an appropriate adaptive function that inhibits aggression or protects the individual from unnecessary personal exposure"
(Hartling and Luchetta, 1999: 263).

My puzzle about why my father should feel shame started to make
sense. It was a way of protecting himself from being reminded of the much
more powerful experience of being humiliated, not only as a result of his
refugee experiences but also by the shock of his internment. It was a way
of avoiding the rage of feeling powerless in the face of gross injustice, protecting himself from risking further humiliation. Now in retrospect, the
question on agricultural policy he posed in the Deutsches Bundestag to
the German government representative, was not only revealing, but also
intensely courageous! I wished I had understood it earlier.

Something profound has changed in me. Recently looking again at
a photo of my father accompanying me on my Wedding Day, I see for
the first time a proud and loving father. He no longer seems so remote as
I begin to understand the pain of humiliation he had carried with him
from not so long before I was born. I had always known about it but could
not give it a name until now. Making sense of his agitation, I realized that
the feeling left with me on his departure was another example of his unbearable trauma being transmitted into me. I began to realize that this was
how he had always felt, distressed and alone.

It is difficult as a child to make sense of growing up with a traumatized
parent. It can take a lifetime to disentangle how and who they are, volatile,

Figure 5.3. Teresa with her father on her wedding day in December 1963 (From family collection).

unpredictable, yet confusingly also intelligent, loving and thoughtful. The result is that I no longer carry his pain as if it were mine but instead, I can feel my own sadness for him.

Bibliography

Bartrop, P., with Eisen, G. (eds) (1990). *The Dunera Affair: A Documentary Resource Book*. Melbourne: Schwartz & Wilkinson with Jewish Museum of Australia.

Bollas, C. (2018). *The Shadow of the Object: Psychoanalysis of the Unthought Known*. Abingdon, Oxon: Routledge.

Hartling, L. M., and Luchetta, T. (1999). 'Humiliation: Assessing the Impact of Derision, Degradation, and Debasement', *Journal of Primary Prevention*, 19, 259–278.

Leask, P. (2013). 'Losing Trust in the World: Humiliation and its Consequences', *Psychodynamic Practice*, 19 (2), 129–142.

6 Mein shtetele Turek

Growing up with stories of a mythical place

I am very much a Londoner. I grew up in London and have lived there all my life. But like many people in London, my family originates from somewhere else, in my case Poland.

Both my parents were Polish Jewish refugees. My mother, Rose Marber nee Keh, arrived in London from Wiesbaden in Germany in July 1939 on a domestic visa when she was 18 years old. Her parents grew up in villages outside Dabrowa Tarnowska, a small town that is now in Southeast Poland. Their families had been peasant farmers.

My father, Kuba Marber, grew up in a small town called Turek, west of Warsaw and just off the road between Warsaw and Berlin. It had been in Russia before the First World War and became Poland on its independence in 1918. His father manufactured bed linen and towels. His mother's family were farmers, owning several large estates in the vicinity of the town. Kuba came to the UK (United Kingdom) with the Polish army in 1943 via Lithuania, the USSR, Japan, India, Palestine, Iraq and Libya. He was 22 years old.

As a family we lived a very Jewish life in an area of northwest London with a large Jewish population. My sister and brother went to Jewish secondary schools, we weren't allowed to write, watch TV or travel on the Sabbath or high holydays, we didn't go to school on Jewish festivals and attended a synagogue that was 100 metres down the road. My mother came from an Orthodox family. Her mother, who lived with us, had worn a *sheitel* [wig] in Germany.

I have visited my parents' hometowns and my mother's family villages several times now and each time there have been different very memorable experiences. Visits have been with family, friends doing family-related visits nearby and local people with an interest in Jewish life in their home area before the war. In this piece I will be focusing on the four visits to my father's hometown in Poland, Turek. The first was in 1977 during communist times, the last in 2012. Visits were always with others, twice together with my husband, Bernard, and twice with my father. On one of the journeys with my father we were accompanied by my sister Susan, and on the other by my son, Rupert.

As children my sister, brother and I grew up with stories of Turek and of my father's travels escaping his hometown after the German occupation. We heard less about what happened to his maternal grandparents, mother and sister, all murdered, and brother who survived during the Holocaust. Turek was a kind of mythical place. On the one hand it was associated with lively relationships with family and friends and feelings of happiness and childhood freedom. On the other, it evoked loss – family members who were 'not there' and buildings and a geographical location that were no longer accessible.

1977 culture shock

I find it difficult to explain why Bernard and I decided to visit Poland and Turek in 1977. I think it may have been to experience the country and town that my father and his family had loved. My father and, I think, probably many in his family, were great Polish patriots. Poland was re-established as a country only a couple of years before my father was born. One of his uncles had fought with the Polish cavalry in the Russo Polish war after the First World War. Another had been in a border cavalry regiment in the 1930s. My father was steeped in Polish history and literature.

Another possible reason why it is me rather than either of my siblings who feels the need to investigate my family's origins in Poland is that I was born relatively soon after the end of the Second World War at a time when the murder of Jews, including many family members, by the Nazis and collaborators from occupied countries across Europe was coming to light.

I was named after my grandmother, my father's mother, who was murdered in Bełżec, an extermination camp in Eastern Poland. I knew this from a young age. According to family members I also looked like her. This may be responsible for making me one of Wardi's (1992) memorial candles.

At the time of our visit to Turek in 1977 Bernard and I were the first members of my father's family to visit his hometown after the Second World War. Poland was behind the Iron Curtain and visiting required visas as well as exchange of currency for each of the days in the country. We had little money and travelled there in our Morris Minor. The steering wheel shook if it went faster than eighty kilometres an hour, so an uncomfortable and long journey.

The carburettor had to be adjusted for the petrol on sale in Poland. We spent nights mainly in campsites.

We arrived from Berlin on the road that went close to Turek and were greeted by two friends of my great aunt Tusia. She had kept in contact with them despite now living in Paris. Tusia had survived the war in hiding with another friend's mother after escaping the Warsaw Ghetto. Marisa and Eugenia showed us around the town. We saw the house on the main square where my father grew up as well as the houses lived in by both sets of his grandparents when in town, the school he went to, the main synagogue (now a cinema), the houses lived in by the shochet (slaughterer for Kosher meat) and the rabbi, the fire station (for some reason this was important) and the town hall where my grandfather had spent a lot of time as town councillor. We took many photos of the outsides of buildings but had no access to the insides. The photos found their way into the treasured possessions of my father and his surviving uncles, aunts and cousins in Israel, France, Belgium and the United States as well as into his brother's memoirs. It seemed that the town had changed little in appearance since late 1939.

One experience in particular felt very close to that of my family before the Second World War. We visited one of Tusia's friends in her room. This was in the house she had grown up in. After the war it had been divided into many units and she had been given one room. When my father lived in Turek there was no running water. The flat he grew up in was on the second floor. Water carriers came frequently to bring water to the kitchen. Being a water carrier was a job. The toilet was a privy in the backyard. This was shared with rats. I'm not sure how the water that made the tea we drank in Eugenia's room came to the kettle. It may have been drawn from a well. I did, manage to brave her privy – a very unusual experience for someone who had always lived in sewer-efficient and mains water connected suburban London.

We stayed one night in Turek and I don't remember feeling any great connection to the town or its people. Communication was difficult since we spoke no Polish and had to get by with broken German that I suspect the Poles we met spoke reluctantly. One encounter will live with me. We stayed the night in a guest house. It was early September and hot. The owner wore short sleeves. She had a number tattooed on her arm. When it came to paying, the guesthouse owner refused to take any money saying, with a lot of emotion, that she had never expected to see a Jew again and it was so wonderful having us in her house. We never asked her how she came to be in Auschwitz. On our return home we told my father the story and he was surprised. He recognized the guest house owner's family name and thought her brothers had been fascists. This was the first of two encounters with Polish people in the town who were not Jewish that indicated extreme hardships experienced during the Second World War. On a subsequent visit to Turek I met a friend of another of my father's aunts whose first husband had died in Auschwitz. Many Poles were sent to forced labour and concentration camps because they were thought by the Nazis to have been involved in helping Jews or in the resistance. As an example of this on one of the two visits with my father we walked around the church in the centre of the town and came across a plaque in memory of one of my father's friends. He had been executed with his brother for being in the Polish resistance.

Visits to post-communist Poland with my father

The next two visits, in 1997, with my sister, Susan, and in 2003, with my son, Rupert, were with my father. Both were post communism and involved us flying to Poland and renting a car. Being with my father meant not only that we were able to communicate with people and therefore find people who remembered his family or who had heard of him but also, we were able to experience the visit to some extent through his eyes. We went to places that were important to him. On the way we met many people who were helpful to us. Only a few are mentioned here.

There are many Polish Jews living outside Poland who have avoided returning. My father was very keen to return and very excited on the journey out and on arrival. It felt like he was experiencing a home coming.

In 1997 we approached Turek through the hamlet where my father's mother had grown up. My great-grandparents had lived in a farmhouse there and farmed land nearby. After they left it was discovered that below the surface was lignite, brown coal, that was accessed through open cast mines. The farmland and farmhouse no longer existed but we had arrived just before the final houses in the hamlet were evacuated and were able to talk to a man who lived there. He proved very excited by the fact that we came from the UK and knew about the channel tunnel in a lot of detail. My father was very impressed by his knowledge and interest saying that in his time people living in the hamlet had little connection with and knew little about the world outside. Life had moved on in a positive way. On the trip in 2003 we met a man in another village who as a young teenager had worked bringing in the harvest for my great-grandfather. He reminisced about how this was done and about his contact with my father's family. This meant a lot to my father as did the fact that the farmyards in the village looked the same as when he was a child, with long, crane-like structures for bringing up the water from the farmyard wells, chickens, ducks and tied up dogs.

A friend of my father, who then lived in Berlin and visited Turek frequently, arranged for us to meet a woman in the Turek Town Hall who was in charge of the archive. She brought out several photographs of people she thought were Jewish to see whether he could identify them. It may have been that there were few people left in the town whom she could call on for help but at the time it felt more like the town had been divided so there was little contact between Jews and Catholics and Protestants. Since only the Catholics and Protestants remained no one was able to identify the Jews in the photos. This made me feel uncomfortable. Very few Jews from the town survived the Second World War. It seemed like the memory of their existence as individuals had been erased. I realize that being remembered is important to me.

My father was given a copy of one photo to take away by the Turek archivist. It was of his sister and brother (twins) and their class at school. The archivist was also able to provide information on the flat my father grew up in on the Rynek, the town square. On both visits with my father, we were able to walk up the stairs to it on the second floor. To my disappointment, I was unable to see inside it on any of my four visits. On three of them it was visibly empty. The archivist informed us that it had been used by the Polish secret police as their local interrogation centre. By the time my husband and I went in 2012 the whole building had been turned into a *Galleria* [shopping centre]. We were there on a Sunday and it was shut.

Our visits to the second floor were via the back staircase, accessed from the backyard. In the backyard had been the privy. It had been turned into accommodation. My father, son and I were listening to my father reminiscing about the rats in the privy and how he and a friend from the flat below used to shoot them, when the woman who lived in the flat that had been the privy came out to find out who we were. Luckily, I don't think she understood English.

We were only able to access the inside of one flat lived in by a member of the family. My father, son and I were looking up at the flat on the main square that my father's maternal grandparents lived in when they came to town from the countryside. Below it was a shop selling denim clothing. The shop owner noticed us standing outside looking up and offered to ask the woman living in the flat whether we could visit. The woman came down from the flat and told my father that she thought she had some photos of his family and that we should come up and have a drink. I could tell my father was getting more and more agitated. We entered the flat and then left almost immediately. The photos and some of the furniture currently in the flat were left behind when his grandparents were resettled in Bochnia in southern Poland. They, and other local landowners irrespective of religion, were forcibly moved early in the German occupation so that their land could be confiscated to produce food for the Third Reich. The population

Figure 6.1. Elaine's father, Kuba, in the doorway of his grandparents' apartment building (Photo taken by Elaine's sister, Susan Devan 1997).

of the town they were sent to was mixed when they arrived but soon Jews were moved into a ghetto. In 1942 my father's grandparents, mother and sister were transported to the extermination site of Bełżec and murdered. We had probably met the person whose family had taken over his grandparents' home in town and their possessions. I have to admit that the full impact of this didn't hit me immediately. I had been more interested in the very beautiful, tiled stove in the living room. The reality of the situation would never have occurred to me at all if I had visited the flat with someone who, like me, had never been there before.

In the meantime, the shop owner had shut her shop and gone home to see her mother. She thought she recognized my father's maternal grandparents' surname, Szajniak. We had arranged to meet at a café up the road. A car drew up and a very elderly woman emerged carrying a tiny photo. It was of one of my father's aunts, Michal, who had emigrated to Palestine in the 1930s after her marriage. Before she left, she had given her best friend, a non-Jewish Pole, a photo. This best friend had kept the photo for over sixty years, through the Second World War and communist times and was sitting next to us. I was in tears.

Post-script: My visit in 2012

On my last visit to Turek, much had changed, not only in Turek itself, but also in the rest of Poland. One aspect of change has been the way in which communities and individuals have attempted to revive the memory of the Jewish past in Poland. Often this has been done through initiatives to restore and renovate Jewish cemeteries and synagogues.

I visited the site of the Turek Jewish cemetery on three occasions. The first time was in 1997 with my father and sister. It was set among relatively new houses on the edge of the town with no gravestones and high grass. What had happened to the gravestones? Their destiny came to light over several visits. In 1997 my father, sister and I visited Chełmno; the site of the first use of gas by the Nazis to murder Jews and Roma. Chełmno is not far from Turek. It has a very accessible communist era memorial. On the day we visited it had many visitors, as it was a traditional day for visiting cemeteries during Easter. A section of the memorial contained unbroken gravestones from the Turek cemetery. This felt good; reassuring in that the gravestones had been saved and were being seen by many people. By the time of my visit in 2012 the Turek Jewish cemetery site had been enclosed using funding by Jews from Turek who lived abroad including my father. Some gravestones that had been taken from the site and used to pave farmyards and build houses had been reclaimed and a memorial to the Jews of Turek had been built. Visits to other towns and villages across Poland have demonstrated this is relatively common practice. In some cases, it is the people of the town rather than Jews from abroad who have paid for and raised the memorial. To me this shows an affection and wish to remember that I value.

As previously mentioned, when we approached Turek in 1997 we drove through the hamlet where my father's mother had grown up. At the time, the hamlet was in the process of being demolished to make way for an open cast lignite mine. By the time my husband and I visited in 2012 the lignite was exhausted, and the scar left by the open cast mine had been filled with water to form a lake for leisure pursuits. This transition demonstrates among other things a post-communist focus that goes beyond work and home and mirrors in many respects that of Western European economies. Amazingly, those wind surfing on the lake kept their equipment in a ship container. This was marked with the logo for ZIM [a shipping line that originated in Israel] in Hebrew and Latin script. One of my father's cousins, who had frequently visited his grandparents in Turek, worked for ZIM in Israel for most of his working life. For some reason this felt very significant – like a circle had been completed.

My feelings for Turek now

I feel that through meeting people in the town of Turek and in the countryside nearby who knew something of my family I have found out more about their lives. This has been helped also by visiting places where they lived, shopped, worked and went to school. I was very lucky to have been able to visit with my father. His interests directed me to aspects of his life that were important to him and gave me an impression of the town from his perspective. Through him I was able to meet people with whom I would have been unable to communicate otherwise

However, Turek has changed a lot since my first visit. Change appears to have been most rapid after the fall of communism. The town I saw in 1977 was very recognizable to family who left in 1939. The central square has mostly the same buildings, but the overall feeling is more opulent and well-tended. The fields my family farmed have evolved from pasture to coal mine to leisure lake. It is not the same place that my family lived in. It has moved on.

I haven't come away with any feeling that Turek is my home. The place to me was about its people and there are different people living there now – it belongs to others. I belong in Britain with the people, sense of humour, architecture, countryside and values that, on the whole, I understand and love.

Bibliography

Wardi, D. (1992). *Memorial Candles: Children of the Holocaust*. Routledge: London.

7 The only house that was built for me

Train to Berlin

On the train to Berlin
I sit facing myself
awakening
in the previous century.
My grandmothers turn somersaults inside me.
In slow motion
the train spins on its axis
returning to the land of my forefathers
traveling backwards
on the journey of death
from Lowenberg to Elbing
the ground scattered with remains –
returning to the work camp
no one named, between the trees,
continuing to Stutthof,
stopping for a moment, moving on,
Bejji alights, sits down next to me, her face frozen,
continuing on to Birkenhau, Auschwitz,
stopping for a moment, moving on,
my young grandfather and grandmother alight,
their fur coats lined with gold coins in secret pockets,
they do not recognize me, sitting down on the bench facing me,
then Yehoshua and David, the children,
they see Mama Bejji, embrace briefly,
everyone polite, restrained,
the train continues, returning all the way
to beloved Oradea, everyone gets off at the last stop

and climbs onto the trucks in which they came, traveling to the pickup point
in the centre of town, the place where it began,
then everyone gets off, even the girl who was shot,
the one with the prosthetic,
and they walk home.

I blink hard. Reshuffle the dream cards. The house
is empty. The house is full of strangers, the house
is gone. I want to warn them, but I miss the truck. Miss
the stop. Everyone gets off, even the girl who was shot,
the one with the prosthetic,
and I continue to Berlin.

In my poem, *Train to Berlin*, I succeed in returning to the place where it
all began. But in the real world, my mother never wanted to go back to
where she came from. I can understand why. But for me, I feel there is a
sharp hiatus in my biography. I have a strong sense of identification with
my 'Mother', with what she had been through in her childhood and later,
during the Holocaust. In many situations in my life, I get a flashback as if
I suffer my mother's memory. One of those situations is described in the
next poem.

Legacy

For now I drag along
what was once my body
with the precision of a bad habit.
My limbs are shackled to a journey

of hunger, trailing behind
a faint shred of existence.
I do not notice the clouds
transmuting over my head

or know where I am going. Pain
is familiar to the soles of my feet

frostbitten and festering on
the burning shore of Tel Aviv.

For as long as I can remember, I felt very close to my 'Mother' and empathized with her unthinkable early life. I was unsure about my own life and who I was, so felt a need to discover more about her past. Without knowing that, I felt as if I had no identity of my own. I'm named after my grandmother who was murdered in Auschwitz and always felt a very strong linkage to my great-grandmother. We called her *Savta Pipike* at home. [Savta in Hebrew is grandmother. Pipike was her nickname]. Her real name was Rachel Rosa Rosenzweig. She was the grandmother of my mother, the mother of Judit, my grandmother, after whom I'm named. So, in a way, I was the daughter of Savta Pipike, because I was also called Judit. The Poem *Judit* describes my feelings about it.

Judit

I crystallized in the womb of my great grandma
and she almost gave birth to me.

Great Grandma Pipike was very wise
and lucky for me at the very moment
of birth
she came to her senses
and my grandmother emerged –
Judit
instead of me.

And when my mother was born
her mother wanted it to be me
but engrossed in other things, she erred
and part of me remained in there.
Wherever she went I went with her.
An educated woman, an activist
with a factory for corsets and bras

with twenty-five workers, all female,
she ordered the village cook to pack up the house
transfer all valuables to the summer lodge,
walking proudly, suitcase in hand,
boarding the train to Auschwitz.

My mother somehow survived
and when she arrived in Israel
I was born
for the third time –
Judit
and I did not know
if this was a sign that now
I must really be
me. Nor did my mother know
and just to be sure, named me after her own.[1]

And so, being folded into previous generations and having almost no identity, or name of my own, I had to ask my mother again and again to take me home, to where it all began. Until 1989, she always had some good excuses about why we should not go there. But once the government changed and one could enter Romania, there was no question. My mother had already been sick and I wanted to go there while she was still healthy enough to survive the journey. I wanted to get there, and it was important to get there with her beside me.

Luckily, my mother was an energetic person, who liked to travel. Despite everything she had been through, she was an optimist, and I could always trust her whenever I approached her with an idea. I did this again and again. And more importantly, she loved Budapest, where she had spent many vacations with her family in childhood. I had to put extra pressure on her by recruiting my brother and sister to help me convince her and at last she agreed to go to Budapest, with the three of us to show us the places she loved. Although she had finally agreed to the journey to Budapest, she had not yet agreed to the possibility of going on to her birth town and home place, Nagyvárad, now called Oradea, in Transylvania, Romania but, once

---

1   All poems in this chapter are written by Diti Ronen and translated by Joanna Chen.

we had arrived in Budapest, she agreed to consider the possibility of going there. This was important as this was where she had lived with her parents before the war next to all her aunts, uncles and siblings, and where her grandmother, Savta Pipike, had built a house for our family.

We booked the flight to Budapest, packed with a lot of good mood and there we were with my mother, my brother, my sister and me, going to Budapest. On the second day we went to the train station and checked if we could book a return ticket to Oradea, in Romania where grandmother's home had been. Yes, they said it is possible and there was no need to buy it in advance.

We had a very good time in Budapest and after a few days came the day of our trip to Oradea.

Everything on the way to Oradea was so weird that the only reaction we could muster to all the absurd situations we encountered was to laugh, partly because we were all so stressed and focused on the goal of the journey. The train was very, very old and very slow. We laughed. The first-class cabin we had booked had wide open windows that could not be closed and the bathroom had no door. We laughed. It was cold and a strong wind came through the windows. We hugged each other huddling up as close as possible to one another, covering ourselves with everything we had, and we laughed. The soldiers on the border, the long stop in the middle of nowhere on the way, the person who came and told us he could take us in his truck for five dollars (and we believed him and left the train with all our suitcases and followed him to the far road behind the train station, realizing it was a cattle truck with no chairs). Everything was funny. Even the taxi driver who took us from the train station in Oradea to the hotel, was drunk, singing loudly while driving with his eyes closed, and the hotel, the only one in the city those days, a very communist one, with a heavy smell of cigarettes and dark carpets everywhere, with a locked reception and our room with torn sheets and a broken window. Everything was weird and funny, and we laughed all the time.

The next morning, when we woke up, we realized we were on the bank of a beautiful wide river. The city was spread out in front of us with its beauty. I wanted my mother to point at some rooftops and say, "This is the Lună Church. This is the Reform Synagogue." But she recognized nothing. It was all very strange for her.

We were very excited. We had a photograph of the house that my great-grandmother had built in Oradea. It was a postcard, with the name of the family firm and my great-grandmother's name on the roof and above the front door.

Postcard of the house

Figure 7.1. Safta Pipike's House in Oradea (Postcard from the early twentieth century (From family collection)).

I had seen this postcard many times and had always imagined myself standing on its second-floor balcony. I was impressed by its tower, that goes up to its top at the street corner, with its round lotus ornament opening up at its base. It was covered with a beautiful *paluto* [decorative turret], engraved with delicate roses that still catch my eyes. The whole beauty of the house standing tall on a street corner, with the name of my great-grandmother on the roof, was a strong image that always haunted my heart and my soul as if implanted in my memory. It had carried the notion of a lost home.

My mother used to tell us how she loved being there, spending time with her grandmother, being with her grandfather and her young uncles. She told us about the *Magen David* [Star of David] on the front doors, and about the stone, which was buried under the entrance, the stone that was brought especially from Jerusalem.

We had a quick breakfast and left. Where were we? My mother didn't recognize the place. We walked along the river. She seemed to be lost. Nothing was familiar. I think now about what she had on her mind: all her childhood memories seemed to have disappeared. The roads that she used to walk along, all seemed to have been erased.

But then, at a certain moment, she saw a passage, the Passage. It was next to a great corner building, very beautifully decorated, with two wide entrances. She quickened her steps and we almost lost her. "Here", she said and pointed at one of the big shops, "This is where Bezi (her beloved aunt, who lost her two children in Auschwitz and then lost her mind and died in Stutthof) had her shop!" She ran into the passage, then passed through it to the other end. We followed her, breathless, trying to cope with her intensity. "Here", she said, "Look, this is where Bezi lived with her family, this is the balcony where I used to sit with the children", and she continued running, saying "Come, come, we are almost there", running between buildings, crossing back yards, "Come, come, I go home, come!"

The small path ended up in a road. She stood there, taking in some air, pointing at her home and said, "This is the window of my room." As the gate to the backyard was open, one could see the old elegance of the building. The gate wall was covered with many mailboxes. "We were only two families living in this building and look what's going on now!" … she said. We passed through the gate and entered the backyard. A few tenants opened their windows and looked out. My mother tried to tell them what she was doing there, but the windows were firmly shut again without reply. We felt unwanted and left.

At the exit, we turned right and only then did we see the beautiful orthodox synagogue, standing tall and wide, with its beautiful stained-glass windows, its inviting gate turned towards us. My mother knew exactly where she was. It had all come back to her. We went into the synagogue, touched the leftovers, the neglected beauty. Some prayer books were there. Some broken windows. It was very sad. We prayed and left.

We were all waiting for her to lead us to the house of her grandmother, the house that we used to see in the old city postcard, but she took her time now. She walked slowly, explaining to us where the border of the ghetto was, crossing the park, showing us where the gathering point was, the place from where they were taken by trucks to the train-transport to Auschwitz, the place where the guards shot the crippled girl who was unable to climb into the truck.

Then we went back to the main road. She was really into it. She knew exactly where she was, as if nothing had changed. We crossed the beautiful City Hall Square, passed the old building on our left, then we crossed the wide bridge with its engraved balustrade, and in front of us stood the big neoclassical State Theatre, that was designed in 1900 by Austrian architects Fellner and Helmer, who also designed the Vienna Opera House. "Here", she said, "The *paluto* house of Savta Pipike is just here, next to the State Theatre."

We went into *Teatrului Strada* [The road of the theatre] and there it was, huge in size, tall and wide, yet faded in its discolouring, surrounded by unpaved roads. Pieces of plaster, with painted roses, were falling apart. It was very neglected, very sad, its decorations almost unseen. But surprisingly enough, the Magen David was still on its gates. So was the stone from Jerusalem. We counted the mailboxes: over thirty. All of them of families living in the house that my great-grandmother Savta Pipike built for her family, for my grandmother, Judit, for my mother, for my brother, for my sister, for me.

At home or hide and seek

1.

Before I came here
My land belonged to others
Who worked it with love.
Before they came here
Their land belonged to others
Who worked it with love.
Before my parents left their homeland
They lived in their own home
That they built with love.
Before you left your homeland
You lived in your own home
That you built with love.
Let's deny history. Imagine
We were not here before you
And you were not here before us.
Instead of playing catch
We'll play with words.
I live in a home that was built for others.
The people who lived in my home
Left to live in a home
That was built for others.
You live in a home that was built for others
The people who lived in your home
Left to live in a home
That was built for others.

2.

The only home that was built for me
Is settled now by people
Who speak my parents' language
My own mother's tongue
That I don't understand.
On central city streets
Of Paris, Madrid or Rome
I walk and recognize
The sign of my people
And hush.

3.

> I take the sky
> And pull it over my head
> To have a home
> But where do my feet go.

We took photos, hugging each other.

The sun hid itself under a cloud. The street was quiet. No one laughed. Rain started to fall. We opened an umbrella and gathered under it. One family that had been able to survive in front of its glamorous sad past.

We stood there, hugged together. A circle of my mother's life, and in a very deep way a circle of my life, tended towards closure.

I looked at the house, knowing I will come back to it.

I came back to the house a few more times. Again and again, I returned like a pilgrim to "the only home that was built for me". On one of my visits, I met people from the municipality to check the name of the architect and to learn more about the house. They said it was built by a renowned architect in 1910, following my great-grandmother's directions regarding the tower, the roses, the *paluto* and the special round inner opened patio that occasionally became a great *Sukkha* [a booth or shelter used on the festival of Sukkot, feast of Tabernacles]. The documents say that after the house was built, my great-grandmother dedicated it to her beloved husband, Shlomo Goldstein, and that is why until today the building is known as Salomon Palace.

As I have written in my poem Judit, which was written much before the first journey to the house, I already had the feeling that it was my great-grandmother who gave birth to me. I was her daughter. So, in a way, I am my grandmother, Judit, who died in Auschwitz, or perhaps I am the revival of Judit.

After visiting the house and learning about its geographical place, the visuality of its architecture, its surroundings, its design, its structure, its smells, – I knew I belonged there much more than I had ever imagined. I identified with my great-grandmother, Savta Pipike, in a very deep way. I felt and understood her presence in the house. I felt her being in the house, in her corset and bra shop that was downstairs at the front of the building, and I felt her walking to the other shop, the bigger one, that was in the middle of the elegant pedestrian area at the heart of the city. And I felt the need to walk the way she walked, back and forth, to the shop and back to the House.

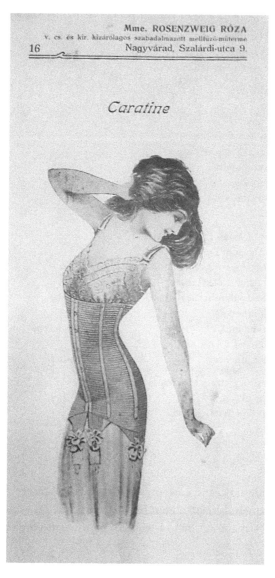

Figure 7.2. A page from Safta Pipike's corset catalogue (From family collection).

Salomon Palace, Oradea

Like to a home port
I row to the house where
I will never be able to dock.
Seven times I surround it
Waiting for its walls to fall.

In spite of the past
You are here. I
Walk your way
From the shop to your home
From your home to your shop
Counting one hundred
From edge to edge
Paving the memory
By my steps.

The house still stands in its glamour.
The big two Stars of David in its gates.
The engraved roses in its columns
Carry your name, Rosa Rachel.
The decorated paluto at the top
Raises itself now taller
Looks over the square
Above the crowd
Defying your absence.

Turn and turn I surround the house
Counting its towers
Paying attention to its strength
Saying its name
For the sake of telling
To the last generation.[2]

I read this poem now, and I ask myself if I wish to conquer the house, like Jehoshua conquered Jericho. And my answer is yes. I do want to conquer it, but not in a material form. I want to conquer it emotionally. I want

---

2   Tehilim (Psalms) 48, 14– 19.

to conquer it mentally. I want to conquer it symbolically. To have its Archetype in my story. I want to have the house in my personal history, in my own body of remembrance. And for this I do not need to purchase it, to buy it or to get it back from the authorities that took it from my family. I do not want to take its inhabitants out of it. This is history. Things move on. Houses change hands, change inhabitants. I only want to have it in myself, my own piece of the house.

Strange enough, it is only now, while writing about this first visit and the visits that followed, those repeated rituals of pilgrimaging to 'the only home that was built for me' by Savta Pipike, it is only now, while writing about my thoughts, that I realize how much it has affected my life, my inner life, my identity. This symbolic conquest, achieved through 'paving the memory by my steps', is now paving my self-assurance, my present identity, the person that I have become, the person that I am now.

I realize that ever since my early childhood I have been fascinated by the stories about Savta Pipike, about how she left her poor mother's home in South Hungary, when she was only 14, and managed all by herself with almost no money to reach her rich and childless aunt, far North in Ostrava in the Czech Republic. She then married her 'Mother's' young brother settling in Oradea where they could start their own business together. My mother's stories about her grandmother's strong and practical yet very spiritual personality always enchanted me. She was broadly educated yet religious, the centre of a family of eight children and yet a hard-working woman, who earns enough money to build such a house for her family to come, being intuitively opinionated, insisting on her ideas and making smart decisions all through her life. All this left a strong impression and the image of Savta Pipike became embedded in me.

When I was already in my 30s, I read her diaries, translated into Hebrew. The translation from Daitch [Judeo-German] was poor. Names of places and people that she mentioned, disappeared and it was hard to follow the details. But the intensity of her writing was there and her courage, her high values and views on family morality and the willingness to do good in this world, her passion to leave a mark on history, it was all there, and I felt very close to her.

And yet, while intuitively I felt a strong connection to her, I never noticed how much she was indeed a role model for me, how much her image directed me in my life. And it is only now that I see how much I followed her in my life.

There are so many similarities between us even though I do not have eight children, but I do have five children. She worked every day of her life, until she was very old, worrying about shelter and food and education for her family, and she succeeded in her work, initiated not only the house but she also had a very successful business that she started from really nothing with no help from anyone. I am not a businesswoman and nor do I sell corsets and bras, but I always worked to have a home and education and enough earnings for my family for all its needs. All my life it was important for me that I still work and thank God I'm doing very well. Savta Pipike was a very good cook. Her recipes were passed around. Her food was always appreciated. I also love to cook. And more than all, Savta Pipike wrote her memories in several notebooks in magnificent handwriting, in very organized sentences and in a form that makes you want to continue to read on and on, to the end. I hope I succeed in making my writing as interesting as my grandmother's.

All these similarities, all these characteristics that we share, are revealing themselves now in my thoughts. I had never thought about it before. As a child I always missed a grandmother. I adopted some, and some grandmothers adopted me but I had no grandmother from my mother's side.

I believe now that unconsciously, I adopted the figure of my great-grandmother, Savta Pipike, to be both my grandmother and my mother. Yes, it appears already in my poem Judit, but like other poets, I understand what I have written a long time after I write.

Why do I understand it all only now, and not before?

Because now I write this chapter and while writing about the visit to the house that she built for her family and hence also for me, I get a better understanding about my deep connection with Savta Pipike. This process of understanding things through writing, is very familiar for me, as a writer. I think it is one of the reasons why I write. In this way, I get a better understanding about who I am, about my acts, about my life.

So here we come to the retrospective introspection. The journey is endless. The journey is a spiral. It begins in a cycle, that one wants to close, but it never ends, because this cycle cannot be closed. It starts ages before you are born and continues after you die in your children and grandchildren's journeys.

I went out to the first journey to the house, because I wanted to learn about myself through my ancestors and I learned much more than I expected. The journey began as a physical geographic journey. It led me to a deep inner journey and this inner journey continues to resonate long after the physical journey has ended and now it reverberates in everything I do.

These journeys continue. The visit long ago and revisiting several times later, was one kind of journey, more physical journeys that continued a previous movement, an emotional-visual movement but the writing about it now is another journey and I want to thank David Clark for the opportunity he gave me to take this journey.

Salomon Palace is 'the only palace that was built for me'. It is where I begin. It is where my roots lie. They lie there and grow now with the memory of Savta Pipike, who initiated the house, who always inspired me, my role model, my Big Mother, my Big Grandmother and my Great-Grandmother.

Now, surrounded by luxury hotels, the house is renovated very beautifully. I go there from time to time when I need to find myself. It is the place where my story begins, it is the place where it will never end.

PART II

Journeys without a survivor or refugee parent

8 Terežin 2000

As I walk the right way through the gates of death
and I pass all you souls walking the wrong way
I silently call out through time:
"It's all right! I am here! We are here! it is all right!"
but you keep walking the wrong way
because I am both crazy
and useless
and so, although no one can hear me I shout
more loudly than I have ever shouted in my life
with deafening silence power known only to us
the second generation
"You! walking the wrong way! know this:
I have seen you
and I will speak about you for the rest of my life!"

If this was only the vaguest fragment
of a whisper
on a faint wisp
of a slight breeze
as you passed,
it is all I can offer.

My first visit to Czechoslovakia was in 1992, just before it divided into Slovakia and the Czech Republic. My father had died in 1985, before the Velvet Revolution. I did not know that he had been Jewish. He had fled Czechoslovakia in 1939 with one suitcase and got to England where his eldest sister Marie had already settled in 1938 after marrying an Englishman. Their younger sister Helen also managed to escape to England, but tragically his mother Růžena and his two brothers, Egon and Mořic were all murdered in Auschwitz, Treblinka and Sosnowiec. I found out these details decades after the events. I knew they had died, but that was the extent of my knowledge, just as I did not know that there seem to be no records anywhere of my grandfather's, Pavel Schönfeld's, fate.

My father, born in 1910, had taken out Czech citizenship as soon as he was old enough. When the Germans invaded Czechoslovakia, he applied for a visa for England. He went to the passport office daily and joined the ever-increasing queue of Czechs desperate to flee. One day he reached the counter just before closing time. The official told him he was too late. My father flattered and cajoled the official, who eventually agreed that if he could find his passport in the cupboard behind the counter piled floor to ceiling with passports, within the next five minutes, he could take it. Fortunately, there was another official at the counter who overheard this exchange. He remembered my father's daily visits and that very day had come across his passport and put it aside. Reaching over the counter he handed it to my father. As my father left, he met his younger brother Egon waiting in the queue. Egon never got his passport.

My father had never been able to talk to about his family after the War. The stories I heard were told by my English mother whom he'd met and married in England 1942. He talked then because he lived in hope that he would find them alive after the War. I grew up being told his family had been killed as part of the Nazis' genocidal policy against the Slavs, but I had no idea where they were killed. It was only after tracing the wife of one of my murdered Uncles, after my father's death, that I was able to piece together a puzzle which had troubled me all my adult life. I wrote about all this in my book entitled *Finding Relly: My Family, the Holocaust and Me*, which was published at the end of 2018. The book finishes at the point of my planned return to the Czech Republic in 2012, with my eldest brother, to take our father's ashes and scatter them outside Olomóc, his birth town. We felt our father had never been able to return to his beloved country himself, after escaping it twice: once from the Nazis, and then from the communist regime after he returned in 1945. He had planned a visit in 1968, but then the Russian tanks invaded.

So, in 1992, I knew very little about my father's family and history. I had not even been aware of Theresienstadt. Czechoslovakia was just opening up, and I went in November with a German friend for a few days to celebrate our joint 40th birthdays. We lapped up as many of the very affordable cultural offerings as we could: a symphony concert in the Rudolphinium, a Black Light Theatre show, a champagne breakfast in a hotel, something which neither of us would ever have been able to afford in our respective countries. We explored the Jewish quarter, where at that time it was not necessary to buy a ticket to do an official tour of all six synagogues.

My friend and I had arrived in Prague from Germany in the afternoon by train and been greeted when we alighted at the station by a woman and her younger teenage sister who showed us photos in the binder she was carrying of their family apartment where they let out a room as a bed and breakfast. My friend and I thought it looked fine, which it was, and that was our base for the next few days. It was about a half an hour's walk to the centre of the city, and my friend and I walked into Central Prague from our bed and breakfast the next morning. Many of the buildings en route were still covered in the Soviet grime which had accumulated over forty years of neglect, but the architecture and fantastic external architectural features, the fascia, cornices, cresting, friezes, carved images of human and imaginary creatures, blew our minds to such an extent that by the time we reached the centre, our jaws had dropped. When we went to sleep that night, we started hallucinating as we closed our eyes, such was the visual stimulation which every visitor to Prague, a city so fabulously rich in exquisitely, sometimes nearly microscopic, detailed design, must experience. We spent our first evening at the Europa hotel café, in Wenceslas Square, a glorious art deco building where a violinist played on the dedicated plinth/stage and the old system of buying a ticket for one's drink was still the practice. I recalled my mother's stories of my father doing just that in his student days in Brno, making one drink last the whole evening. My friend and I were both quite shocked to witness the arrival of what must have been one of the first stag parties from the United Kingdom. For them it was a good choice: very cheap, central and cheap beer. But it marked the beginning of the end for the exquisite Europa. On my next visit with my partner in 2000, not only had the violinist gone, but the café had moved to the basement. On my third visit, in 2012 when my brother and I took our father's ashes back to the Czech Republic, the building was boarded up completely.

My search for my Aunt Relly began four years after my first trip to Prague. I had joined the Bristol second generation group in 1994. After the first year or so of attending meetings, I resolved to find out whether Relly was still alive and if so, where in the world she was. The second-generation group was emotionally and practically hugely important in my search, particularly Zuzana Crouch, who herself is Czech and whose family came from the same town as my father: Moravská Ostrava. After searching for several years, finally, in 1998, I discovered that my Aunt Relly was still alive and living in Sydney, Australia. I began communicating with Relly and her family, first of all by letter. Relly was by then 85. Before our first phone call I sent her a recorded cassette of me talking, so that she would be accustomed to my voice before we actually spoke to each other. Although Relly's son, daughter-in-law and I began to use the relatively new practice of e-mailing, Relly and I continued writing letters and speaking on the phone.

My first of five visits to her before her death in 2010 was in 2000, and this prompted me to make my second visit to what had become the Czech Republic. My partner and I hired a car and had seven specific places, including Prague, we wanted to visit: Olomóc (my father's birth town), Moravská Ostrava, where my father had spent his childhood and school years; Brno where he had studied Civil Engineering; Theresienstadt; Luhacovice, the spa town where my Aunt Marie had worked and met her future husband; and Jistebnik, a village outside Ostrava, where Relly's family had lived, owned a shop and bakery, and which they left, after the Nazis invaded, for Valašské Meziříčí, our seventh destination where Relly, her parents and my Uncle Mořic went to live in the hope of being safer by being further away from the Eastern border. My uncle Mořic, Relly and her family lived on savings, no longer being allowed to work. Mořic, who was a gifted artist as well as a doctor, painted. They went for bicycle rides. Whatever they did, they knew at any minute they might be deported, which Mořic, Relly and her parents ultimately were. I did not know it then, nor did I know it when my eldest brother and I visited it in 2012, but there is a memorial there for the Jews who were deported from Valašské Meziříčí, including the name of my uncle. All the Jewish people there had made a desperate attempt to find safety. When I visited again with my eldest brother, he said Valašské Meziříčí was the saddest of all the significant places we visited.

After we picked up the car from Prague and started driving to Olomóc, we stopped in a small town to find some lunch. One way of coping was not to make notes, and I can't remember now which this town was. We found a nice-looking café and had lunch there. Part of the building was in a state of refurbishment. As we were leaving, I pointed out to Marianne the beautiful wooden balustrade of the staircase which was only partly covered up. A Czech man connected to the renovation overheard my comment, realized I was interested in interior architecture and offered us a tour of the rest of the building. It was extraordinary. Upstairs was a beautiful theatre, with the gorgeous rich colours, detailed shapes and designs which characterize so much of Czech design. He showed us the biggest private box and the other box behind that box. The easy-going kindness and friendliness of this man who was clearly very proud to show this extraordinary theatre to two interested strangers, felt typical of the Czech character, and reminded me of my father.

I have a photograph of me standing under the village sign at the entrance to Jistebnik, which I sent to my Aunt Relly. It felt to me an act of rather puny and much too late defiance; a statement of "I have come back. I am still here. You did not annihilate European Jews to extinction as you had hoped."

We stayed in Olomóc overnight in a lovely hotel on the edge of the town, within walking distance or a short train ride to the centre. It was summer and hot. Everything, including hotel prices, were still remarkably low. It soon became clear that the hotel was frequented by well-heeled Czechs who dressed either semi-formally or formally, not casually. We realized too late that wandering around in shorts was actually a bit of an affront to the relaxed yet respectful ambiance. A television screen in the foyer ran black and white Czech films from the 1930s, the heyday of Czech cinema, all day. That was a time when the Czech film industry was on a par with Hollywood. We stopped wearing shorts in the hotel.

I arrived in the centre of Olomóc completely unprepared for any delving into official records which might contain information about my father's family, such as an address. I had done none of the requisite painstaking and time-consuming research which is necessary to access official files. There were several reasons for this. One was that at that time, the year 2000, not all communication was done by email, making any pre-visit research very time consuming. Another was that then, the second language for most Czechs over 40 years old was Russian. Not everyone spoke English, so both phone calls and letters could be problematic. Yet another reason was that the erratic and sporadic release of this kind of information which had been hidden for decades under layers of anti-Semitism and Soviet control, tended to go to Prague first. So, when I simply tried my luck by making an enquiry at the Tourist Information Centre, I really appreciated it that the official, or clerk, to whom I was directed, treated me more seriously than my casual tourist like behaviour warranted. At the beginning of the twenty-first century, they were just beginning to get more people like me coming there to try to find information about their families. As I have found in all my searching about my father's family, sometimes the first attempt fails, and during this visit I was not able to glean any information about my father's family.

We had a coffee sitting outside a café in the town square. There is a wonderful clock tower there, a kind of take on the astronomical clock in Prague with its calendar, parade of twelve apostles and a skeleton. Olomóc also has an astronomical clock in the square, but its exterior was destroyed by the Nazis. It was replaced with Soviet images and small sculptures of proletarians at work, for example, hammering an anvil. My Danish partner had started a conversation in German with an old man (my German at that time was poor). When she asked him about the name, Schonfeld, he immediately said, "Oh yes, the Yiddish family", so we invited him to sit with us and bought him a coffee and cake. I still don't know whether this man was genuine, or a local eccentric, or whether he just saw two Western tourists he could probably get a coffee and cake out of, but it was the first time I felt I had made some living connection with my father's family, tenuous, dubious, fanciful as it might have been. There were other such memorable moments during this trip. For example, in Brno, we went to the Jewish Cemetery, a huge walled area where the last burials occurred in 1939. The official on duty there was as helpful as he could be, given that he spoke no English, I no Czech or Russian. But we did find three Schönfeld graves. Whether they were relatives of my father I did not find out.

It was my next visit in 2012, taking my father's ashes back, when the emotions kicked in with a vengeance. I am a professional musician and singer, and until I was able to identify and work with the legacy that many in the second-generation experience, I had great difficulty doing the deep

breathing which is essential to all singers when practising. For years I struggled with the onset of tears which would flow when I tried to focus on my
breathing. According to the Chinese system of acupuncture, the lungs are
where we hold grief. For years, I felt I was never reaching the full poten-
tial of my voice. I eventually found a singing teacher who was also healer,
and who more or less located precisely where in my body I had a physical
block. Eventually I overcame this affliction, but my lungs remain a weak
area for me. If I catch anything going around, it goes to my lungs, despite
being a very fit and physically active person. I ended up in hospital once
with trachea-bronchitis and this is what kicked in two days before my trip
to the Czech Republic with my father's ashes. I couldn't cancel. My brother
was flying from Brussels, and we had made appointments in Ostrava with
Liba and Michel Salomonovic, two remarkable people who had become
involved in an ever-expanding Ostravaks group, comprising descendants
of Jewish Ostravaks living in the UK and other countries, and were themselves from Ostrava.

Liba is a retired municipal archivist who, upon retirement, has devoted much of her time to tracing, uncovering and unearthing information about the fates of the Jews from Ostrava. Michel was an Auschwitz
Survivor. They both would meet families, such as my brother and me, on
pilgrimages and take them around the city to key places. For us, Michel
took us to the Municipal Archive where there are, among other documents,
my father's school records and records of the attempts my grandmother
made to escape; took us to the memorial statue erected by the train tracks
from where the deportations left for Theresienstadt and the East; took us
to my father's family apartment building in Moravská Ostrava where my
grandmother had run a small fish canning factory, and outside which we
have had a *Stolperstein* laid for her; took us to the pub opposite where we
had lunch and which, Michel pointed out, my grandmother had probably
supplied with tinned fish from her little factory. The waiter learned why
we were there. He lived in the same apartment block. He offered to take
us to his flat so we could get a sense of what one of those flats was like. We
went up three flights of stairs and he ushered the three of us in, much to
the graciously concealed surprise of his mother. After we parted company
with Michel, we met Jiří Jung an academic researcher in Ostrava, who

helped Liba in her archival endeavours. He took us up to the roof of the town hall for a view over the city, and from where we could see Vitkovice, the mining town whose hospital was where my Uncle Mořic had worked as a radiologist before being forced to resign by the Nazi occupiers. We have also had a *Stolperstein* laid for him, outside the hospital. A second-generation friend of mine does not want *Stolpersteine* for her parents. She does not like the idea of people walking on their names. I understand this, but I also know how effective they are in bringing home the point, to those who see them, that the number 'six million' does not refer to one mass of faceless victims; it is made up of individuals who had lives, families, stories to tell and were part of communities. My brother and I chose to have just one *Stolperstein* outside the apartment block where my father grew up. We could have had seven: one each for his parents and five for the children. But to us that would appear more of a memorial, and not a 'Stumbling Stone', which is there to nudge people's consciousness. For that reason, we chose to place Mořic' *Stolperstein* outside the hospital in Vitkovice, where he had worked as a doctor. According to my Aunt Relly, he had to stay on for six months after the German invasion, so that he could train the German doctors who would replace him.

Throughout this visit, I coughed incessantly, relentlessly. I coughed all night. I coughed through all the meetings, through our visit to the Ostrava Archives, through lunch, through our visit to the apartment, as we stopped next to the memorial by the train track. I felt I was coughing right down to my toes. The others were remarkably tolerant and polite. I just couldn't stop. I would leave the room in the hope I could have one final cough and return quietly. It was hopeless. I couldn't take in the information and records we were shown. I could barely eat lunch. Cough, cough, cough, cough. I coughed while my brother and I drove outside Olomóc to find a small woodland stream which eventually joined the Danube. I was coughing so much I simply watched while my brother had to practically dig out my father's ashes from the urn (they'd been in the urn for nearly twenty-five years) and scatter them in the stream. He calculated how long it would take for them to reach the river running through town and we then went to main bridge to be there at the approximate time our father's ashes would be flowing by. I had brought the urn in my suitcase, not declaring it through customs. My father had died in Canada, and although we had his cremation certificate, I would not have been able to bear it if some officious 'jobsworth' at customs or security either in England or the Czech Republic decided I couldn't take it through. It felt fitting. My father had fled Czechoslovakia with one suitcase and he was returning in my one suitcase. When my brother and I drove from Ostrava back to Prague, we removed the name plate from the plastic urn and deposited it in a rubbish bin at a motorway station. My coughing was beginning to abate.

I have been back to Prague a few times now, joining my partner after she has attended academic conferences there, for a few days' break. Because of Brexit, my brother and I decided to apply for, and have managed to 're-claim', with the extraordinarily kind help of the Czech Embassy in Brussels, our Czech Citizenship. The process took nearly two and a half years. One of the documents we needed to supply, and which we fortunately still have, was the very passport issued to my father over the counter by the kind passport clerk, facilitating my father's escape.

My father, my brother and I have all been helped by the kindness of Czech civil servants, complete strangers at first. All my life I have felt that if there is any such thing in this world as 'security', it is having two passports so one can leave a country immediately if necessary and get into another one. Suddenly feeling unsafe in Britain, where I am a citizen, because of the rise of the extreme right disguised as Brexit, my Czech passport makes me feel I have an escape route. How ironic to feel that the country from where my father had to twice flee occupying forces, is now the country to which I would be able to flee, and whose citizenship gives me the right to live in any of the twenty-seven EU countries. If events in Britain, which echo far too clearly 1930s Germany, gather pace: relentless propaganda (fake-news and lies); the rise of the far right; xenophobia; the undermining of democracy; the active and passive complicity of both population and government in all of these, then I need my escape route. I campaigned against Brexit and against current Conservative policies, because I believe in being active against things that one knows to be both dangerous and wrong. But just as the Holocaust happened in arguably the most highly cultured and scientifically advanced European nation, many people here simply refuse to acknowledge the horrendous swing Britain has taken to the extreme right, and how dangerous that is. My partner is Danish, and spending time in Denmark gives me a perspective on Britain, particularly England. What is happening here is extremely worrying, and it could well be that we end up living there. In the meantime, I am carrying on writing music and giving talks about my book, with the aim of helping to give the Holocaust contemporary relevance, just as this present book does.

Bibliography

Schonfeld, R. (2018). *Finding Relly: My Family, the Holocaust and Me*. Elstree, UK: Vallentine Mitchell.

9 Exploring German Jewish roots in Berlin

Introduction

As I grew up, my parents told us a few stories, mainly the more dramatic and exciting ones about their actions in the resistance movement in Nazi Germany. We were very aware of our 'differentness' from other English children – our parents' German accents, their ignorance of English classics, the food we ate at home, our lack of cousins, aunts and uncles.

My parents avoided any journeys back to Germany, although my father went skiing in Austria most years, and we had a family walking holiday in Austria in 1954 when I was 11. On the way we stopped in Munich briefly to visit my father's old nanny. For my mother, there was no 'going back there'; Germany had rejected her and England had become her home. Any German person entering our house had to be politically vetted before being welcomed. My mother loved travelling to Mediterranean resorts, frequented by many Germans, who would ask how she came to speak such good German. She would reply, "Oh, I studied in Berlin" and then change the subject.

I could understand my mother's attitude, she had suffered so much at the hands of the Germans. But I have never tried to hide my origins. At school there were two other girls with German surnames, one from a Jewish background, one not, but it was never a subject of discussion. At university many people asked me about my name, and I would say, "My parents were Jewish refugees from Nazi Germany" and be open to further discussion if the other person wished. When I got married there was a perfect opportunity to hide my origins, but I decided to keep my name, partly for professional reasons, but also because I wanted to continue the discussion about origins. I felt that unusual names should be acceptable – and over the years 'foreign-sounding' names have become quite normal.

Although academically I was following in my parents' footsteps, specializing in science, knowledge of my background led to an interest in other situations of oppression and disadvantage and much of my non-science reading was around these issues. I made a resolution to try to make the world a better place. I did not want to carry forward my parents' understandable prejudice against all Germans. I thought my generation needed to start again – otherwise, how could all this hatred and discrimination stop?

This led me to want to visit Germany and see what this 'dreadful country', that had done such awful things to my parents and their families, was like. My mother asked a good friend to search out suitable opportunities. She knew an older couple in Lüneburg who had resisted the Nazis and wanted to do anything they could to atone for Germany's terrible treatment of the Jews. So, in my gap year between school and university I went to stay with them for two months as a paying guest. It was a good opportunity to improve my German, which I had studied up to O Level at school but never spoke with my parents.

Lüneburg 1961

The couple I stayed with, Gertrud and Karl Heine, lived in a large house on the edge of Lüneburg near a forest. During the Nazi times Karl was a history teacher and, refusing to teach the Nazi curriculum, was thrown out of his job and had to make a living selling coffee under cover. His two young sons carried parcels of coffee through the forest. One day the younger one slipped into a river and drowned. The older one who was with him at the time, suffered mental health issues as a result, thinking he should have looked after his brother better. I was very moved by the Heines' story – my parents had no choice because they were Jewish, but here were non-Jewish people who suffered greatly, when they could have chosen (as many did) to look the other way. The Heines also hid Jews in their house on their way to escape and looked after their books, showing me their deep bookshelves with space for a second row behind.

After the war, politicians in Lüneburg were looking for the few people with clean records. They asked Karl if he would be mayor. He said, "No thanks, I'm not a politician, I'm a teacher – but I would like to be head of the newest school." This was a *Volkschule* [Elementary School] for 6- to 14-year-olds. I went with him a few times. Along the way, people greeted him respectfully, "*Guten Tag, Herr Heine, wie geht's*? [Good day, Herr Heine, how's it going?]" When I commented on this, he said, "Don't believe any of that. When they get behind closed doors, their opinions are still the same." I was shocked.

Gertrud had been a social and community worker and was very proud of being chosen to represent Germany in one of the first visits of a women's group to the UK, again because of her clean record and work in the community.

I had so many questions to ask! And the Heines patiently answered them as far as they could. They also gave me books to read. One book which impressed me greatly was called *Das Gewissen Steht Auf* [Conscience Stands Up] – short biographies of other people who stood out against Hitler when they didn't have to, and suffered for it, often being killed for their principles.

When I returned home, my mother and I tried to talk German to each other, as my German had improved considerably. But it felt strange and stilted – it was not our shared language – and we soon stopped. She was interested as a parent in my experiences but had no wish to know more.

My mother's memoirs

My father died when I was fourteen, so I never had the chance to talk to him about his life. But I did have occasional conversations with my mother, especially after my visit to Germany. I really wanted her to write down all the stories she had told us as children, but life took over. Then when she was 60, just after she retired, she had a heart attack. I worried that she might die, and I would never know about the important events in my background. It took her several years to recuperate enough to take up any activities. Then, with my prodding, she made several attempts at writing things down, but she was not happy writing. We found people to help her, but she just ended up falling out with them, especially when she felt they were imposing their own ideas.

With her 70th birthday on the horizon, I thought helping her to complete her memoirs would make a good birthday present. I set aside a week and sat with her and a tape-recorder. When she dried up, I simply asked another question. After a friend of mine had typed it up, I spent a year literally cutting and pasting our conversations into a coherent document, clarifying and filling in the gaps with weekly 'editorial' sessions with my mother over the phone. Her 70th birthday present was finally ready by the time she was 71. She chose the title: *We Kept Our Heads – Personal memories of being Jewish in Nazi Germany and making a new home in England*.

I enjoyed the process, and it brought me closer to my mother. I began to forgive her for her mistreatment of me as a child – she would lose her temper and hit me from time to time. I saw what a tough life she had experienced, both from her family and in suffering anti-Semitism, and appreciated how well she had managed in the circumstances.

We made a few copies of the memoirs for family and friends, but to my surprise all my friends wanted to read it, so we made fifty extra copies. In 2006 my cousin Henry put it on computer, and I still occasionally send it to people who ask for it.

Visit to Berlin 1977

As soon as I had finished the memoirs, I wanted to go to Berlin to see if I could find the places my mother had mentioned. Fortunately, I had an old school friend who lived in Berlin and was willing to host us (I was accompanied by my husband Mike). I also wanted to visit Gertrud Heine, now on her own after Karl's death. So, in February 1977 we spent five days in Lüneburg renewing our friendship.

Before I left, my mother gave me a copy of my great-grandfather Louis Badt's memoirs, which had recently come to light, typed up from the original handwritten manuscript. I thought they would be interesting to read while in Berlin and did so, German dictionary in hand. These memoirs documented the way the family moved around central Europe in the 1800s before Germany became unified as a country in 1871. They settled wherever they could run a small store which gave them a living and moved from place to place as opportunities waxed and waned, finally ending up in Berlin.

After Lüneburg we went to Berlin for eight days. Our friends met us, and we spent the first two days getting our bearings in Berlin, finding buses, visiting the National Gallery, Tiergarten and the Reichstag, where we saw an exhibition entitled *Frage an die Deutsche Geschichte* [Questions about German history]. We saw the Berlin Wall and had a glimpse of East Berlin. I continued reading Louis Badt's memoirs.

The next day we started the hunt for addresses in my mother's memoirs. We went to the *Jüdisches Gemeindehaus* [Jewish Community House] where there was a map of Jews killed in Berlin and a small exhibition. Then we walked down Kurfürstendamm, a famous shopping boulevard in Berlin, looking for number 100, where my mother's family had lived at one time. It was now a boutique and a hotel! We duly photographed it. We went to Sybelstraße to see if my mother's school was still there. We found two schools there, so photographed them both. We weren't sure which was the correct one.

We returned to the Reichstag to see more of the exhibition, particularly the sections on the Weimar Republic and the Nazi times. We then headed towards the Hansaviertel, another area where my mother's family had lived. This area had been completely rebuilt in 1945. It was a weird feeling to see that former lives of my family could be wiped out as if they had never existed. It added to the feeling of disconnection from my family who had lived in Berlin.

Our hosts had procured tickets for the opera in East Berlin. This involved catching the S-Bahn to the Friedrichstraße checkpoint, where we were checked at four different stages by officious guards who looked down on us from elevated positions and examined our ears, eyes and whether we had any seditious literature with us. We had carefully left any leaflets behind. It took forty-five minutes for our passports to be checked. I found the whole experience quite frightening. It reminded me of the way in which my parents must have been treated, and how much more frightening it must have been for them, with much greater consequences riding on the results of such an inspection. Fortunately, the opera itself was superb and worth the hassle; and the Opera House had been rebuilt since the war in its original style and was a magnificent building.

Next day we went to Wilmersdorf to find Wilhelmsaue 136, where my mother had a flat for several years and then shared a larger flat with my father after they married. It was their last address before fleeing Germany. The house was large and contained many flats and was the only one in the road which had not been restored – it was rundown, with peeling paintwork and a lobby with brown and yellow décor that looked as if it had remained untouched since my parents left in 1937. It was an emotional moment as I felt I was staring my own history in the face. I climbed the stairs hesitantly to the first floor and almost knocked on the door of a flat that could have been theirs. But I wasn't certain – there were several flats that met my mother's description. So, we took lots of photos of the outside.

The next place on our list was Wannsee, a lake which is part of a series of lakes in south-west Berlin. This lake was significant because my parents had their own small sailing boat there, which they used as a weekend escape from the pressures of Nazi rules and intimidation. They felt less identified there, as Jews were not thought of as 'sailing people'. I was surprised because in England sailing is generally the preserve of rich or at least well-off people, and my parents were pretty poor; however, my mother explained that sailing in Berlin then was something that poor people could easily do. They never had the money or the opportunity to take up sailing after emigrating to England. Our walk round Wannsee took place in February chilly drizzle and twilight, not the sunny sailing season!

We had another day in East Berlin. This time the checkpoint crossing took place in daylight hours and did not seem so frightening, but this reminded me how easily we can get used to barbaric rituals and accept

Figure 9.1. Marian's mother's apartment building, Berlin, in 1977 (Photo taken by Marian Liebmann).

them as normal. We wandered round many streets and landmarks that would have been part of my parents' Berlin. The whole area seemed shabby and rundown, with queues for every shop – a great contrast to shiny West Berlin!

On our final day we visited a few more memorial sites: a church in Charlottenburg, another district where the family had lived, in the shape of a concentration camp, "Poor congregation!" I thought; and the

Gedenkstätte Plötzensee, a memorial to political prisoners on the site where they were killed by the Nazis for such things as listening to radio broadcasts.

Returning home, of course my mother was interested in my experiences, and especially the house where her last flat was. But this didn't make her want to go back to see that or other familiar haunts at all. I was very glad I had taken the opportunity. It gave me a feeling that I knew where I had come from, even though I had no intention of living in Germany.

Mediation and restorative justice

My professional career started with a degree in physics and maths, followed by a teaching qualification, some school teaching, then educational writing. My next job as educationalist in a day centre for ex-offenders brought me into the world of criminal justice. After a break for family, I took a job coordinating Victim Support, then a very new concept. It seemed strange that the worlds of victims and offenders were kept very separate, so when someone handed me a slip of paper with details of a mediation course in London in 1984, saying, "I think this is for you", I dropped everything and went. Mediation was a concept that was instantly attractive to me, as it provided a space where my ability to see both sides of everything was an asset rather than a liability – I had often felt unable to campaign and protest because of this. All the lights went on in my head, and I took the ideas and skills with me to my next job as a probation officer, where I facilitated victim-offender mediations when I could.

I also got involved in Mediation UK, the national organization for mediation, and became its director, then projects officer for seven years. In addition, I was a founder member of Bristol Mediation (for neighbour disputes) and through Mediation UK helped to establish about 100 similar services around the UK. Attending conferences brought me into contact with the wider role of conflict resolution and peace-making work.

Although I did not set out consciously to do this specific work, when I looked at myself with hindsight, it seemed perfectly appropriate. My love of art also led me to train as an art therapist and I have pursued both of these in parallel for the last thirty years. I am not unique in this. Many second-generation people have had careers as therapists or similar professions. I think our history leads us to have a greater need than others to 'help put the world to rights'.

My mother's memoirs revisited

In my mother's memoirs she related the deaths of her family in her usual matter-of-fact way. Her father Albert Badt had died of 'natural causes', her mother Emmy and sister Ilse of pneumonia ("It was a great killer at that time", she said), and her brother Erich, to whom she was very close, of a bike accident at the age of 14. I just accepted this, although I did think that her father's death at 57 from 'natural causes' was a bit surprising in 1926.

In 2009 I took part in an art therapy conference in Israel and visited my cousin Henry in Jerusalem. At the time, he was busy with documents he had received from a relative in Berlin relating to his mother Ilse's death, which was said to be pneumonia, which I knew from the memoirs. Henry's wife Judy told me that Ilse had taken overdoses because her husband was unfaithful, and the second of these led to pneumonia and her death. Judy also told me that Erich had hung himself at the age of 14. She knew all this from Ilse's best friend, now living in the UK, but had never told Henry, thinking it would be too much for him, so I was sworn to secrecy as well. Only recently she let me know that she had finally told him, so that I no longer have to keep the secret.

I was already thinking, "Is the other pneumonia death the same kind of pneumonia?" On my return I wrote to my second cousin in the UK, who told me that Albert and Emmy had also committed suicide. She wrote, "Your mother made me promise never to tell you that they all committed suicide but as others are now gossiping, it is pointless keeping the truth from you." For several weeks I felt as if a big rug had been pulled out from under my feet – what else in my mother's memoirs was not true? But as I assimilated this new knowledge, it made sense of many incidents and attitudes that had puzzled me. It made sense of my mother's anxiety when I became depressed at university, or later when I was ill with anything. She must have been thinking, "Here comes the family pattern again, maybe my daughter will commit suicide." I experienced her anxiety and over-protectiveness as a real pressure, and I stopped telling her if I was ill or was having a bad time.

My mother died twenty years before I discovered these truths, so I will never know why she lied about her family's deaths – was it to protect me, or to protect herself? I was sad she could not tell me the truth, as I would have appreciated being able to discuss those deaths and how they affected her.

Then came the dilemma of what to do with my new knowledge. I really didn't want to tell my daughter that her lovely Granny had not always told the truth in her memoirs, which I knew my daughter had read. But I was determined that the secrecy had to stop, it was corrosive. Truth can be difficult to bear but lies and secrecy are worse. I picked my time on a visit to my daughter, when her young children had gone to bed, and we were having a cosy mother-and-daughter chat. I told her and held my breath – what would her reaction be? It came in the form of a question, "So do you mean that Granny was the only one in her family not to commit suicide?" "Yes." "Cor, what a survivor." I breathed a huge sigh of relief. I hadn't thought of it this way before and was very grateful for her reframing.

Visit to Berlin 2010

I had often thought of going back to Berlin after the Wall came down in 1989. There would be more I could see, including various Holocaust memorials. I was impressed by what I read about German efforts at reparation and re-education. Life was busy and it remained an intention until I received an invitation from a young woman from Berlin whom I met at a conference. I made a four-day visit in March 2010, accompanied again by my husband Mike, now 81 and needing some support. I was 67. Despite

Mike's infirmities we walked around the central areas of Berlin and used public transport to reach other places.

We visited the Tiergarten and the Brandenburg Gate, which had divided East and West Berlin, the rebuilt Reichstag with its replacement glass dome, the Kuppel, with a spiral walkway up to the top viewing platform and an interesting historical photographic exhibition on the way up. We visited many Holocaust memorials – for me it felt like an obligatory pilgrimage. High on our list was the Jewish Museum designed by the architect Daniel Libeskind; apart from all the usual Jewish artefacts and photos related to the Holocaust, the internal architecture of strange dead ends and unexpected twists led to feelings of disorientation and being trapped, entirely appropriate.

One of the other most memorable memorials was the Memorial to the Murdered Jews of Europe (also known as the Holocaust Memorial), a maze of 2,711 concrete slabs of different heights, widths and lengths – again I felt lost and trapped. We visited the New Synagogue (new in 1866) in Oranienburgerstraße, badly damaged on *Kristallnacht* in 1938 and the war; and taken over by the Nazis for storage in 1940; because it was in East Berlin, restoration could only start after the collapse of the Berlin Wall in 1989. We saw many other memorial and Holocaust-related sculptures on the streets or in small parks.

I was curious to see my parents' old residence again, at Wilhelmsaue 136, to see if it was just the same. I was quite unprepared for the total transformation. The whole building had been done up in smart grey and yellow, with a new door and inside a smart metal plate listing the flats and a new-looking lift instead of the wide stairs. I slipped in after a resident, feeling like a trespasser.

Outside in the cobbled pavement we saw three sets of *Stolpersteine* (a six and two fours). The large number of *Stolpersteine* we saw in front of number 136 contrasted with just one set or none outside other similar buildings in the street. This was because the landlord was Jewish (I knew this from the memoirs) and more willing to let to Jewish tenants. The Stolpersteine didn't include my parents' names, as I thought that *Stolpersteine* were only for people who had been murdered, not for those who had escaped. I wished my parents could join the others in the pavement.

Another important pilgrimage was to the Weissensee Jewish Cemetery in the Weissensee district – this would have been in East Berlin before

Figure 9.2. Marian's mother's apartment building, Berlin, in 2010 after it had been renovated (Photo taken by Marian Liebmann).

1989, therefore difficult to visit in 1977. The cemetery is the second largest Jewish cemetery in Europe and contains 115,000 graves. I thought it would be difficult to locate any family graves in such a large place, but the cemetery had a very efficient microfiche system, which enabled staff to provide us with plot number, row number and precise position.

Figure 9.3. Marian's husband looking at the *Stolpersteine* outside Wilhelmsaue 136, Berlin 2010 (Photo taken by Marian Liebmann).

What was surprising was the different state of care for different plots. The nearest grave on the diagram was that of my grandmother, Emmy Badt. We couldn't see anything, only some humps completely submerged in ivy. With some difficulty we scraped several layers away to reveal only the partial dates of their deaths, as the names and the rest of the numbers had disappeared. We saw that this gravestone was not only for Emmy but also for Erich, her son.

By contrast, my grandfather Albert Badt's gravestone and my aunt Ilse Lichtwitz's gravestone were in an excellent state of repair, in a clean plot containing other family graves. We were unable to find out the reason for this difference as the office had shut by the time we returned to the entrance. We wondered whether the difference was due to the fact that both Erich and Emmy had committed suicide (a taboo in Judaism). Visiting the cemetery was a sombre experience. My mother had never mentioned the family graves (possibly because they were inaccessible on my previous visit), and because they received such different treatment.

Other visits to Germany

I have never thought of Germany, or more specifically Berlin, as 'home' or a place to 'go back to'. Rather I have thought of it as a country and city 'to go to', a place to explore my history. It was never a country that either attracted or repelled me.

I made two other visits to Germany for work conferences, one to Trier and one to Hanover. In Trier I attended a European working party contributing UK experiences of restorative justice.

In Hanover I attended a peace-making and conflict resolution conference and was seen as typically British in my attitudes with an 'island mentality'. Although this was hurtful, it preserved my identity as a British person. Just one or two people remarked on my German name, and when I told them my parents were Jewish refugees from Nazi Germany, there was an embarrassed silence, with neither of us knowing what to say next. My discomfort was about inadvertently opening up a topic which many people in Germany feel very ashamed about. It was more comfortable maintaining a British persona, but I was not prepared to cover up to achieve that. My poor German, of which I am not proud, probably helped to identify me as British.

The story continues ...

When I discovered that my cousin Henry, who had escaped on the Kindertransport, had included himself in his family *Stolpersteine*, I realized that they were not only to commemorate those who had been murdered by the Nazis, but also those who had escaped. Feeling that I owed it to my parents to commemorate them properly, in the right place, I made enquiries and learnt that I could indeed apply for *Stolpersteine* for them. So early in 2017, I applied and received a reply in June 2017 that I had been placed on their 'long, long waiting list' and might expect to be contacted in 2019.

As 2019 was drawing to a close, I had heard nothing. As I was about to write to the project, I noticed that, in the Bristol Festival of Ideas 'Festival of the Future City' October 2019, there was a panel session entitled 'Beyond Apologies: Past Guilt and Urban Futures – How should cities deal with guilt?' Members of the panel spoke about how various cities had addressed the slave trade, the Holocaust and the French colonial past. The speaker on the Holocaust was Anne Thomas from the *Stolpersteine* Project. I approached her at the end of the session and asked what had happened to my application. She promised to enquire and very soon another staff member wrote to tell me I would be included in their list for 2020. A wording for the *Stolpersteine* was agreed as follows:

> Hier wohnte
> Gerhard Liebmann
> Jg. 1906
> Januar 1937 Flucht
> Frankreich
> England

> Hier wohnte
> Dora Minna
> Liebmann
> Jg. 1906
> Januar 1937 Flucht
> Frankreich
> England

2020 was ravaged by Covid-19, so I was surprised to receive an email on 28 October scheduling the laying of our *Stolpersteine* less than a month later on 24 November. This provoked panic-stricken attempts to see if travel was feasible, then a further email two days later on 30 October cancelled the event due to lockdown in Berlin. A rollercoaster of emotions, so near and yet so far!

I am hoping for an opportunity in 2021, but that is still very uncertain. By 2021 sixty years will have elapsed since my first visit to Germany. In the meantime, I have been busy writing biographies of my parents and finding photos for the *Stolpersteine* Project website.

Conclusion

As with any journey it is often difficult to know whether the journey itself is more important than the destination. This journey has been emotional and full of unexpected twists and turns. It has helped me to bridge the gap over the stark divide of the buried past and the living present, resulting from my parents' abrupt dislocation due to the Holocaust. Now I feel more connected to my heritage, giving me a feeling of belonging to a family I never met. I also now understand why many other people, born in the UK of parents who migrated to the UK, decide to visit their parents' countries. This is important as the feeling of belonging is what is missing for refugee families the world over.

Our history is part of ourselves, not something to be disconnected and alien. Part of belonging is belonging to ourselves and to our history.

VIVIAN HASSAN-LAMBERT

10 Letter from Bratislava: 1976

For as long as I can remember, I have always known about my mother's past. She'd survived the war in Czechoslovakia as a Jewish child in hiding. So had her sister, Kitty and her mother, Alice. Her father, Sigmund, was a well-respected doctor in Bratislava. But by 1939, laws were passed prohibiting Jews from practising medicine. No longer able to work, and seeing how bad things were getting, he left Czechoslovakia and went to London where the family had relatives. There, he hoped to set up a life for himself, get a job and lodgings, with my mother, her sister and my grandmother soon to follow. But before long, the borders in Czechoslovakia closed and my grandmother, then in her mid-20s, was separated from her husband for the rest of the war. It wasn't until seven years later, in 1946, that the family would be reunited on the docks of New York harbour.

Throughout my childhood my mother told us fairy tales – Grimm's, Hans Christian Anderson and her own creations – and the stories of her early years from both before and during the war, mingled with the fairy tales. There was darkness and there were moments of joy; there was adventure and escape. I could imagine the rat-infested basement where she'd hidden, the orphanage she'd stayed in, the snow she'd trudged through alone, her pockets stuffed with cash to take to the partisans while the Hlinka Guard were rounding up Jews in the nearby hamlet.[1] I could picture the beautiful fields of cornflowers surrounding the mountain village where she, her sister, mother and aunt went to live temporarily, and the loaves of home-made

---

1   During the Second World War, the Hlinka Guard in Slovakia, the militia of the Slovak People's Party, were like the SS in Germany. They were directly responsible for the rounding up and deportation of Jews to concentration camps, in appropriating Jewish-owned property and violence against Jews.

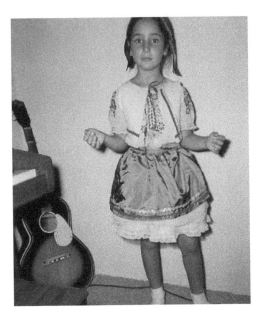

Figure 10.1. Vivian in Slovak costume (From family collection).

bread she lusted after and relished. Everything she told me was so much more vibrant than anything I had ever experienced in my safe, middle-class, Los Angeles childhood.

And yet, in all her storytelling with its sense of longing and nostalgia, there was always something missing. These were only stories: not quite real; my mother expressed no emotion, no outward sign of fear. But what was untold or unfelt worked its way into me. Sometimes I had dreams where I was being chased by Nazis. Other times, I would lie awake in bed terrified, imagining a shadow by the door to be a wolf ready to devour me. I would see my sister, two-and-a-half-years younger, across the room, her chest slowly rising and falling in the rhythm of sleep, and I would be paralysed, afraid to move any muscle for fear that the wolf in the corner would spot and obliterate me.

I remember a scene. I was probably 6 or 7 years old. We were watching TV as a family, something we often did on a Sunday evening. Suddenly, there was a picture on the screen. Though I didn't know it then, it was a picture of the ovens at Auschwitz. My mother was in tears. I was perplexed and tried to ask her why. She wouldn't talk about it; she couldn't talk; and even at the age of 6 or 7, I knew, not the details, but I knew, as sure as the doors of those closed incinerators, there was something bolted up inside her, I couldn't reach it even though I wanted to.

My mother never used to think of herself as a 'survivor'. Even after the film, *Schindler's List*, came out in 1993, and she was interviewed by the foundation Spielberg set up to record and archive testimonies of Holocaust survivors as a collection of videotaped interviews, my mother still had difficulty in thinking of herself in that way. She reasoned – there were people whose experiences were so much worse than hers: people who'd been in the camps; relatives like her Aunt Lily, who died in Ravensbrück; or her cousin Grete who had been medically experimented on in Auschwitz by Mengele; and people, like her uncle Tivadar, a former judge, who had survived Buchenwald, only to be forced after the war in his native village, to sign a paper with the words – "I have to die like a pig because I am a Jew" – before being murdered by anti-Semites.

For a long time, I've been collecting information about my mother's past. But, like so many other second generationers, I have found it difficult to contain everything. No matter how many times I've been told about or researched something, dates get jumbled, facts get forgotten and how people are related to me gets confused. All the information is tangled in my mind, and I've had the ongoing desire to one day hold everything down, organize it, put it in its place, make a narrative that I can communicate to others, or even physically hand on to my daughter, niece, nephew and cousin.

Recently, I finished a novel I'd been writing for several years and was in the process of developing a new project. By January 2020 I had finally begun, settling in to two pieces of work: one fiction with two characters based loosely on my grandmother and Aurelia Plath, the mother of American poet Sylvia Plath; and the other, an attempt to finally sort out my mother's family history. The two projects often overlapped and at the Wellcome Trust Library where I was writing, I would alternate my days between them.

Then, in early March 2020, Covid hit. The nation-wide lockdown put an end to my library visits, and I found that daily life needed so much attention that it was impossible for me to escape into the fantasy world of fiction. I decided, "Now is the right time; I'm sixty-three; what am I waiting for? I'll immerse myself in the family history."

A few years ago, I went to a second-generation workshop led by an experienced therapist. The session was only ninety minutes long, but it was a revelation to me to be amongst people who had similar experiences. I had always felt so different from most other Jews, an outsider amongst outsiders, but here, at last, I was with people with more of a shared background, and for a while, the experience of that workshop fed my desire to continue finding out about my family's past.

Two years later I had the opportunity to join a twelve-session, weekly group led by the same therapist. It was a small group, we were of a similar age, and, as fate would have it, we had all grown up with at least one parent who had survived the Holocaust as a hidden child. There was so much that was understood, so much emotional baggage that was common, or, if it wasn't common, we could almost completely understand. It felt like family. It felt energizing and freeing.

So, during lockdown, when I finally began my family history project in earnest, I had the emotional impact of that group behind me and made the bold (to me) decision to contact the therapist and see if she would work with me on a one-to-one basis.

Over recent weeks during our Zoom meetings we've spoken about many things – family dynamics, history, the effects of suppressed emotion. In one of these sessions, I talked about a period of intense anger I felt towards my mother in my early adolescence. I suppose many teenagers have bouts of anger, but somehow, on reflection, mine seemed so miserable and sudden. My mother had worked full-time as a doctor; she ran the household; looked after my disabled brother and had little space to be available for all that I was going through as a teenager. I told the therapist about a letter I had written to my mother when I was 13. I described how I sat on the bed next to her one Saturday afternoon and read the letter aloud with tears streaming down my face: the feeling of being hurt, of desperately trying to communicate with my mother, of wanting to be heard and recognized, wanting her to feel what I felt. But, for the life of me, as I recounted all this to the therapist, I could no longer remember what I had been so hurt or angry about.

I keep all my letters, even, sometimes, copies of the ones I've written. After that session I began searching for that childhood letter, but without success.

Then, a day or two later, I received a call from my mother. "I found it", she said. She was crying, which was unusual for her. "I found the letter."

I took a huge gulp. I was horrified. She'd found the angry letter I'd been searching for. But how was this possible? I hadn't told her about it.

"The letter", she repeated. "The letter you wrote to me from Czechoslovakia in 1976, when you went to see Anna. It's so beautiful."

I was amazed – both by the strange and irrational fear I had just experienced, and then by her response to what she'd found, not my early-adolescent letter, but a letter I'd written as a 19-year-old when I'd gone to Bratislava for two days, the town of her childhood, to visit Anna Igumnová.

Dr Anna Igumnová, I had heard about her for most of my life. She was a Russian scientist who had been working at a research institute in Piešťany, a famous spa town not far from Bratislava. Anna Igumnová, who during the war had risked her life again and again to help save others: my mother included. She had smuggled food to my mother and grandmother when they were hiding for three months in an abandoned hotel; she had convinced wealthy sympathizers to surreptitiously donate funds; she had been the lynchpin that kept people safe. She was a hero in our family.

So, in 1976, on a gap year between high school and university, armed with a backpack and an Interrail pass, I travelled around Europe and Israel for five months, and at the end of that trip, made my way from Vienna to communist-controlled Czechoslovakia to see Anna. As a result of that meeting, I wrote a letter to my mother. It journeyed over 6,000 miles to California, rested for nearly half a century, and this summer it came back to me.

The Letter: Bratislava 1976

Zdravstvujt² Mama!

I am in your land. I came on a night train from Vienna. All that I know of this place is ground into my deepest parts. I see in the compartment next to me: a fat woman in huge layers of skirts, a scarf on her head, a whining voice; a man in shabby clothes, yellow hair, eyes closed, mouth open, drunk and snoring.

All that I know of this country is from a past era. I feel in me the bright dancing peasants. I remember the Halloween costumes you once sewed for us: shining blue skirts with red rickrack at the hem, colourful embroidered shirt that was once yours and, in our hair, red ribbons and fresh flowers. That autumn, we collected more candy than ever before.

There is a way of breathing that is ingrained in me, through you: your *Bože moj, yois, popši nek³*; the food we ate spiced with paprika; the tastes we have; the colours we choose; smells we like. We were not raised in an 'American' air: white bread, *Oreo cookies*, apple pie. And all the time I listened with large eyes to your stories of dark forests, drunken peasants, long thick braids, school; then you watching through a window, German boots, fellow class mates passing to school and you staying home; becoming a temporary Christian orphan; hiding in large abandoned pipes; wondering about your mother, about Kitty, *Tatko*, your father; wondering how all this could be happening to someone so ready to play in the streets with other children. Every contact I make with this past brings to me a drastic pain, which passes my brain without thought, without realization, and suddenly I am in tears. For me, it is only a shadow, something I never lived, and yet I experience a deep fear.

So, this land, and all that is with it, is a part of me somewhere, like a past life. I shudder with the closeness I feel.

The train has stopped now [border crossing between Austria and Czechoslovakia]. Men in thick boots and green uniforms make crunching sounds on the gravel outside. I look through the window into a black sky: a double-thick fence covered with barbed-wire, and occasional armed watchtowers. How strange to keep a country full of prisoners, several countries full of prisoners. I try to imagine why.

---

2   *Zdravstvujt* is a Russian greeting for 'hello' which many people in Czechoslovakia used at the time this letter was written.

3   *Bože moj, yois, popši nek* are Slovak terms of endearment. Though my mother spoke very little Slovak to us, she often used these terms. Literally they mean: my God, ooooh, little bottom.

The men in thick boots ask questions and rummage through suitcases. They do not bother with me. Mostly they direct themselves to the Slovak passengers. The men pull out items: a book, nightgown, skirts, blouse. A childish looking woman with sad blue eyes and a mess of old hair, whines to him at every question. The peasant woman next door follows an official out of the train, also whining. I watch them through the window. I am reminded of something: the gravel-crunching sound, the barbed-wire fence, the armed guard on a tower, the simple woman following a man in uniform, the bright spotlight in a dark sky, the silenced train infested with soldiers.

The train arrives [in Bratislava] late at night. No one speaks English. I take a bus to the wrong hostel. I am almost crying, tired, trying to struggle in a language I don't speak. No one understands. Some very nice young Slavic boys accompany me, demanding to carry my luggage to a comfortable hostel. And I spend the night under a thick down comforter.

It is morning. I take the address of *Teta* Anna, [*Teta* means aunt in Slovak and is an endearing sign of respect]. I have exchanged telegrams with her and hope that she expects me. I find her building. I am in such awe of this woman and I have not yet even met her. Everyone who knows her talks of her with great love. All my life I have heard her name as a magic pair of syllables. I am half afraid. I feel silly and awkward. My finger presses a red doorbell button. There is no beaming eye through a peephole. The door opens. I am no longer meek. I am in the arms of a warm feeling in grey hair. Oh, what a beautiful gleaming smile this woman has. How can anyone help but fall, enchanted by her? She is beautiful in every way: strong, aware, alive. She does not study or judge me. We are old friends at once. She is petite, vibrant. She is wearing a royal blue silk suit, and has soft white hair, huge eyes, nothing fancy, completely without vanity. Her one room is without any evidence of age or gender. It is simple but not bleak: a bed, a table, a bookshelf, vases of dried flowers, a teddy bear three generations old. I have constant urges to hug her, sing to her. I call her *Babushka* [grandmother in Russian] and she loves this. She tells me of her life in Russia, before, during and after the revolution. Of how in 1921 she went on a two-week vacation from Russia, leaving her young baby in the care of a friend, and then suddenly, not being able to return, not seeing her daughter again until after a horrible war, until 1956. We walk through a nearby forest, by a castle, through the streets of Bratislava. Here I am, running on the same cobblestones that you once ran on. I come to a street and begin to laugh. I have been here many times before, the tall clock tower, the crowded street. I am standing inside a painting *Tatko*, [my grandfather], once painted.

I want to tell you many things. How much I love you, more every day. How I think you are one of the strongest women alive, how I long to be like you. What strength it must have taken for you to come back here.[4] It is beyond anything I could ever

4   My mother finally returned to visit Slovakia and Anna Igumnová for the first time in
     1975, twenty-nine years after she left. Subsequently my mother made sure to register
     Anna with Yad Vashem in Israel, as one of the 'Righteous Among the Nations'.

write. I want to tell you of all the wild-flowers I've seen, of the snake-like Danube and the green forests. It is you that are an amazing wonder. I think that you understand people, you know how to live. I wonder at this strength and dignity in which you do everything. I will come home in a few days and I will see you and hug and kiss you, but I will never, in all my life, in anything I ever do, be able to equal all the love and gratitude I feel for you. Thank you for keeping us all strong.

Forty-four years later can I say what happened as a result of that visit or of writing that letter? How the travel and words changed or impacted me? I was young then, on the cusp of adulthood. I know I wanted to please my mother, to connect with her and with a part of her past, and that the visit to Bratislava was one step of many towards my life-long journey of understanding who I am in terms of the Holocaust and an almost lost history. I wanted to meet Anna Igumnová; I wanted to prove to this remarkable woman that I existed; I wanted her to see my mother in me; and I wanted to show Hitler that he hadn't won, that generations of Jews had continued and that I was one of them.

After those travels, I returned to Los Angeles as a different person, more grown-up and ready for the next stage of life. I went to university, took classes in science, literature and creative writing. I did my final year as an exchange student at the University of Sussex, studying Virginia Woolf and other British authors. There I met my husband-to-be.

After finishing university, I moved to the UK. I felt I was moving back to something, closer to the world my family had once inhabited. But I was only looking in from the edge – a position that is familiar to many whose parents are refugees or migrants. I married my university sweetheart. I worked in theatre and staff-training, wrote and made visits to the US, and all the while I remained embroiled in my mother's history and how her past, the past of so many Jews in Europe, those who were murdered and those who survived, have affected me.

When I think back to that angry letter, the one I wrote aged 13, I wonder if the intensity of my anger was to do with my mother's lack of feeling, or at least her unexpressed feeling, about her past. Perhaps she was incapable of fully recognizing the pain I had inside. After all, there was no room for the expression of anger for a child in hiding. By the time she was 13, she had learned to suppress her feelings in order to survive; a cry or whimper could have been a matter of life or death. And perhaps I picked up on those feelings and, without knowing it, absorbed them inside.

As a child, I did express my anger, in fits of screaming, torrents of tears, or arguments with my sister which my mother did not really know how to handle. I had inner rages and I had fierce joy. I longed to be seen for who I was – a feeling, sensitive, deep-thinking, complex, artistic person.

As I entered my later teens, I was hungry for my mother to share her emotions with me, and in turn, to validate mine. I became good at listening. If I could be her confidant, if I could get her to communicate her feelings – it was a way of being close to her.

The skills I developed in late adolescence became useful skills in later life and even shaped the work I did as a group facilitator and writing coach. Always observing and watching from a distance, taking things in, I explored the undercurrents of what is said and unsaid in my fiction writing. We have a lovely daughter who is now grown up and as a parent, I made sure there was a vocabulary in our home that made it possible for my daughter to develop an ability to understand her feelings and the feelings of others.

Figure 10.2. Vivian with her mother (From family collection).

My mother is a survivor in more ways than one. Within eleven years of her arrival in the US, she had learned English, graduated high school and medical school, met my father and given birth to me. She has had a distinguished medical career. She has raised two daughters and a profoundly disabled son. She has three grandchildren. She has had a long marriage and, with my father, ran a beautiful home. Her positive attitude during the Covid isolation period has been remarkable, evidence of her resilience and an example to us all.

For many, this time of Covid-19 is a traumatic period. For some, it is a time to look back at decades of life. For others, it is a time to look forward, wondering and worrying about what the future will bring. So, it has been for both my mother and for me. She has answered my ongoing plethora of questions, filling in details, so that at times I feel I am rebuilding a lost world piece by piece. Memories bubble up to the surface, little facts, thoughts, or feelings and sometimes we even share our emotions. I still long for that recognition, a kind of mirror to see my reflection in, but I am much more accepting now. Of course, what happened to her during the war shaped who she became; and it has shaped me too.

11 The dawn of realization

My parents knew each other already when living in Berlin. My Jewish mother Ruth met my non-Jewish father Erich when they were both members of a Jewish resistance group which was part of the Communist Party in Opposition (KPO), a splinter group of the main Communist Party (KPD). My father was the only non-Jewish member of that group, having been introduced to it by a Jewish friend, Heinz Sachs.

Even though it was clear early on that there was no future for Jews in Germany my parents waited until the end of 1938 before leaving. My mother hadn't wanted to desert her father, Benjamin Magnus, while her mother had already died from stress-related asthma in 1936, having been sickly for quite a while. They were lucky to get a visa for New Zealand (with Australia also being prepared to accept them) and my mother left Berlin legally in November 1938. It was a different story for my father who would not have been allowed to leave Germany after conscription was introduced there on 1 September 1938. As a subterfuge, he purchased a return rail ticket to Zürich, ostensibly to visit a friend and flew from there to London where he met up with my mother ten weeks later.

In Germany in September 1935 Hitler had introduced the Nuremberg laws which prevented my parents from marrying sooner. Those laws excluded German Jews from citizenship and prohibited them from marrying or having sexual relations with persons of 'German or related blood'. My parents had to wait until getting together again in London to get married. To seal their union they needed two witnesses, taking the landlady of their boarding house with them for one and grabbing the other off the street. Straight afterwards they took the train to Liverpool, boarded a boat to Newfoundland, crossed Canada by train and sailed from Vancouver to Auckland. I was born in July 1944 in Auckland and my brother Peter a year later. As I later learned from other refugee families, our parents wanted to assimilate locally as much as possible. Though we spoke German at home in those early years, that stopped once I went to kindergarten at the age of 3. Neither parent was religious and even the concept of religion was foreign to us. We grew up with a minimum understanding of Jewish culture and German history, but we did take note of the food parcels that my parents sent regularly to my father's family and to two of my mother's non-Jewish friends during the 1948 Berlin Blockade, *Luftbrücke*.

For me growing up involved hearing conflicting stories about Germany: my mother couldn't get over the death of her father and what the Nazis had done to the country and my father suffered from nostalgia for his beautiful home city of Berlin. As a result, I felt it was pre-ordained that I would one day visit the place and see it for myself and that is indeed what I did after completing my university studies. My intention was to stay away for two years as part of my 'OE' [Overseas Experience] that many young New Zealanders engaged in at that time.

What with numerous bureaucratic difficulties in getting both a residence and a work permit in Berlin and with finally getting a good position at the university as a computer programmer for a technical institute, it made no sense to quit after two years. In fact, I did not return to live in New Zealand until twenty years later, in 1986.

So, I arrived in Berlin, or Westberlin as it was officially known at that time, not being part of the German Federal Republic. I was on my own in a new country, at the age of 21, with everyone around me speaking a language that was not my mother tongue. I was picked up from the bus terminal by my father's sister, her husband and their grown-up daughter and whisked off to the family home in Charlottenburg. It was a welcome reception, and I was allowed to stay in their daughter's room. My cousin Jutta was 2 years older than me and lived in her own apartment, working as a sales assistant in a lighting store. From the start I was able to borrow a bicycle to explore the city and to this day cycling is my favourite way to not only get around the city but also to spend leisure time in Berlin's many forests, enjoying the beautiful river and lake scenery – my main occupation now whenever I visit during Berlin's summer months.

In the first weeks after my arrival my focus was on three things: learning the language (I would compile new vocabulary on a daily basis to enable me to carry out conversations beyond the minimum I needed to just get around); exploring the city on my bicycle; and meeting both my father's closest family and then the extended families from a step-uncle and a step-aunt, his father having married again. In the second stage of settling in my focus was directed towards three further aspects of life: finding a place to stay (for which I needed a residence permit); finding a job (for which I needed a work permit); and making friends by engaging in social activities. Without a residence permit I could not get a job and without a job I could not get a work permit and without a work permit I could not get a residence permit. I would spend days waiting in long queues outside the office of the Foreign Police for a chance to break through the bureaucratic stranglehold that engulfed me. That and my relative immaturity, at just 22 years of age, meant that history and Germany's past record did not feature prominently in my thinking. It had not helped me that growing up in New Zealand with my parents' unwillingness to talk in-depth about what pushed them out of their country of birth had left me naïve about the circumstances of their flight.

Some of those factors resulting from the Nazi era were forced on me in interactions with the various relatives and friends of my father. They lay latent in my mind and did not surface until years later when I was settled and had commenced researching and recording local history together with others of my age. To start with, the welcome at my aunt's place lasted only one week – until she discovered hairs in the bathtub and asked me to move out. I guess my free and easy New Zealand ways did not fit in with their more rigid 'German' way of thinking. There may even be some truth to the supposition that she was uncomfortable to be in such close proximity to someone of Jewish descent. I next moved to my step-aunt's family in one of the outer suburbs and stayed there for six weeks and could probably have stayed longer. But I felt I needed my own space.

'Flatting' as it is called in New Zealand did not yet exist in Berlin where it was customary to get a 'room with landlady'. My first endeavour in that direction was a dismal failure and I was given notice on the day I moved in. I learned that it was expected that I stay in my room and interact only with my landlady and her family. Instead, I dumped my two suitcases in the room and skedaddled off to spend time with another of my relatives.

When I returned there was a written notice waiting for me on my bed. The second such attempt was no more successful and I couldn't wait for a further month to pass before finding a place where I could live independently and permanently.

In time I discovered it was mainly only with new contacts and friends that I could be myself and feel unrestricted. With my immediate family I always felt a bit constrained, trying hard to please them and my father, who wrote letters twice a week, seemed to be telling me how I should behave. With the extended families, there was my step-aunt's family with three daughters at the time and a husband who was some political bigwig in the city – I never did find out exactly what he did.

After struggling through my first three months in this completely foreign environment, three things happened within just a few days and my whole outlook changed. First, I found a job as a research assistant and programmer at the Institute for Hydromechanics and Hydrology of the Technical University. Then with a letter containing a promise of employment signed by the Institute's professor who was highly respected with multiple PhDs (the same professor who later once said to me, completely unsolicited, that some of his best friends were Jews), I received the red-carpet treatment at the Foreign Police headquarters. And finally, I picked up a card at the student accommodation centre where I was able to rent a single room with its own entranceway. Even though that room was only twelve square metres in size it felt like paradise to me.

It is worth noting that in all my early bureaucratic struggles it mattered not one pfennig that my parents were originally German and had been forced to leave Germany to escape Nazism. So-called 'guest workers' from southern European countries including Italy, Turkey and Greece would have had no such problems getting the required permits but as a New Zealander I did not feature on the officials' radar – and the fact that my parents had become naturalized citizens of New Zealand and accepted as residents counted against me. Ironically when my younger brother moved to Berlin twelve years later and asked for a residence permit he was told that "German citizens do not require a residence permit". It seems a new law had been passed declaring that all descendants of German refugees were 'German by birth'. It no longer mattered that those original refugees may have adopted the nationality of their new home countries, rescinding their German citizenship in the process.

Meanwhile, Henry Sachs, my father's friend mentioned at the beginning of the chapter, and his wife Hanna had found a new home in New York and while I was living in Berlin they would come on regular visits every year. I felt they truly cared for me, becoming very much how I would have wished my parents to be. They were not controlling and accepted me for who I was. My father, on the other hand, seemed to care more for his Berlin family members than for me and yet not one of any of them ever spoke about the Nazi dictatorship. For me I would have appreciated some acknowledgement around the past, some acceptance of how most of the population could be conned into going along with Hitler's ravings and be so gullible in taking his madness on board, and even some admiration for the many acts of resistance that had been performed – whether open sabotage or secretly aiding those being persecuted. While I was not expecting to hear confessions of guilt, it certainly grated with me that those twelve years were simply being swept under the carpet as if nothing had happened. Of course, at the time I was too young and naïve to voice such feelings.

As for my mother, to what extent she was ever religious I do not know, but I do believe that she held 'God' responsible for what happened during the Nazi era and wanted nothing more to do with religion. Whenever I tried to ask questions about her past, she would recall her own father who at 74 years of age died from the conditions in the Theresienstadt, Terežin, concentration camp in November 1942. She tended to break down in tears and my brother and I learned very fast not to touch that topic. She became a very bitter lady as she aged – and family friends would frequently comment on that. As for Heinz Sachs mentioned at the outset, he and his wife Hanna had managed to escape to New York where he changed his name to Henry. After the war he returned to Germany for a short time to work as an interpreter at the Nuremberg trials. I so much wish now that I had asked him a lot more about his role in that capacity as well as about his and Hanna's whole life stories.

That was all about five years after my first arrival in Berlin. During that period, I got caught up in a first marriage, lasting three years. I was doubly drawn into that liaison, and it was probably what I needed to advance my maturity. On the one hand Nina related to my status as a 'returned Jew', telling me about her Jewish mother protected by her father, an SS officer, who had hidden them in an apartment in Paris during the war years (Nina was born in 1942) and on the other, Nina was my first real contact to the opposite sex. The relationship was doomed because of our lack of openness and lack of knowledge around mental illness that existed in those days. I understand now that Nina was suffering from bipolar disorder or manic depression. She had already survived one suicide attempt at the age of 16 or 17 and claimed she needed me and my easy-going Kiwi ways to maintain her hope in life.[1] I heard years later, from her daughter from a subsequent marriage, that the story of her Jewish mother and the Paris episode was not true. Could it have been wishful thinking on the part of someone living with the burden of German guilt on her shoulders?

As for the members of my father's extended family, once I felt I had established myself in Berlin they ceased to exist for me. Over the years the only one who stayed in contact and reached out to me was my grandfather's second wife, a simple woman of Polish stock and Catholic background. So much for what my father had tried to instil in me, that "blood was thicker than water", was a lesson I never did manage to learn. My step-grandmother was not a blood relative.

Having grown up without an extended family, it was not a big deal for me that nothing had changed in that respect even if it took a number of months before I realized that I could not relate to my father's motto. In time I accepted them as bystanders during the Nazi era and not as upstanders. For what it's worth, if I had felt then what I feel now I would certainly have been more challenging in discussions about the past than I was at the time. Even so, I doubt I would have made much progress with one family member in particular, my aunt's volatile husband. When I would spread margarine/butter thinly on my bread he would scream there was no need to do that, war time had long passed. Or when I mildly suggested that not everything in the east of the city (under communist rule) was necessarily

---

1   Kiwi is a familiar term that refers to people from New Zealand, including their language and culture.

'bad' he would explode and say if I didn't like it in the West, I could go over and live in the East.

Anyway, at the beginning of the 1970s with a good job under my belt and comfortable independent living secured, I began to find myself reflecting more on how I had got to be where I was. One day a copy of the *die tat* [the Action] fell into my hands and I immediately took out a subscription. Its editor Emil Carlebach was Jewish, a communist and active in the resistance against the Nazis. Arrested in 1937, he spent the entire war years in Buchenwald concentration camp where he was a member of the camp's resistance team. His pungent prose, he called a spade a spade, spoke to me as if from the heart. He wrote about resistance acts from the past, the commemoration of victims of Nazism and the continued presence of former Nazis in current Germany as well as the ongoing discrimination against communists. It was from the newspaper itself that I gained much of my knowledge of the Nazi era.

Together with others in 1947 Carlebach founded an organization made up of surviving resistance fighters and former victims of Nazism. That organization, the *Vereinigung der Verfolgten des Naziregimes* [Union of Victims of Nazism] (VVN), still exists today and at the time I first heard about it the doors to younger members had just been opened while the name was expanded to include people generally of an anti-fascist persuasion. I joined up immediately and felt right from the start that this was where I belonged. I continued my membership through the 1970s, attended meetings and learned about the dedication to keeping the memory of victims alive, to commemorating acts of resistance and honouring the memories of those who lost their lives fighting the Nazi regime and to combatting modern-day forms of fascism (the term 'Holocaust denial' was not then part of everyday language). I met many of those who had worked in the resistance and survived, most of whom had spent years in prison or a concentration camp. I learned about many of the crimes committed by the Nazis as well as about the various actions undertaken by resistance groups. I felt it was an honour and a privilege to be party to their stories.

After having spent twelve years in Berlin during which time I completed postgraduate studies and after a further three years in Nigeria where I obtained a posting at the Ahmadu Bello University in the north of Nigeria.

I returned to Berlin in 1980 and started IT work in the commercial sector while seeking some form of 'justification' for remaining in Germany. It was therefore most appropriate for me that a subgroup of young people in the VVN, all around my age, decided towards the end of 1980 to work towards the goal of producing booklets in time for publication two years later to mark the fiftieth anniversary of Hitler having been handed power to rule the country on 30 January 1933. Westberlin at that time was made up of twelve boroughs, *Bezirke*, and our group initially consisted of about twelve people, so we each selected our 'own' *Bezirk*. Each of us took time to study our region and gather information. We carried out our local research under the heading *Nazi Terror and Resistance Activities*. We held regular meetings and while we did not fully achieve our initial goal, we did manage to produce booklets for about six of the boroughs.

In my own case this period was one of intensive reading and research – a steep learning curve. The more I read the more I found to read. In the end I could not stop and with arguably excessive care for detail I ended up compiling a book with over 150 pages of small print. At the time I was of course working full-time. I had married again, and daughter Sara was born in 1983. I worked through my daughter's early years right up to the month before departing from Berlin to return to New Zealand, only just getting the booklet completed, published and distributed on time.

I considered myself lucky to end up investigating the central borough of Tiergarten which although small was the centre of much of the Nazi administration machinery. Central to the Nazi takeover was the burning of the seat of government, the *Reichstag*, presumably orchestrated by the Nazis themselves in order to consolidate their dictatorship – firstly to discredit and arrest major opposition politicians in the Communist Party but later also to remove and arrest members of the Social Democrat Party still in Parliament. Before then Tiergarten had been the scene of the murder by right wing paramilitary units of the most famous socialist leaders at the end of the First World War: Rosa Luxemburg and Karl Liebknecht. During the war years the *Volksgerichtshof* [Peoples Court], also located in Tiergarten, placed itself above common law by abusing all its privileges and passing countless death sentences for 'crimes' such as telling anti-Hitler jokes or harbouring Jewish people trying to live underground. Almost a third of the book was devoted to acts of resistance, much of that being undertaken by ordinary people individually or in clandestinely organized groups. Tiergarten was also the scene of the shooting of the chief collaborators in the 20 July 1944 failed assassination attempt on Hitler – in the *Bendler-Block*, today the site of a memorial museum. Finally, the central organization for euthanasia killings (200,000 in Germany alone, 100,000 in other European countries), the *T4 Aktion* [T4 Euthanasia Programme, officially instituted from 1939 to 1941] had its headquarters in Tiergarten.

Figure 11.1. Oliver's booklet on the Tiergarten district (Provided by Oliver Hoffmann).

One of the biggest shocks to me after I gained a stronger appreciation of the courage of those who had stood up against Hitler was when it dawned on me that those who spent years in prison or concentration camps during the war years often received a *Berufsverbot* sentence [professional ban] excluding them from the civil service and teaching positions. This was in the 1950s when they faced the same judges who had condemned them under Hitler. The anti-communist hysteria that had marked pre-war Germany was still prevalent in the then German Federal Republic.

For sure, were I living in Berlin today there would be at least one event every week that I would endeavour to participate in – whether at a protest against the latest neo-Nazi provocation or a commemoration of some anniversary of a resistance activity from the Nazi era. Instead, I am reduced to following the news from a distance, keeping abreast of developments from a new bi-monthly newspaper called the *antifa* and sharing some of the items from that publication with our local second-generation group on a regular basis and more infrequently at Auckland's annual *Limmud* event [Festival of Jewish learning]. Since retirement, I find myself reading all kinds of Holocaust-related literature – at least five books a year. Every single one made for fascinating reading.[2]

Reading about developments in Berlin – seventy-five years after the defeat of fascism – is still a roller coaster ride for me. The negative news from Germany never seems to cease. The most recent scandal is the decision of Berlin's Inland Revenue Department to withdraw the charitable status enjoyed by the VVN, the organization that continues to fight for peace and recognition of the victims of Nazism, an organization that is and has always been working in the public interest. Inland Revenue's twisted thinking claims that the organization's motto, 'fascism is not an opinion but a crime', is designed to incite violence and attack the Constitution. The positive news is that a large outcry resulted with immense efforts being undertaken to ensure that the officials retract their decision.

So what else was it like to be 'home' again in New Zealand? After spending so many years immersed in a different culture it's not surprising that my emotions ran the whole gamut from deprivation (lack of vibrancy)

---

2   These books are listed at the end of the chapter.

to joy and relief (friendly environment). No longer did I have to put up
with rudeness and typically abrupt behaviour, but suddenly I found myself
having to put up with vagueness and lack of commitment. Gone were many
close friends whereas old university friends from twenty years earlier had
changed. One plonked me down in front of the TV where we partook of
our evening meal; another grabbed a stick to beat his two daughters to bed
after a relaxing chat during dinner. I found myself looking for a range of
new activities and new friends to match my new position in life, a house
in the better part of the city, an easy job as a systems analyst and caring
for my daughter who was soon to start school. My first 'political' activity
started a year later when I joined the local Peace Foundation and became
active in a campaign to get the government to transfer One Day's Military
Spending towards 'peace-making' (ODMS).

I should add that my father Erich died in 1968, just a little over two
years after I left New Zealand. When he received his cancer diagnosis, he,
who had never expressed any religious views in his life that I recall, turned
to religion, Christianity, in his final months. He wanted and would have
paid for me to visit him before he died – but not for my then wife Nina
from whom he felt a certain antagonism. That marriage had been just one
way for me to assert myself and free myself from my parents' control – but
of course I had at that time merely slipped from one control to another. My
father disappointed me in other ways too, for instance in the early 1960s
he became an ardent fan of German's first post-war chancellor, Konrad
Adenauer. Adenauer, a fierce anti-communist, was instrumental in pursuing the separation of Germany into two parts by failing (unlike Austria)
to adopt a military neutral stance and that he kept his State Secretary Hans
Globke in his administration even after it was revealed that Globke had
played a major role in drafting the anti-Semitic Nuremberg Race Laws.

My mother Ruth lived until 2004. From her seventieth year onwards,
she started visiting Berlin again for about six weeks every European summer
until one year, about 1998, she simply did not return home. She lived independently in Berlin for another two or so years until she ended up in a
home, a prey to dementia.

It was many years before I heard that there was a second-generation
group holding regular sessions in Auckland. In the 1990s I was running

a small private bridge club – and two Holocaust survivors (Helen Erdos and Olga Romer from Hungary) were regular attendees. One day Helen happened to mention the group and put me in touch with the group's convenor. Many more years passed by before *Limmud* became a regular local event. Initially I was happy to help as a volunteer but subsequently I was twice accepted as a presenter. Even now I prefer the general atmosphere and the volunteering aspect rather than attending presentations, particularly with many of the topics being around Judaism, which was not something that had featured in my upbringing.

I've also been asked why I returned to New Zealand at all after having enjoyed life so much in Berlin. There are two main reasons for that. First, one of the best periods of my life had come to an end. My contract as a research assistant at the Technical University had lasted nine years. I enjoyed the liberal atmosphere offered by the university environment and loved the freedom that local society offered, the more so since pubs in New Zealand still closed at six in the evening, infamously known as the 'six o'clock swill', when I left the country. The dedication of a parent-children's *kinderladen* initiative where I participated with my girlfriend at that time meant a lot to me. This initiative like many others was set up by the parents themselves as a collective. The name was derived from kindergarten but mostly they were hosted in shops (Läden), hence the name *kinderladen*. Our group would meet on a weekly basis, starting at nine in the evening, and conduct serious discussions around educational issues connected with individual children. After the meeting we would continue informal discussion in a nearby pub until midnight (completely unheard of in New Zealand). The group would celebrate holidays together, go on picnics and organize annual trips – all with the children. I have not encountered anything like that in New Zealand but even in Berlin ten years later such initiatives no longer existed.

It had never really been my plan to live in Germany permanently. Berlin as a separate political entity to the German Federal Republic was for me a special case where it was acceptable to conduct my life. But even in Berlin I used to say that my New Zealand passport as well as the Berlin wall were my chief assets. The one would allow me to leave the place at a moment's notice, the other stood as a security symbol to prevent any

Figure 11.2. *Stolperstein* for Oliver's grandfather (Photo taken by Oliver Hoffmann).

further wars and served a reminder of what had occurred in the past. On top of all that came the long, cold winters – not a serious deterrent if you spend most nights until 4 o'clock in the morning in a cosy corner pub, but with increasing age and a young daughter those alternatives were coming to an end. I think I also missed the 'bush' even though one third of Berlin is recreational area.[3] Also, I felt that New Zealand was a better place for children to grow up in, so we left Berlin when daughter Sara had just turned 3.

Finally, in July 2012, together with my brother Peter we celebrated the setting of a *Stolperstein*, stumbling stone, as a memorial to our grandfather Benjamin Magnus. I gave the talk and Peter, together with a friend, provided the musical accompaniment on flutes to a gathering of about sixty people in front of Benjamin's last home in Joachim-Friedrich-Straße 49, Charlottenburg. I'd like to think that Benjamin and his wife Valeska would have been proud to know what became of their two grandsons.

---

3   Bush refers to native forest in New Zealand.

On reflection, I realise that historical events are far too important to be ignored, whether they occurred eighty years ago or just two years ago. It was a big shock for me to be made aware that racism does not just belong to one people's domain and that even tiny, isolated, New Zealand is not immune from the grips of hate speech and white supremacism. I refer to what is now known as the Christchurch massacre in March 2019.

Bibliography

Avidan, I. (2017). *Mod Helmy: Wie ein arabischer Arzt in Berlin Juden vor der Gestapo rettete*. [Mod Helmy: How an Arab Doctor in Berlin Saved Jews from the Gestapo]. München: dtv Verlagsgesellschaft.

Bade, J. (2005). *Im Schatten zweier Kriege: Deutsche und Österreicher in Neuseeland im zwanzigsten Jahrhundert*. [Shadows between Two Wars: Germans and Austrians in New Zealand in Twentieth Century]. Bremen: Temmen.

Batalion, J. (2021). *The Light of Days: Women Fighters of the Jewish Resistance – Their Untold Story*. London: Virago Press.

Engelmann, B. (1990). *Wie wir wurden, was wir sind: Von der bedingungslosen Kapitulation bis zur unbedingten Wiederbewaffnung*. [How We Became What We Are: From Unconditional Surrender to Unconditional Rearmament]. München: Goldmann Wilhelm.

Ferenc, B. (2002). *Less Than Slaves: Jewish Forced Labor and the Quest for Compensation*. Bloomington: Indiana University Press.

Gross, L. (1999). *The Last Jews in Berlin*. New York: Avalon.

Hoffmann, O. (1986). *Deutsche Geschichte im Bezirk Tiergatern, Naziterror und Widerstand 1933–1945*. West Berlin: VNN.

Lipstadt, D. (2006). *Denial: Holocaust History on Trial*. New York: Harper Collins Publishers.

Müller, I. (2014). *Furchtbare Juristen:* Die unbewältigte Vergangenheit der deutschen Justiz [Terrible Attorneys: The Unresolved Past of the German Judiciary]. Berlin: Tiamat.

Wichtel, D. (2017). *Driving to Treblinka: A Long Search for a Lost Father*. Wellington: Awa Press.

12 Into the stream of history

It wasn't until 1987, over twenty years since we left for New Zealand, that I returned to Vancouver. It's where I was born into a post-war, post-Holocaust world. We lived there until I was 13. It's where I last saw my father.

Figure 12.1. Diana's father in 1947 (From family collection).

The idea was to take our reconstituted little family – my partner Chris and his son, Ben; me and my son, also called Ben – to America. Disneyland for the kids, San Francisco, to meet up with my brother Jeff and his girl-friend. They were studying in Iowa but refused to let us visit them there in snowbound mid-winter. Vancouver? Well, we were going to be on the west coast. We might as well. I didn't admit it – the door to the life there had long ago slammed shut – but, filled with dread and yearning, I needed to go back.

The panic kicked in immediately. I insisted we get a taxi to stop in the dark so I could leap out and take a photo of the family home where we were happy, the one I still dream of. When I got it developed, the paper was blank.

I ran up and down Pender Street like a madwoman, looking for Dad's tailor's shop, *English Textiles*. I could still see it: the rows of fabric; the ornate cash register [...]. I knew it couldn't be there. The stores and immigrant tenements in that part of the street had been tidied away. But I was unable to stop myself from expecting to find my father more or less where we left him, standing outside the shop, smoking a cigarette, watching the world go by.

He died alone in 1970. Was it in Montreal, where he was when he sent the only heart-wrenching letter from him that I still have? Or Ontario, the place my mother mentioned before she decided she had to forget everything in order to carry on?

Mum, a Kiwi girl, had come to Canada, aged 29, on her travels. She went to work for my father.[1] Within a year she was pregnant, then married. He was 10 years older and had lost everything. He wasn't messing around.

If I asked Dad about his life before Canada, my mother was inclined to shut it down. "Don't upset your father." What did I know? That he was a Polish Jew. He was in the Warsaw Ghetto. "You would wake up in the morning and the person next to you was dead", he said when I sat with him in our Vancouver living room, stunned, watching the first documentary footage on television. I would later learn that his grandmother, Brandla,

---

1   Kiwi is a familiar term that refers to people from New Zealand, including their lan-
     guage and culture.

died of starvation in the ghetto in 1941. She gave her rations to the little ones. None survived.

I knew Dad jumped from a train carrying his family to Treblinka. I was told he hadn't been married but I have just found a record of his sponsored application to come to Canada that lists him as "widow". His wife may have been on the train, too. He had a photograph of his mother, Rozalia, by his bed. "How could you leave her?" I asked when I was small, not understanding what a terrible thing that was to say. "They would shoot you", was his reply to my questions about why he didn't fight, why everyone didn't just run away. The only option he had then was to choose the manner of his death. "I rolled down a bank and waited to be shot."

Finding himself miraculously alive, he took off into the forest. In July 1944, he was liberated by the Soviet Army with partisans near Lublin. Apart from one brother in New Jersey, who left Poland before the war, an aunt in Queens who emigrated in the 1920s and a few cousins we never saw, his Wichtel and Jonisz family of over 100 were systematically murdered. How did he know they were all dead? I once asked. He said, "I went back." Going back didn't seem like a good idea.

Things fell apart in the early sixties. By 1964, my mother later told me, when my father left for work, he was no longer going to *English Textiles* but sitting in the park feeding the birds. He was ill, physically and mentally, though I didn't know that then. Not really. When school finished for the summer my mother took me, my sister and my brother back to New Zealand, taking from the whole once solid-seeming edifice of our old life, just what we could carry. I know now that Mum's big Catholic family had mounted a rescue mission. Dad was meant to pack everything up and follow. He never arrived.

We ended up shipwrecked in a leaky *bach* [a vernacular Kiwi holiday cottage] on Auckland's Milford Beach. "Where is your father?" my new friends asked. It was a mystery. There were letters at first that became increasingly strange. In some, Dad seemed to think we were living the high life with his brother Sy in New Jersey. Then the letters stopped, as far as I knew. On our first Christmas in Auckland Mum rang him from a phone box near the beach. He said, "Come back, Diana. It's snowing in Vancouver." I was angry. It was the last time I spoke to him. I was a bitch. He knew that I loved the snow.

On that 1987 trip back to Vancouver we took the boys to Stanley Park, where Dad would take us on Sundays, his only day off, and buy us hot dogs and toy windmills and pony rides – "The sky is the limit!" It was thrilling to see a squirrel. Suddenly, the grass was seething with them and it felt like a bad dream. Going back to Vancouver: too many squirrels, too many ghosts.

We had arranged to meet Dad's oldest Jewish friends, who, for want of real relatives, we called Auntie Rose (scary) and Uncle Harry (legally blind and affectionate). We had dinner at a restaurant with them and Rose's sisters, Auntie Ethel and Auntie Ida. Ethel drove us to the restaurant through a city lit for Christmas. Dad never allowed Christmas lights, I told her. "Of course, he didn't. He was Jewish", she said. I didn't remind her that he wasn't big on Hannukah either and that the biggest Christmas tree in the street stood in our front window.

After dinner we went back to Rose and Harry's little house. There was the piano on which Rose taught us to play Heart and Soul. There was the chair where Dad would sit, smoking and arguing about politics. I excused myself, went to the bathroom and took a tranquillizer.

Rose didn't want to talk about Dad. Harry took me aside and whispered what he knew. He had offered assistance. Others had, too. It was refused. Dad left Vancouver, went east, disappeared. Harry wanted me to know he had tried. I gave him a hug.

It's a common thing in families with secrets and silences: we often leave it too late to open that door, to ask more questions. Dad's brother, Sy, had died by the time I reconnected with his widow, Mollie. She and my cousin Linda came from New York to visit us in New Zealand. She told me they tried to help him. She told my mother that leaving was the right thing to do. But I knew this terrible thing: my father lost everything and everyone, twice. He didn't abandon us, as I thought as an angry 13-year-old. We abandoned him.

Going back: that's how many of the second generation, children of Holocaust survivors, catch ourselves speaking of visiting the place we have never been, except in nightmares and imaginings so vivid they seemed like our own memories. The place our displaced parents came from. In 2010 we travelled to the UK when Chris had a three-month press fellowship to the University of Cambridge. Haunted by my preoccupations, he included the architecture of murder and memorial in his studies. "We will go to Poland", he declared. I can't now believe how reluctant I was. To me it was a graveyard, the place where my father was hunted not just by the occupying Nazis but by some fellow Poles. Anti-Semitism in Poland didn't start or finish with the War. I didn't hear my father express much bitterness, but he made it clear that was a particularly bitter betrayal.

We stayed first in Kazimierz, the old Jewish Quarter of Kraków. Our hotel had a mikvah, a ritual bath. There were stores with little wooden figures of stereotypical Jews, some holding money bags. For good luck you tipped them up so the money might come your way. This couldn't be right, I thought. We ate at a restaurant made up of old shops knocked together, still featuring the names of the Jews who had owned them. "Sit down at the original carpenter's workbench. Touch the flywheel of an ancient sewing machine", urged the menu. I turned over the page to see what had happened to those who once owned the shops. Nothing. We asked if the place was owned by Jewish people. "No." This weird mix of nostalgia for a vibrant lost culture and something not so cosy has been referred to as 'shtetl chic' and 'Jewrassic Park'. It's funny. It's deeply disturbing. Going back in reality outdid anything I could imagine.

In Warsaw, we picked out the traces of the ghetto. We joined the crowds of 'dark tourists' and went to Auschwitz. "You will see the industrialization process of murder by the Nazis", my father's first cousin Joe, keeper of what family history we had, wrote to me from Pennsylvania. "It is an education like no other." History felt so close. Too close.

It's amazing the narratives you get used to. My father was lost. I tried to find him but couldn't. Nothing to be done. One day my daughter, Monika, and my niece, Nicola, got sick of my kvetching [whine or grumble] about this futile quest. "You can't not know where your father is buried. It's not acceptable", they said. "Mum, it's not normal." I discovered then that it is possible to make a conscious decision to stop not knowing, if not for me then for the generations who came after and deserved to have their history.

Around that time, I had managed to wrangle a phone interview with American classicist and writer, Daniel Mendelsohn, about his epic memoir tracing his family's Holocaust history, *The Lost: A search for six of six million*. I took the opportunity to get some tips on the search for my own lost.

"Insert yourself into the stream of history", he advised. "Open the door to the past for good, knowing there's no closing it again."

My late brother-in-law, Jim, a lawyer, had been quietly applying his forensic mind to my situation. He sent me the name of an archive in Ontario. I filled in the forms, expecting the usual sort of reply. We regret to inform you that there is no sign your father ever existed. They came back with additional questions. I sent what I knew and held my breath. "We have found your father", they wrote.

I expected a few index cards. What arrived was a large envelope straining to contain 158 pages charting his last three years of life, at Brockville Psychiatric Hospital. I sat down, read the pages and wept. It was the story of a man who found himself alone again, betrayed, back in the forest, fighting to survive, still trying to get some justice.

He believed there were forces arrayed against him because why wouldn't he believe that? In psychoanalyst Stephen Grosz's collection of case studies, *The Examined Life*, he writes of a patient who, when she returned home after a work trip, was convinced the door was wired to blow her up. It emerged that this was her way of dealing with returning to a cold, empty apartment. To think that someone is after you is better than to feel forgotten. "Her paranoia", writes Grosz, "shielded her from the catastrophe of indifference."

That, in the end, was my father's catastrophe. His stay at Brockville began when he was picked up wandering across a bridge in the direction of the US border. Was he trying to get to New York, thinking he would find us at Uncle Sy's? Among his effects was a 'Jewish cap'. By the time he died, he seemed to be claiming to be Catholic. Maybe it felt safer. There was a priest who visited him. It is also recorded in his notes that his Polish family had died during the war in an "accident". By then, perhaps it was easier to believe in bad luck.

He died on 26 November 1970. The funeral was on 30 November, my birthday. The worst sentence in a devastating file: "Friends and family present: none".

What had I done? This tragedy to which I felt like an accessory would have to be shared with my family. Chris and I were planning another trip to Poland. We hastily added a stop in Ontario where, incredibly, my brother was now living two hours away from his lost father, and a visit to a grave with an institution plaque, the name wrongly spelled, in a Catholic cemetery in Brockville. Daniel Mendelsohn wrote, "There is only looking, and finally seeing, what was always there."

In Poland again, I visited the Emanuel Ringelblum Jewish Historical Institute.

They had found small fragments of my family: my father's registration card from after liberation; my great-Uncle Paul's; addresses where they had lived. On that trip, the past suddenly lived.

We trekked through the overgrown ground of Warsaw's Jewish Cemetery (me on a knee damaged on the train from Berlin, my psychic pain made physical) and found the graves of my grandfather and great-grandfather. I found myself embracing their shared stone – hello, Jacob Joseph and Chaim Dov Wichtel – and pressing my face to its sun-warmed surface. To our amazement there was the grave of my great-grandmother, Brandla Jonisz, who starved to death in the ghetto in 1941, when funerals could still be permitted, to give an illusion of normality. One crazy day, Chris drove us to Treblinka. Tour buses slowly rolled into the car park. The Nazis destroyed the camp in 1943 so there are only representations – symbolic train tracks, a symbolic cremation pit – of its horrors. An estimated 870,000 people were murdered. "They destroyed this beautiful family, beautiful people", wrote my cousin Joe. "You go to Treblinka, there are no graves. There are symbols of stone but they simply represent the dust. That's what the Germans accomplished."

I have friends who would never set foot on that soil. But after all those years of resisting going back, here I was. I had to fight the urge to lie down on the ground to get as close as I would ever get to my family whose ashes were there. We left stones with others on a memorial, and a message listing all the names we knew, knowing the rain would soon wash it away.

One day a publisher sent me an email. She had read an essay I had written about the business of going back to Poland. Did I want to write a book about it? By now there was no closing that door. I said yes and proceeded painfully to add to the genre of family Holocaust memoirs with the word "search" in the title: *Driving to Treblinka: A long search for a lost father*. I applied for a writing award – the Grimshaw Sargeson Fellowship – and somehow got it. We moved into a small flat in what had once been stables at the University of Auckland. Every day I wrote at a big desk at a high window. Four months in a sort of altered state, going back: to the houses where we lived and the singalongs and the happy times before everything got broken. My father visited me in dreams. It was only after the book was sent off to the publisher that there was a severe anxiety attack about putting it all out there combined with, perhaps, a measure of long-delayed grief and transmitted trauma.

What had I done? It was so ... personal. It had to be. It was my version of a story that not everyone in the family sees in the same way.

In the end there is always more than one story. I know now that the past isn't safely back there somewhere, out of reach. It flows alongside the present. Dip into the stream of history and things can change. Since the book, I've connected with family I didn't know. Strangers have got in touch. There are those rare ones – from Australia, from Peru – who are Jewish and have 'Wichtel' in their family tree. "We must be cousins!" I have come across others whose fathers jumped from a train to Treblinka. A childhood friend turned up to my event at the Vancouver Jewish Book Festival. Some of the third generation – my daughter, my nieces – have explored their Jewish heritage. They have changed my narrative – one of unremitting, unalterable tragedy – about their *zayde* [granddad in Yiddish]. As my daughter said, after reading about how he survived: "That's some Tarantino shit." He jumped. He ran. He fought. They have returned him to me as a hero.

There are attempts, too little and too late, to try to repair the past. When we visited that small, overgrown plaque at the cemetery where my father lay, it seemed so wrong. We have to dig up the grave and take his bones back to New Zealand, I said. Chris and my brother Jeff thought I had gone mad. We can make a new headstone, they said.

In June 2016, our family from New Zealand, Canada and the United States gathered in Brockville to unveil the new stone. In Canada, my cousin Linda pointed out, it was Father's Day. Because of a glitch at the cemetery and because, in our family, even the solemnest occasion has its farcical elements, we found the stone covered in a black rubbish bag with a festive red ribbon. My father might have found that funny.

For years it had seemed that his story ended like that of almost every one of his family in Poland. He was erased. The stone now tells who he really was: "Benjamin Hersz Wichtel, May 16, 1910 – November 26, 1970. Holocaust survivor, survivor of the Warsaw Ghetto, fighter in the forests of the old world who started again in the new." It is inscribed with the names of all of his descendants, so he is no longer alone.

One morning, back in New Zealand, sitting at breakfast in a hotel in Hamilton after a book event, tears dripped into my congealing scrambled eggs as I read a message from my niece, Jocelyn, in Ontario. The family had been passing Brockville. "We stopped in to say hi to Ben Wichtel, of course." She noticed people had been placing pebbles on the stone. There were two lanterns that hadn't been there before, with burned tea candles, and the stump of a smoked cigar. She returned with candles, a lighter and a note, which she left in a jar. Soon she heard from a man, call him Frank, who had been drawn to my father's grave and liked to spend time with him. My father, a dedicated smoker, would have appreciated the cigar. In 2019, when our family gathered again in Ontario for my stepson's wedding, we visited Dad's grave with my brother and met Frank. He had the same build as my father and my brother, Jeff. I thanked him for looking after my dad and gave him a hug. "Your father has been a good friend to me", he whispered in my ear.

Then came an email from Jan, another complete stranger from Brockville. She had been out on a solitary Covid isolation walk. "I came across the gravestone of your father, Benjamin", she wrote. "The Star of David was glowing in the April sunshine and drew me over." Now she visits him often. On his birthday, 16 May, she called by and laid a stone. My father, always charming in life when circumstances permitted, is still making friends. A little community is forming around him.

"Our inability to be with him in his final years, when he needed us most, is a scar our hearts", my brother Jeff had said at the headstone unveiling. He was talking about the guilt. It can be an indulgence. Sometimes it's easier to imagine that you could have done something to make things turn out differently than to feel you were entirely without agency: helpless. "You were a child", my cousin Jill said to me. "You didn't have a vote." But I'll hang onto the guilt. It's what I have to offer. You must have closure now, people say kindly. Well, no. I don't want closure. I'm keeping the door open, staying in the stream of history. It's where my father has always been.

I used to be so envious of those who were able to go back to Europe with parents who escaped before the war or survived it. I would never have those conversations. Then, while I was writing the book, doing my random searches for 'Wichtel', I discovered a piece by Professor Emeritus at the University of Maryland, C. Fred Alford, about transmitted trauma. The professor had read online an essay I wrote about my father. It mentioned a game I had made up to play with him. He always came home late. The table was set, beautifully, for one. On a dark night when he would arrive at the back door, my sister and I would muss up his hair, turn up his collar, cast him as a homeless wanderer seeking help. We would bring him in from the cold and lead him to the table. It was a strangely satisfying ritual. Alford (traumatheory.com, 2015) saw this as an acting out of his Holocaust experience.[2]

> We neglect the degree to which the child and adolescent needs to know and feel the inner reality of the parent, even if this reality includes horror. Without this access, everything feels phony, unreal, including the child him or herself. If the parent has been horrified, then the child needs to be horrified too if they are to be securely attached.
>
> He and his children seem to have been able to play-act his duality, his frightening strangeness that was also a closeness, in a way that worked to contain the horror. Had this part not been shared, the young girl would have been less attached, not only to her father but to life itself.

2   A different version of this story is told in, Alford C. F. (2016: 64–65).

Figure 12.2. Family Portrait Christmas 1951. Diana is on her mother's knee and sister Rosalind standing (From family collection).

There are many ways to interpret my story, Alford concludes. "One is that her father gave her a great gift." In our house of secrets and silences I was trying to ask my father about the past he couldn't talk about – at least in part because no one wanted to listen – and he was trying to tell me about it. It meant we had a relationship. It meant we shared a journey. We were going back, together.

Bibliography

Alford, C. F. (2015). *Daddy Mad Face and Daddy Angel Face: Trauma and Attachment.* <https://traumatheory.com/daddy-mad-face-and-daddy-angel-face-trauma-and-attachment/>.

Alford, C. F. (2016). *Trauma, Culture, and PTSD.* New York: Palgrave Macmillan.

Grosz, S. (2014). *The Examined Life: How We Lose and Find Ourselves.* New York: Norton.

Mendelsohn, D. (2008). *The Lost: A Search for Six of Six Million.* New York: Harper.

Wichtel, D. (2017). *Driving to Treblinka: A Long Search for a Lost Father.* Wellington, NZ: Awa Press.

13 Shards of the past

The train from Kraków to Auschwitz was a socialist achievement of discomfort and inconvenience. You would think that fifteen years after the
Fall of the 'Iron Curtain' these old trains could have been replaced with
something more modern. Still, there were probably other priorities. The
train proceeded cautiously on the worn-out track making British rail-
ways seem like a world class example of smoothness and efficiency.

My husband Martin and I were on our way to Auschwitz-Birkenau to
retrace the footsteps of my parents who had spent six months there, to pay
respects to my relatives who were murdered there and to find the suitcase
that used to belong to Mitzi, my mother's cousin. In our small rucksack
we had my parents' slim war memoirs, a box of matches, several memorial
candles, my mother's old tablespoon and a small plastic box.

It was July in 2004, eleven years since my mother's death and sixteen
years since my father died. It was also sixty years, almost to the day since
my parents had survived Dr Mengele's selections for the gas chambers and
were sent to other camps instead. And it was sixty years since my father's
brother, my uncle Max was sent together with almost 4,000 other Czech
Jews to be gassed during one night in March 1944. I have always known
that one day I will have to make this pilgrimage.

Now was as good time as any but my body did not want to go to
Auschwitz. I started feeling ill days before our departure from Bristol, with
headaches and horrible nightmares about vicious dogs.

We arrived in Kraków the day before and settled ourselves in a hotel
room with papier-mâché sheets on the bed. We were in the Kazimierz district where the Jews of Kraków used to live. Szeroka, the main square, was
used by Spielberg in his film *Schindler's List* and had several charming little
restaurants decorated with carved wooden figures of orthodox Jews with
flowing beards and clutching violins. Klezmer music came softly through

the speakers and the Central European Jewish cuisine that was offered was delicious and reminiscent of my mother's cooking.

There were tourists including Jews and Israelis, but local Jews were absent. It was like visiting the paraphernalia of an extinct North American Indian tribe. I became aware of my sense of desolation which was made worse by the feverish state of a bad cold. The world reached me through a fog of muffled sounds that ricocheted in my brain. My reactions felt slow, unreal and underwater.

The train was drawing closer to the small town of Oswieczim which was about a kilometre from the main Auschwitz camp. The buildings could have been there from the 1930s or earlier and though I knew that my parents could not have seen them from their sealed cattle train, the buildings would have witnessed the 'Jew trains'. If only buildings could talk, I thought, not for the first time.

We walked through the infamous *Arbeit macht frei* [work sets you free] entrance to the Auschwitz base camp and went to the archive buildings which were immediately on the left. A pleasant young man called Simon Kowalski asked for my parents' Auschwitz tattoo numbers, their full names and date of arrival in Auschwitz. He then pulled out their registration cards and told us their precise dates of departure from Auschwitz. Oh, the wonders of the German sense of order and organization! They might have murdered millions, but it had to be properly registered! And so, we discovered that my parents left the death camp only days before thousands of their fellow Czech Jews were sent to the gas chambers. Looking at their Auschwitz registration cards, my parents' six months existence in the camp and their survival against all the odds became more real than ever before. Simon photocopied my parents' memoirs and asked about their lives after the war. I was deeply touched by his genuine interest and felt a curious sense of pride that their lives continued after the horrors, that they were able to enjoy life, to laugh and to tell jokes, that they had me and later also grandchildren whom they adored and who loved them in return, that they led happy lives well into their old age.

My parents, Otto and Ella Deutsch, were married before the war. They were the only survivors of their extended families of whom some eighty members had perished. My parents were unusual in post-war

Czechoslovakia as very few Jewish couples had both survived. After the war my parents had returned to Prague, to the same block of apartments from which they had been taken in 1941 and did their best to start a new life. Despite their barely comprehensible losses they had a positive outlook on life and a deep love for each other. When, two years after she was liberated from Bergen-Belsen, my mother became pregnant at the age of 37, she was initially horrified, assuming that the baby was going to be born damaged as a result of her experiences in the camps. She later described to me vividly how she had tried to get rid of me. A month before I was born the communists took power in Czechoslovakia and many Jewish survivors left for Palestine. My parents had neither the energy nor the will to emigrate and to start all over again. They stayed and I was brought up in a communist country. My mother talked about her experiences in the camps openly, eloquently and frequently. Her 'Auschwitz verbosity' sometimes bordered on the embarrassing. While waiting for her in a public toilet she could be heard shouting from her cubicle: "It's like Auschwitz here, there is no toilet paper." The women waiting in the queue were probably wondering whether the infamous horrors of Auschwitz were about the lack of toilet paper or whether the shouting woman was a lunatic. My father rarely made any comments about the war but about a year before he died, he suddenly started talking and could not stop. Later he wrote down his memories and they proved to be a remarkable record of facts, names, dates and events. My mother added her short war memoir to fill in the gaps left by my father. My mother's memoir is more about feelings than my father's, and she often describes events from the female point of view: for example, how quickly women lost their menstruation, how women were forced into sex or sold sex for bread and survival, their own and sometimes their mothers' too, how often women were tougher than men and survived longer.

Five of my parents' many cousins managed to get out of Czechoslovakia just before the war broke out. They went to Palestine, the USA, Africa and Australia. After the war my parents maintained regular correspondence with the cousins and I am to the present day in touch with some of their children who are roughly my generation. A distant relative informed me that one of the suitcases on display in Auschwitz was the suitcase of her aunt and my mother's cousin, Marie Kafka, known in the family as Mitzi.

My mother grew up with Mitzi and her six siblings and I heard a lot about her during my childhood. Simon checked the veracity of the suitcase, and it was indeed as my relative said. Mitzi arrived in Auschwitz the same day as my mother but perished in the gas chamber. The suitcase was right behind the glass panel of the display box with her name chalked on it, staring me sadly in the face. I thought of the tall 35-year-old Mitzi with her large brown eyes wrapped in a long black coat which together with her suitcase and her life was soon to be ripped from her. The suitcase was the only tangible witness of her existence.

We had no more time to spend in the base camp (Auschwitz I) as the main task of tracing my parents' footsteps lay still ahead of us. We now needed to get to Birkenau (Auschwitz II) which is 3 kilometres from the main camp. We decided to take a taxi. The loquacious taxi-driver's chat in a mixture of Polish and pidgin English was truly irritating: "I give special deals. I take people to many death camps. There are many death camps in Poland. You want to see Treblinka or Sobibor? Very good. Me take you. Very special deal for you."

"No, thank you", said my husband crossly.

On entering Birkenau, we followed the train tracks which led under the main entrance and its observation tower. We climbed to the top of the tower and suddenly there it was in front of us, unadorned and unsanitized for tourists, brutal and shocking in its vast reality. Stretching towards the horizon were brick chimneys each surrounded by a rectangular outline of the foundations.

Apart from a few reconstructed barracks these were the remnants of the prisoners' barracks. They were in rows, separated by barbed wire fencing, which were originally charged with electric current and sentry towers. I had seen photographs of Auschwitz-Birkenau in the past: the entrance, the ramp, the rail track. I knew that the scale was enormous but this apocalyptic sight with its grim brick fingers accusingly pointing to the low grey sky was offensive to the soul. We could see in the distance the birchwood, after which the camp was named, and which hid, we knew, the remnants of the gas chambers.

Having consulted our map and my father's memoir, which acted like a guidebook, we realized where the Czech sub-camp would have been.

The entrance to it had a gate with a loose chain across it. We looked surreptitiously around and broke in. The main road stretched ahead of us, roughly made and uncomfortable to walk on. The chimneys of the buildings and their foundations were on each side. Thirty-two barracks, wrote my father in his memoir, with 400 prisoners in each. So, this was the road on which my father was hit in the face by the *kapo*, [prisoner assigned by SS to supervise forced labour or carry out administrative tasks] Arno Boehm, a slap, he wrote, that was like a kick by a horse. I stood there, thinking of my father's lovely face, his large friendly ears and deep brown eyes full of Jewish wisdom and sadness; and what those eyes and those ears that I loved so much must have witnessed.

We found where the block number six, the former latrine, used to be and where my parents used to meet in secret. Here, one day, my father had a surprise for my mother when he untied his trouser leggings, stood on his head and his few stolen, half frozen potatoes rolled out.

They had a forbidden potato feast and risked their lives for it. I walked up and down block number six, whispering private thoughts and private fury and my grief at it all, and marvelled at my parents' survival and understood why they called me a miracle baby when I was born. I was a miracle because after all the suffering that they had been through, physical and mental, a healthy baby was born unto them. A symbol of new beginnings, a renewal, life re-born and a replacement for all those children in their families who had been murdered or had no chance to be born. I have always been aware of this unspoken responsibility to make good again, this shadow that has been following me throughout my life. Sometimes I forgot its existence, sometimes I struggled with it and sometimes I delved into its dark corners trying very hard not to get lost.

Not far from the Czech enclosure there was a sunken footpath about three meters wide with barbed wires on each side. It was the road to Gas Chambers IV and V along which the Jews were forced to walk or to run. I was staring at the Commandant's headquarters which was straight ahead of us and suddenly realized that my parents would have been able to see that too, as well as the main entrance tower and the woods with their not so well-hidden deadly secret. As we approached the birchwood we saw the ruins of a building which was all that was left of *Krematorium V*.

My uncle Max was murdered there, together with almost 4,000 other Czech Jews during the night from the 8–9 March in 1944. The gas chamber could not cope with so many victims and they were made to wait their turn in the birchwood. They sang the Czech national anthem and *Hatikva* [the Jewish national anthem]. Their singing from inside the gas chamber could be heard until there was no more singing.

We were completely alone. The tourists were elsewhere and there was an eerie silence. It was the middle of July and we were in a woodland but we heard no birdsong. There seemed a tangible sense of evil in this place but perhaps our imagination went into overdrive.

We took out the candles: two yellow ones for my grandparents who died in Birkenau of starvation and disease and a white one for Max who was only 24 years old when he was murdered. We also had several nightlight candles to represent all the other members of my family who had perished in the Holocaust. Martin helped me to light the candles and find a place for them that somehow seemed right. It was cold, windy and grey. I started saying my own version of Kaddish as I did not know the real thing and mumbled my own prayer for them all, all dead now including my parents, all having suffered tortures physical and mental that we, the second generation, despite having been brought up in the shadow of the Holocaust, cannot fully understand. I told my family that here I was, sixty years later, and that they were and will be remembered. A cage of sadness and grief came down on me. My cold had suddenly gone to my chest and breathing became difficult. I started to cry and realized that this was the very first time, at the age of 56, that I was able to cry for my murdered relatives and for my parents' suffering, as well as for my own sorrow at having had my grandparents, uncles and aunts and cousins stolen from me.

The soil in Birkenau is still mixed with human ashes and using my mother's old tablespoon I scooped up a little of it into our small box. The soil was going to be put into my parents' grave in Bristol – a symbolic re-union with their lost loved ones.

It was only after my parents' deaths that I felt able to verify their written accounts of what had happened to them, put up plaques for my murdered grandparents and uncles, visit Auschwitz and find the very place in Bergen-Belsen where my mother discovered that my father was alive and that life was worth living again.

In July 1944, after my parents had got through the Mengele selection, my father was sent to a small labour camp called Blechhammer which was one of the satellite camps within the orbit of Auschwitz. In mid-January 1945 he escaped from Blechhammer and thus avoided the so-called Death March on which thousands of famished, sick and exhausted prisoners perished. Somehow, he managed to walk through the front line of fighting between the German and Soviet armies and after an odyssey journey of several months he arrived back in Prague in May, shortly after Prague was liberated by the Soviet Army.

Meanwhile, my mother had been sent to a concentration camp in Hamburg in July 1944 where she, like many others, was used for slave labour to repair the damage done by British bombing. In March 1945 she was taken to Bergen-Belsen concentration camp where she was liberated by the British on 15 April 1945. Like thousands of others, she was suffering from typhus and was close to death. She was moved by the British to the hospital block and, although well looked after she was not recovering. In late June a letter arrived for her. My father, back in Prague, had discovered that my mother was still alive and had sent her a letter through the Red Cross. She always claimed that it was the only love letter she had ever received from him. "Darling, you are alive!" it began.

There was a sudden miraculous recovery: my mother's will to live had returned. She ran out with the letter, down the steps of the hospital building and into the nearby wood to have a private moment with this unexpected happiness.

By 2015 I had translated my parents' memoirs and was using them in schools in my teaching of the Holocaust and on Holocaust Days. My job was history teaching in schools and the teaching of the Holocaust was a part of the syllabus. I taught it at different levels including A level. My students needed a primary document to help them to understand what the experience was really like for the prisoners. My father, who as I said earlier, only started talking about his experiences towards the end of his life, was persuaded by me to write everything down. I then promptly translated his war memories from Czech into English, and almost immediately started using them with my students. The manuscript had an enormous impact on them because they knew that their history teacher was the daughter of the author. It all became very real to my students and I felt a huge sense of achievement that my father's voice was reaching them.

It took a few more years for me to find the time to translate my mother's memoir. Although it was much shorter than my father's, it was difficult to translate as the format was in the form of a letter to me and had references to people that only I knew. I wanted the document to be accessible to wider readership and therefore it needed sensitive editing and putting into a context.

In 2015 I decided to donate my mother's memoir to the Bergen-Belsen concentration camp archive. For several weeks I corresponded with the Deputy Archivist, Bernard Horstman. Quite unexpectedly he invited Martin and me to join the forthcoming commemoration of the seventieth anniversary of the liberation of Bergen-Belsen.

One of the commemorative events was an evening with long speeches and a short concert in the City Concert Hall in Hannover in the presence of the German Federal President and hundreds of guests which included some eighty survivors. The following day we visited the site of the camp with its infamous mass graves. There were more speeches and some interesting encounters. We talked with two Germans of our age who stressed how their generation, despite everything, hadn't really been told by their families what had happened and how they felt the guilt and responsibility as Germans. I spoke to several survivors, one of whom was liberated as a 3-year-old!

Then we went by bus convoy to the British Hohne Camp Roundhouse, still occupied by the British Army. This was originally the base for the SS from which they had controlled Belsen. The centre of this army camp was a handsome circular building with a huge reception hall, all originally built by the Wehrmacht. Now, in April 2015 the British Army was hosting all these hundreds of people with a proper British roast lunch.

I knew that somewhere here was the place where my mother had been recuperating from typhus and where she had received my father's letter. She must had been here, in the very same place, I thought.

The Deputy Archivist met us on the steps outside the main hall. I handed over my mother's memoir and asked him where the hospital was in April 1945. "Exactly, where you just had your lunch", he answered. The steps she ran down clutching my father's letter were exactly where we were standing and in front of us was the wood where she went to hide, dreaming about life starting again. This was an overwhelming experience and I felt deeply moved. I wanted to tell her that I have translated her memories and that they have come a full circle, back to the place where they were born and that I was now able to feel her joy at being alive in the Spring of 1945 and knowing that she will see her husband again.

I have deposited my parents' memoirs in the archive of the museum Beit Theresienstadt in Israel and I have also donated them to the Jewish Museum in Prague. The archivists in Prague added the documents to their collection of similar documents and recorded an interview with me as a member of the second generation who grew up in socialist Czechoslovakia. We, the children of Holocaust survivors were a small group who felt affinity towards each other which we could not express and only understood as adults. After the Soviet invasion of Czechoslovakia in 1968 many of us left the country and went into exile for political reasons. Most of us could not return to Czechoslovakia until 1989 when the 'Iron Curtain' collapsed. Since then, every three years we gather together some 200 people who are now dispersed all over the world, and remember our unusual and yet normal childhood, we laugh about the bizarre antics of the communist regime, tell jokes and talk about our different lives in different countries. We call ourselves 'The Children of Maislova', the name of the street where the Prague Jewish Town Hall is and where we used to meet as children and as adolescents. We come home to remember our past, our parents' past, our ancestors' past.

But it is the past and I, for one, have come to terms with my awkward Holocaust inheritance. It is always there, like a scar that one gets used to and notices only occasionally, but it no longer hurts.

My journeys into the past were revealing, sometimes traumatic, always interesting and very healing. As a secular Jew I don't feel that I really belong to the Jewish community in Britain but strangely I feel that my soul is Jewish. I cannot imagine ever living in Prague again and yet Prague is in my heart.

The Czech national anthem opens with the words "Where is my home?" Where indeed? I used to wonder about belonging and I still think that my European roots are deep and that I could be at home anywhere in Europe, if only Brexit would let me. "A citizen of nowhere", as a certain politician said.

But the truth is simple: my home is where my family live, including my children and grandchildren and that is England and that is what is really the substance of my life. My parents and my ancestors would agree.

14 Black milk and word light: To Latvia, Siberia and back

Reachable, near and not lost, there remained in the midst of the losses this one thing: language. It, the language, remained, not lost, yes, in spite of everything. But it had to pass through its own answerlessness, pass through frightful muting, pass through the thousand darknesses of death bringing speech. It passed through and gave back no words for that which happened; yet it passed through this happening. Passed through and could come to light again, "enriched" by all this.

– Paul Celan, 1986: 34

It's 30 October 2020 and I am sitting at my desk waiting for words to come. I have done everything possible to make this writing time free and now I sit, and I struggle to voice feelings to impressions, thoughts, recaptured memories that perhaps I have not even realized I had until now. I feel as if I am being put into a washing machine and soon, I am meant to step outside the rotating buzz, shake myself down, be hung up to dry and wait to be ironed, neatly. But life is not neat I hear you say, and you are right.

I was born on a cold winter's day in 1964 within reach of Bow Bells (The bells of St Mary-le-Bow: a reference to those born in London's East End). I am a Londoner you could say but my DNA says otherwise, indeed my roots come from the frozen north: Norway, Latvia and Russia and Germany, too.

My father, Ernst Josef Loewenberg, born in 1922 in Halle an der Saale, in Germany but whose passport stated Latvian, as his father David Levenbergs was born in Liepaja, Libau, Latvia, managed to get out of Nazi Germany with the help of the ORT school (Organization for Rehabilitation through Training, a Jewish agricultural and craft training school) three days before the outbreak of war. His mother, my grandmother, Marianne Loewenberg née Peiser, a professional violinist and opera singer from

Leipzig managed to get out on a domestic visa six months before, the rest
of my Jewish family did not.

My mother, Rosemarie née Lessing, born in 1935 in Luckau, Germany,
is not Jewish but Christian. In 1946 at the age of 11 and after the Russians
had arrived on their estate and my grandmother Ruth Redlich had been
raped, the family fled. With her mother Ruth, her handicapped brother
Günter and her older brother Dieter, my mother swam across the river
Elbe for the West.

My grandmother died of breast cancer when I was 6. My last memory
of her is picking red currants in her beautiful garden in West Germany,
a rundown field into which she poured all her dreams. Once back in the
kitchen we put the ruby berries into a bowl, poured milk and sugar over
them and ate until the bowls were empty.

My mother's father Günter Lessing, my grandfather, a man I loved
and looked up to, was a 'Junker', an estate owner from a very well-known
German family of artists and publishers: the Lessings. The most famous
of my Lessing ancestors was Gotthold Ephraim Lessing, an eighteenth-
century philosopher and playwright, whose books were burnt during the
Nazi period.

My Lessing grandfather had apparently been a high-ranking freemason
and to his funeral in 1977 a number of masons suddenly turned up. With
childlike curiosity, I viewed them as one would an alien. Many years after
his death, I became aware that my grandfather had been a major in the
Wehrmacht [the armed forces of the Third Reich] and to my horror, a
Nazi party card carrier.

Perhaps like many of the upper classes, my grandfather mistakenly
and arrogantly had thought Hitler could be controlled. Perhaps he joined
the party due to social pressures or to avoid harassment as he was a great
nephew of Lessing whose books Hitler was busy burning. Or perhaps he
simply approved of the Nazis at first?

Had he? Such thoughts regularly went through my mind, and I lived
with doubt and fear until I read a diary from a friend of my grandfather
who stated, "*Lessing muss aufpassen*" [Lessing has to be careful]. He had
disobeyed orders and was in danger of being court martialled. Until I read
that diary and had seen *Opa's* [Granddad's] military record from the

Deutsche Dienststelle [German government agency holding the records of the Wehrmacht] I lived with a deep sense of shame.

How could I ever reconcile who I was, where I came from, out of which ashes? My inner turmoil was so great that there were moments I could not see how I could carry on living. Today I am glad that a selfish gene made me hold on to the fact that my grandfather was a man who loved me, a man who loved my father, a man my father called *Vater* [Father]. A man who had fought in two world wars, had lost his hearing in one ear in the first and had a kindness and fairness to him that stood out.

Without wanting to sound romantic, it had been *Opa* who told my parents that I should be raised understanding and embracing both my Jewish and my Christian roots. A man who had carried a Nazi party card. A man who did not deny his past, did not excuse it, did not take pride in it, a man who had clearly felt trapped within a system he could not fight alone, a man who read to me in German, Lessing's plays, my favourite being *Nathan the Wise*, about an interfaith folktale, a ring, a plea for religious tolerance and a happy ending. A man who told his two older children, my mother and Dieter, to leave Germany and make their fortune in Canada and England. A man who died when I was 12. A man I have had to learn not to judge but rather try to understand in the context of facts and German history.

Would I have joined the Nazi party in his shoes? Probably.

"Most people are not brave. Most people are not heroes. Most heroes are not heroes but simply people who do heroic acts. People will do anything to survive and keep their family safe", my father said, "Anything."

My mother came to London in 1959. She met my father at a dance club in Cricklewood and they fell in love. Six months later they were married and discovered that their grandmothers had been school friends in Leipzig. My Jewish and Christian families seemed to be acting out 'Nathan the Wise' before my very eyes.

Figure 14.1. Monica's parents together with Opa Lessing and Granny Lowenberg
(Photo taken by Ruth Lessing).

Yes, I am a *Mischling* [The Nazi term for someone of mixed heritage, especially one who is partly of Jewish descent] in more ways than one. I am a child of war, conflicted and haunted by events that in the main I have not personally experienced but feel deep within my being, who without knowing was fed Celan's 'black milk' but a child who was also fed redcurrants, love and reconciliation.

So, going to Germany, the "land of the murderers" as many people would claim in the 1960s and 1970s, was not my experience. My Lessing grandparents ensured that their home, a rundown flat, stuffed full of wonderful old books at the top of a castle near Cologne, a place that they were given in exchange for my grandfather managing the land for the count, was mine too and my parents and my Jewish grandmother who had visited them. I played with the *Grafen Kinder* [the count's children] in the fields and surrounding forests, drank *Apfelsaft* [apple juice] and was made to feel part of the 'family'.

My childhood home in Germany was, by all accounts, picture perfect, idyllic. But there was the man in the village who proudly displayed *Mein Kampf* [My Fight] in his window. I remember my father recalling that with a strange sense of disgust and despairing acceptance and there was the man I remembered, only thirty years later, who set the guard dogs on to me when I was 4 because he thought it was funny to see them grab my furry toy. I remember my mother screaming and my grandfather deadly furious with anger. Yes, I have good and bad memories, some are my own and others have been passed down to me. The washing machine is spinning.

It was not till I was in my late 20s that my father told me the name of my Jewish grandfather, David Levenbergs. Until that time, his name had never been mentioned. David had a bad temper; David got into rages; David had not been a good husband to either one of his two wives. "What are those marks on your back Daddy?" I remember asking my father one day.

> Nothing, your grandfather was at times a little too enthusiastic with a belt. "When did you last see your father?" A few days before I left for England, I saw him on the opposite side of the street in Berlin. I called out to him, but he ignored me. I had made him angry the last time I saw him in his flat; he thought I was being rude to him and he was upset I was leaving. He could not get out and Paul had already gone with Jugend Aliyah [organization preparing Jewish youth for emigration to Palestine] to Denmark to work on a farm, to then go to Riga and then Palestine. He felt alone and abandoned. He told me to leave.

Silence. I asked no more questions. My father had enough wounds.

But in 2011 things changed. In 2008, Dad had been diagnosed with cancer; he miraculously survived major surgery and was told that he probably still had five years to live. My father asked me to find out what had happened to his brother Paul, my grandfather David and the rest of our Latvian Jewish family. I bought a plane ticket to Riga, Latvia and in October 2011, I flew to the home of the other half of me. The half that had been frozen in time.

I can still see the fish market and the golden sprats flapping their fins and crying for the sea; the oldest wooden house in town, standing defiantly in the midst of a busy street and dwarfed by Stalinesque administrative buildings; the regal white opera house and the less regal production of *Don Giovanni* with singers flirting in bikinis; the State archive with its classroom seating, which introduced me to my Latvian family over the last few days; the amber sellers; the flower sellers; the burlesque night clubs; the pastel-coloured buildings; the cobbled streets; the town hall with its impressive spire with a view of the Daugava river and the house of the Black Heads – a group of unmarried merchants.

And then I think back to my discoveries in the Latvian State Archives the day before, the names of my Latvian family. They are names in black ink on time-stained pages, in Russian, in black leather-bound books. I have ten piled up in front of me and a piece of paper that the archivist has kindly given me with the Russian spelling of the name, Levenbergs. I search the names and scrutinize every sweep of a pen.

Over three days I find them, they come alive and wave to me from the pages, they open a window into a patriarchal world that nurtured traditional roles, dates telling me when they were born, married but not where they died. "Your grandfather's father was called Lazzers Levenbergs, he was an *omem*", the archivist says, "a soldier". "A soldier?" Yes, a soldier who fought for his country and probably proudly, and then he married Minna, Minna Bernstein, and they had eight children and they lived by the sea in Libau and they ran a furniture shop.

They worked hard and they traded as commercial merchants and they hoped that their business would do well so that their children could be educated. They helped my grandfather David go to Dresden University to study engineering and their eldest twin boys Moishe and Abraham, born shortly after they married in 1867, left Latvia as well. Their daughter Gertrud married a German solicitor and moved to Switzerland. But their four other children and his aunts stayed in Libau where they lived by the sea, played in the dunes and kicked the sand.

I am tired, my feet hurt but we can't stop, it's way past lunchtime and most of the restaurants and cafés are no longer serving latkes with sour cream. A hot coffee would be welcome to fight off the cold and I am grateful that I have got two pairs of thick socks on, but we can't stop. Before I fly back to London tonight, I have got to see the place where my uncle had lived, before he was sent to the Riga Ghetto.

"This is Lacplesa St", Aleksandrs calls out. "Paul lived here as well." "Yes, it was part of the ghetto." It's a long street; we walk along it with traffic rushing past, as we make our way through the Riga Ghetto, officially announced on 23 August 1941.

On 25 October 1941, its gates were locked, 29,602 Jews were driven together into custody behind barbed wire in the area where about 13,000 people had lived before. Among them 5,652 children, 8,300 invalids, 9,507 women, 6,143 men and my uncle. "What day is it today?" I ask Aleksandrs, "Wednesday 26 October 2011." When did the archivist solemnly hand me a small rectangular book with Paul's name in it, the black book that neatly listed his address 33 *Mariajas iela* [Mariajas Street], his date of birth and the word *geto* below the date 4 October 1941? Yesterday, 25 October 2011. Time stands still and I freeze.

"How many people were killed?" I asked Aleksandrs, "Paul was a workman, he was nineteen, he was young, he could survive, did he survive do you think he survived?" "Perhaps, I don't know", he replied.

On 29 November and 8 December 1941, the ghetto was annihilated in murderous actions. Approximately 25,000 inhabitants of the ghetto were brought to Rumbula – to the woods a few kilometres out of Riga – where over a thousand Latvian Ārajs commandos robbed them, accompanied them, and guarded them before SS soldiers shot them and packed them in pits like sardines.

Only one in ten Latvian Jews survived, only one.

Aranka, David, Israel, Jossel, Mark, Modechay, Rebecka, Rivka, Fanny, Jenny, Lilia, Minna, Rafael, Rosa, Rachel, Wiliam, Abram, Selig, Scheine, Sore, Rosa, Paul. Albert, Benjamin, Eugenia, Haim, Judith, Lia, Minna, Paul – their names and plaques in the ghetto museum flash past me, all Levenbergs, all taken to the ghetto.

I stare at them, and they look back at me in black straight suits made of capital letters. "Look at this photo: it is the burning of the synagogue, 300 people, 300 Jews were burnt alive in there. Look at this man." "He looks as if he is laughing." "Yes." He is not a German soldier, he looks like an ordinary man, a man who buys furniture and sits and sleeps in it.

"Here, this is Number Thirty-Three Marijas iela." Aleksandrs points to a beautiful old art deco building in a street that used to be a thriving hub for tailors. The street is now called Aleksandra Caka iela. I would never have found it. Inside, a sweeping bannister dominates the landing and on the wall a list of businesses located in the building can be seen. Located in Apartment Number Ten, where a company called Manol now work, the walls around their office are neon yellow. We knock on the door. No one is in but somewhere behind that yellow door, Paul wrote the last words his mother ever received from him.

> Please use the address soon, because I'm waiting for an answer from you with eager-ness! I feel quite well here, I work and earn my living. I'm expecting Vati to arrive

soon. It's my only comfort that Vati is coming, because then I won't be so lonely anymore.[1] I'm always thinking about you, dear Mami! How are you? I hope that the address at Dr Whelen at Horton hospital is still the right one. In case it is not I'm sending the letter to this address as well.

I beg you again to answer as soon as possible, by airmail! I'm longing for an answer from you. How is Ernst? Best wishes to him and tell him, that he will hear from me soon. Dear Mami, I'm so happy that I can finally write to you. My heart is full of worries because of the long separation. If I can even hope to see you again? How happy I would be if I could be with you. In my thoughts I'm always with you dear Mami. When I hear back from you I'll give you more details about me. Until then, this short greeting.

I greet and kiss you many times, your loving son, who always thinks of you! Paul

"Who always thinks of you?", those words they rush through my mind, and I can't let them go and I think of a photo a friend of mine sent me of a plaque inside the oldest ghetto in the world, the Venetian, created in 1516, the very place where the word ghetto originates from. The plaque reads, *Perché le nostre memorie sono la vostra unica tomba*, [For our memories are your only graves]. Did we see a plaque in the former Riga Ghetto? I can't recall.

A few days after my visit to Riga I wrote, I wrote and I wrote. I simply could not stop. Those few days in Riga left an invisible scar. I doubt it will ever heal. It is good if it does not, some things should not be forgotten.

Today, I can still vividly recall the long list of Levenbergs in the Riga Ghetto museum and the moment I realized that they were all cousins, the family I had never known.

I can still recall the absolute feeling of extreme horror, fear and disgust when I went to the Jewish museum on my own and read the letters written in German explaining how the killing of the Jews in Liepaja was to take place.

A series of mass executions, many public or semi-public, in and near the city of Liepāja, (*Libau* in German) on the west coast of Latvia in 1941 where my great aunts and uncles had been murdered. The main perpetrators were detachments of the *Einsatzgruppen* [Nazi death squads] the

---

1   *Vati* [Familiar name for father].

Sicherheitsdienst or SD [Security Service] the *Ordnungspolizei*, or ORPO, [Order Police] and Latvian auxiliary police and militia forces.

Wehrmacht soldiers and naval personnel had also been present during the shootings. "So, the Wehrmacht was not so innocent after all", my inner critic cried out. Photos showed quite clearly how they enjoyed taking snaps, taking part in a form of execution tourism.

I remember having to swiftly leave for a bathroom where I was physically sick and literally wept. I must have been in that bathroom for at least thirty minutes, but it seemed like hours. I remember not being able to move and feeling a pain worse than anything I had ever felt before. Worse than when I had, in the year 2000, gone with my parents to Berlin for the first time and helplessly watched my father get confused and angry trying to find his home, Hansaufer 1, discovering it was gone and finding not so far away the Levetzowstraße deportation memorial which looked brown dirty and rusty and then watch my father lose his temper while my mother and I tried to calm him down. Worse than all the funerals I had been to, all the heart breaks, physical pain and losses I had felt. Worse, even, than when I had gone to Theresienstadt and, on seeing my great-grandmother's name, Fanny Peiser, in the black book, had passed out and worse than the internal trauma I had felt when my mother's younger brother, my uncle Günter, threw my grandfather's Nazi party card at me in his pain and distress. A wake-up call if ever there was one when turning 30.

Yes, it was simply the worst pain I had ever felt, it was as if I was feeling everything my Levenbergs relatives had felt and had left unspoken. "This is something I most feared", my uncle Günter said crying down the phone, shaking with guilt. A guilt that was not his. The pain came in waves so strong I could not stand. And then, without warning, I stopped crying and anger took hold. A fury that seemed to burn and sear the very inside of me with a passion I had never felt before.

I became possessed. There are no other words for it. The stream of work that came out of me, someone who had suffered from writing blockages, amazed even me.

Absolute determination not to allow the victims to be forgotten, not to allow the Latvian government to think that honouring the Latvian SS who had collaborated with the Nazis was an acceptable thing to do in the twenty-first century took grip.

Every free moment I spent researching and applying the knowledge I had gathered for my doctorate (a doctorate concerned with the Holocaust that I had not completed) was fed into my articles as I attempted to halt the Holocaust obfuscation that was quite clearly taking place in Latvia with the tacit consent of the British Conservatives.

My guide from Riga, Dr Aleksandrs Feigmanis, became a friend who translated documents when Google could not. It had been Aleksandrs who had told me that, since 1998 each and every year on 16 March, former Latvian SS men marched down the streets of Riga in Latvian uniforms and had thousands of people, including politicians in smart suits, who presented them with flowers and flags.

YouTube clips of each of the marches made clear that Aleksandrs was not making up stories. Only that year, on 16 March 2011, in Riga, in the heart of NATO and the EU, more than 2,500 people had paid tribute to Latvians who fought on the side of Nazi Germany in murderous Waffen SS detachments during the Second World War! 62,000 Jews, or 90 per cent of Latvia's pre-war Jewish population, were killed in 1941–1942 by German SS and Latvian Arajs commandos, many of whom later joined the fifteenth and nineteenth divisions of the German SS in 1943.

The brutal murder of Latvian Jews by firing squads was the worst atrocity in the Holocaust committed on Latvian soil yet the Museum of Occupation in Riga only devoted a couple of stands to their deaths and Latvian politicians quite openly and unashamedly showered their praise on to their 'heroes'. They had fought against the Russians, yes, they had worn German uniforms, yes, but this was irrelevant, they were heroes.

I contacted Dr Efraim Zuroff of the Simon Wiesenthal Centre who in turn put me in touch with Dr Dovid Katz of Defending history.com. On 20 January 2012, on my Uncle Paul's birthday and seventy years after the Wannsee Conference, I launched the petition, 'Stop the 16-March marches in Riga and Latvians revising history'. In little under two weeks, the petition gathered worldwide attention and over 900 signatures.

A few months later and on 12 March 2012, I went to Riga for the second and last time. I was invited by World Without Nazism to attend their international conference against the SS march. There were around forty speakers: historians, activists and politicians from around the world. I felt honoured to be asked to speak but terribly nervous. I was pleased to see a few friendly faces: Efraim Zuroff, Dovid Katz and Aleks my guide came to the hotel to say hello and give me the Latvian healthy version of Lucozade. I needed it. At ten in the morning, on 16 March, as conference delegates we were asked if we wanted to lay a wreath to the victims of Nazism before the honouring of the SS commenced.

I agreed and down the road to the monument of freedom I walked alongside a German MEP, the president of the European Jewish Parliament (an NGO based in Brussels), the director of the Simon Wiesenthal Centre, an EP deputy for Latvia, the chair of the Board for Associated Diversified Trade Unions (Latvia), the president of the association Latvia Without Nazism and the leader of the European Social Forum, among others. Many photos were taken, but the photo that perhaps spoke more than any other to me was one I was not even aware had been taken. A photo where I stand alone in silent protest staring at the SS.

After we had placed the wreath for the victims of Nazism, the crowds started to collect in their hundreds: Latvians and neo-Nazis from abroad. They looked like normal people, young, old, even toddlers, it was surreal, and I could only think of Hannah Arendt's words, "The banality of evil" (Arendt, 2006). But the protesters with placards showing pictures from the Liepaja massacres did as well so that when a Russian-speaking anti-fascist asked me if I wanted to put on a striped overall reminiscent of a prisoner in a camp, I found myself simply saying, "Yes." Shortly afterwards, I started to find myself being followed by a sympathetic looking policewoman whom despite looking sympathetic I was determined to escape.

The Latvian SS men in their brown Latvian uniforms were smiling as they walked under a canopy of flags, serenaded with Latvian songs and showered with flowers. They marched up to the Monument of Freedom while the wreath to the victims of Nazism was destroyed by a group of young Latvians.

The sight was simply too much. I was incensed. I can't remember how I did it or even why I thought it would be possible, I simply felt I had to escape the policewoman and stand near the Monument of Freedom ready to welcome the SS! Blind fury had led me to that point. If I had thought about it, I would never have done it. I am not brave. The encounter was undramatic but telling to the core. Not a single one of those SS men could look me in the face. Not a single one. The press had a field day, and nobody knew what to do with the furious Riga Ghetto relative from London.

Afterwards I ended up drinking five stiff whiskies with Dovid in a pub. It was a truly crazy day but 'boy it felt good'! Absolute fury had made me courageous and something frozen in me had finally melted. "Do you think there are good SS and bad SS?" I remember a journalist ask me and I replied, "As human beings we can all be good and we can all be bad but as military units, no unit that worked for the most genocidal regime the world has ever known can be good. So, no it is not a good idea to publicly honour such units, it is important to honour and remember the victims, the victims who did not have guns to protect themselves."

Since the petition was launched in 2012 it has gained over 7,000 signatories and has generated hundreds of articles in numerous languages around the world. The BlogSpot continues to have hundreds of visitors each day. The result: the march still goes ahead, and protesters are banned from protesting at the Monument of Freedom.

But ... ministers are now also banned from attending the march, and the march is not an official day despite repeated demands to make it be one. I have had to learn to be grateful for small steps. I remain vocal in my opposition of what is quite clearly a serious affront to the victims of the Holocaust and indeed a lacerating wound to the truth. If I returned to Latvia, I have no doubt I would be arrested. I therefore do not return, only my pen.

Today, I now sit surrounded by mountains of research spanning seventy-five years. I have discovered that over 150 members of my family, over a hundred Latvian relatives and over fifty German relatives, were murdered. My grandmother suffered from serious depression all her life. Only last year, I discovered from World Jewish Relief that she was in two notorious mental homes in Leeds, UK in 1947 after she tried to kill herself.

Later she found some kind of peace; she lived to see 90, spending the last years of her life in the comfort of Leo Baeck House in Hampstead

Garden Suburb, paid for by the German government, while my Jewish grandfather's fate was only revealed following my protest in Riga in 2012.

After years of searching for his father, my father suddenly received a letter from the Russian Federation, on 26 September 2012, about his father David. My protest in Latvia must have placed us on their radar, the arrival of the letter only a few months after my protest did not seem coincidental. Nothing seemed coincidental anymore.

David Levenbergs, an engineer and self-made man, born in Libau/Liepaja, Latvia 1875, whom my grandmother had divorced in 1939, had been not only a victim of Hitler but also Stalin. He fled Berlin on 13 March 1941 to head a machine tool factory in Moscow but then on arrival was accused of being a spy.

For three months he was imprisoned in a building annexed to the infamous Hotel Lux. Later in the July of 1941, David Loewenberg was deported to a gulag in Krasnoyarsk region, Siberia. He survived one winter and died age 67, on 26 May 1942, in Novosibirsk Oblast. Little did he know that he would never see his family again or that forty-seven years later, on 28 November 1989 his file would be reviewed by the military prosecutor's office of the Moscow Military District and his name would be rehabilitated.

The letter contained no apology just the facts. "Well, at least they wrote", my father said. We got together all the documents we had gathered, said Kaddish and I planted an olive tree near the large cypress tree in my garden, which I realized looked like a conifer transplanted from a Siberian landscape. For a number of years, I tried to establish where David had died and where his ashes could be, but I hit a wall. A researcher kindly wrote back following my enquiry,

> I am afraid I will not be able to provide too much assistance. The Soviet penal system was a sprawling set of camps, prisons and colonies. Even one camp could be an entire system with various 'places of detention' covering an enormous territory. Documenting the details surrounding the death of supposed spies (even the location) was not a priority for Stalin's regime, especially during the deprivations of World War Two. This can make finding the place of death of a prisoner quite difficult, as you have learned.

In my mind I float a candle on the Yenisei River. As a child I had always thought of visiting Lake Baikal, little had I known that my grandfather's ashes float not so far away.

One year later, Dad's cancer started to progress, and he died on 26 August 2014, the very day he left Nazi Germany with the ORT seventy-five years earlier.

After his death, I sifted through his papers and I realized that from 1945 to 1948 my father had worked for the American army as one of 250 translators who worked on the paperwork for the Nuremberg trials, he was based in Pullach and Nuremberg. He had never spoken to me or anyone else about his work there.

Until his death in 2014 my father had supported all my efforts to contest the Holocaust fiction that the Latvian and Lithuanian governments have been diligently and systematically re-writing since their independence and had protested with me and my mother and others outside the Lithuanian embassy in 2012 while battling cancer. It became clear to me that my father had known the history intimately even if the Baltic governments did not want to.

Before my father died, I had read a book by a fellow campaigner, Denis MacShane, *Brexit: How Britain will leave Europe*, it became clear to me, after witnessing how Europe was moving rightwards, that Brexit was on the cards. I asked my father if he minded if I got a German passport. He looked at me thoughtfully and said, "One can never have enough passports."

On 20 October 2014, I went to the German embassy in London to apply for dual nationality. My mother waited outside, "I don't want one, I don't need it, I don't want it. I'll get a coffee and see you in an hour", she blurted, "I am ok, get your passport." The embassy was busy; there were no comfortable seats, no cups of coffee or little Anglo German flags offered which other second generation received in recent years.

"Do many second generation apply for a German passport?" I asked the lady at the counter in German. "No", she replied in German, "I think you are one of the first." "As you can see my mother's family records span several centuries in Germany but my father, a Holocaust refugee born in Halle an der Saale in 1922 but whose father was Latvian Jewish, is by German law, despite being born in Germany, not German. I have only three German born grandparents not four, one half is Christian and one half is Jewish. Will that be a problem?" "Ein Moment bitte."

I knew it could be a problem and a part of me wanted to embarrass them, embarrass them for all those years of pedantry when the German government had not given my father a German pension because his father was Latvian, a rule which suited the German government's financial coffers and no one else's.

I started to feel angry again, the woman turned and walked away clutching my paperwork. I stood at the counter and viewed a sign the woman had just passed, it read, '*Nicht Weiter Verfolgt*', not to progress further but it can also mean not to be persecuted, hounded, followed, chased, the Germanist in me called out.

Ten minutes later the woman came back, "*Kein Problem, Frau Loewenberg, herzlich willkommen*! No problem, Ms Lowenberg, hearty welcome! You will receive your passport in around six weeks." Indeed, it arrived in two. "I am not to be, *weiter verfolgt!*" I told my mother laughingly, as I walked out of the embassy. She looked at me quizzically, "Perhaps not for the moment", she replied "Who knows?"

Figure 14.2. Oma Ruth Lessing in Cologne with mother, Rosemarie and Monica in 1969 (Photo taken by Ernest Lowenberg).

Bibliography

Arendt, H. (2006). *Eichmann in Jerusalem: A Report on the Banality of Evil.* London and New York: Penguin Classics.

Celan, P. (1986). 'Speech on the Occasion of Receiving the Literature Prize of the Free Hanseatic City of Bremen'. In R. Waldrop (trans.), *Collected Prose.* Manchester, UK: Carcanet Press.

MacShane, D. (2015). *Brexit: How Britain Will Leave Europe.* London and New York: IB Taurus.

15 Only a two-hour flight, but it took me forty-seven years to get here!

It was only after my father's death in 1991 that I began to contemplate such a journey. My mother had given me one of the folders of forty letters from his parents that my father had made for each of his children. He had never told me about them: they began on 27 June 1939, when he and his sister left Leipzig with the Kindertransport and ended abruptly on 17 April 1941, affecting me deeply. Saying goodbye at Leipzig station was the last time the children saw their parents …

The letters, often long, emotional and loving, are full of hope for a reunion in America, where their cousins lived. The last one, very short, was from the Nowy Sącz Ghetto in Poland: basically, a plea for food – sent to an American cousin. Below is a poem I wrote in 1996.

My grandparents' letters 1939–1941

Words, symbols, connections
   with another world, place, age
These words – my unique bridge
   to my past, my heritage

Words of love, forewarnings, care,
   (unwritten words, thoughts confined)
Chiding, hope, fear, and despair
   how can I read between these lines?

Dreams of what could/should have been
Pictures of what's lost to me

My world has no grandparents
I'm a branch from a broken family tree
                  floating
                     rootless

Had they lived
    I would not be here
Another little brown-eyed girl
    would be running, laughing
    into their loving arms
My light in her eyes

Their dream of a future lives on for me
    In their letters which still plead and hope
Their unwanted gift to me, bittersweet
    unknown
    my right to a living past,
    Angehörigkeit
Now *these* belong to me:

pictures
        of strangers
words
        in foreign tongue and script

untranslatable emotions
with which I can barely express
               my
                self

Background and preparations

My grandparents' letters had enabled me to 'get to know' them for the first time. I meant by '*Angehörigkeit*' [belonging to in this case, a wider family]. Fortunately, my father's sister Helga was ready to answer my many questions, so I slowly started planning a commemorative visit to Poland.

I had always felt excluded when childhood friends spoke about seeing their grandparents and other relatives. My only relations in the UK were my parents and three siblings. All my grandparents were dead. I visited my mother's Catholic family in West Germany when I was eight – with my elder brother aged 12 – but I had never met any of my Jewish father's relatives.

Figure 15.1. Front cover of Rolf Dresner's Polish passport (From family collection).

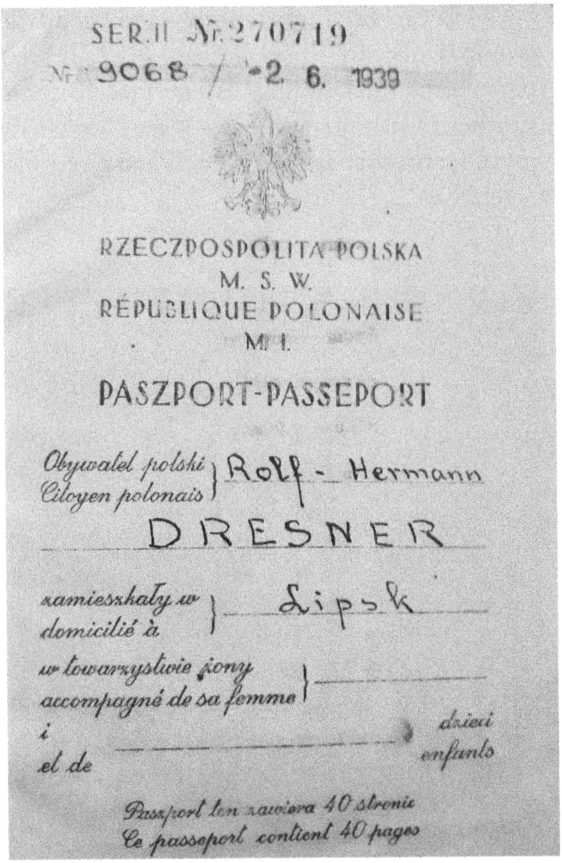

SER. II Nr. 270719
Nr. 9068 / 2. 6. 1939

RZECZPOSPOLITA POLSKA
M. S. W.
RÉPUBLIQUE POLONAISE
M. I.

PASZPORT-PASSEPORT

Obywatel polski / Citoyen polonais } Rolf - Hermann
DRESNER
zamieszkały w / domicilié à } Lipsk
w towarzystwie żony / accompagné de sa femme }
i / et de dzieci / enfants

Paszport ten zawiera 40 stronic
Ce passeport contient 40 pages

Figure 15.2. Inside page of Rolf Dresner's Polish passport (From family collection).

My father, Rolf Dresner, was born in Leipzig, Germany. He arrived in the UK, aged 14, with 16-year-old Helga. Unlike many other German refugees, they were not interned as 'enemy aliens', as they had Polish passports and, during the war, my father was permitted to join the RAF. This passport greatly changed his prospects and he owed it to the goodness of the Polish consul in Leipzig, who gave Polish passports to between 2,000 and 3,000 Jews who had to flee Leipzig and had Polish heritage.

My dad was stationed post-war with the British Occupying Forces in Gütersloh, West Germany, where he met my mother, living nearby in Verl, a small, agricultural village. They married in Kent, where my father had settled, in March 1948. Both spoke sparingly about the war, though my father would say emphatically: "My parents were killed by the Nazis, because they were Jewish", and my mother, "Not all Germans were Nazis."

When I, eventually, realized that our dad's parents were also our grand-parents, I realized that we children had lost relatives in the Shoah too. Our mother's parents had also died in their 50s, from ill-health: her father, verger at the village church, in 1932, her mother in 1937. Although our mother was also orphaned early, at 13, it took longer for me to understand her loss.

She had six older siblings but was sent away to a boarding school after her mother's death. Our dad's only sibling chose to return to Germany post-war, with her communist husband. Both of our parents may well have felt abandoned after their bereavement: these feelings, however, being com-municated non-verbally, which is very common in families such as mine.

When I asked my mother about her family's response to the Nazis, she said her parents, as Catholics, disapproved of Hitler. She had been forbidden to join the *Bund Deutscher Mädel*, the female equivalent of the Hitler Youth. I understood her wish to join the *BDM*, having enjoyed being a Brownie. Our German relatives welcomed us with affection in 1962, allaying any fear I had that they might be anti-Semitic. They appeared to like our dad and I grew very fond of them. We are still close.

I have always felt rather 'proud' of my mixed heritage, of my parents' love for each other – despite their very different backgrounds. I am sure both having been orphaned as young people contributed to their closeness. I felt 'different' when at primary school – but in a positive way, valuing difference.

By 2001, I was close to my Aunt Helga and her son Thomas, having visited them in East Berlin before German 'reunification' and annually after my father's death. Through Helga I learned more about my Polish Jewish family history and our relatives' fate in Europe during the Holocaust. She even sang the Polish national anthem to me, the significance of which I understood later.

As none of my relatives could accompany me to Poland, I put a notice in *Second Generation Voices*, the UK Second Generation Network's journal, inviting readers to contact me about visiting the places where my relatives had been during the war: Kraków, Nowy Sącz, Tarnów and Bełżec.

I was relieved when Elaine contacted me: some of her relatives had lived in that area. Before the trip we met several times, and ate in Polish restaurants, including Daquise, where I had also eaten with my father. She also invited me to my first Passover Seder night meal, at her home. Then Elaine's friend, Sławka, a child Holocaust survivor, whose mother, having been imprisoned, then released, joined her to survive in hiding, suggested accompanying us, as our invaluable interpreter.

I had done much preparatory research before our journey: reading Polish history, before and during the Second World War, gaining information and contacts from friends and from staff at the new Holocaust Exhibition at London's Imperial War Museum. My first visit to Poland was to become enriched by invaluable contacts, support and expertise.

Visiting Kraków

Poland was only a two hours' flight, yet it had taken me forty-seven years to get there.

A few hours after arriving in Kraków, we met Norman Jacobs, a contact via the Second Generation Network, from England. He was working in Kraków with survivor, Bernard Offen who was writing his camp memoirs (Offen 2008), on his book. Sitting with Bernard at a café outside in the main square, *Rynek*, I found it incredible that one of the first people I met was a camp survivor, looking relaxed and calm. Bernard visits Poland every year for several months, to teach young Poles their wartime history. He also accompanies visitors at Birkenau, which he had survived as a teenager, 'walking with them' and answering their questions. He said that Polish students were not taught about anti-Semitism in their own country. I later met a student in her 20s, who was going to attend Bernard's sessions. I was amazed when she said she did not believe there was much anti-Semitism in Poland before the last war. I realized that under Soviet rule, the plight of Jewish people was downplayed, as a way of promoting unity, so he had taken on quite a challenge.

Meeting Norman and Bernard was unforgettable, especially in Kraków, where my grandfather was born, his family having lived there for over 100 years. Bernard's strong, positive personality, generous nature and sense of humour, despite all he had lived through as a teenager, must have enabled him to undertake this work. It still felt unreal, meeting them later to eat in a 'milk bar', although it was like any meeting with new people I liked. We had been welcomed in an unforeseen manner.

This was before I had worked for the Association of Jewish Refugees, with Holocaust survivors including camp survivors like Bernard, and had not imagined they could be such characters. On his website is the title of the film of his story: *Love, Light and Courage*. In what Bernard would call his 'process of healing', it says, "He returned to Poland in 1981 to confront his demons (and soon began) his life's mission of advocacy … spending summers in Kraków remembering, educating and inspiring others."

Elaine and I also ate a lovely, almost celebratory meal with plentiful vodka and *Slivovitz* [plum brandy] with Sławka's friends: a Jewish mother and daughter who had survived there 'passing as non-Jewish' and shared accommodation with Sławka and her mother at the time and stayed in Poland after the war. That warm, homely, experience, with current and former Jewish residents in Kraków was totally unexpected and remains almost indescribably special for me: my relatives having lived there both before and during the Nazi time. It was a mixture of really enjoying myself, while simultaneously feeling a great loss: facing the void of what could have been, for me, my family and so many other families.

By chance, I met another Kraków resident: Anna, in her 40s, who luckily spoke excellent English, and offered to help me search for family records in Kraków's archives. We found records of my grandfather Elias, his father Chaim and his father Izak. It was exciting to see official records of my family and a little of their – and my – history.

I also met a mother and daughter living in a flat where my grandparents had lived after their enforced departure from Leipzig in 1939. The address was on some of their letters. It struck me: it must be strange and challenging when people like me arrive, unannounced. We had heard that some residents would fear such callers may try to repossess their past homes. It felt really odd and moving to walk in the streets to a flat where my grandparents had stayed. Seeing a lovely stained-glass window there, I thought: my relatives have seen this. I still struggle to describe that feeling; both magical and very sad, perhaps. My family must have lived there, consumed by a fear which I can barely imagine. We were not invited in but were treated very politely.

Nowy Sącz: A 'place of dread'

I visited Nowy Sącz with Sławka and with 'Tante Erna's letter' in mind. My father's aunt Erna who had survived, was his uncle Ignaz's wife. She had written to Rolf and Helga after the war, telling them of the fate of their family in Nowy Sącz.

My father's parents, his frail paternal grandmother Ruchel and uncles, Władek and Ignaz, must have been among those forced to move from Kraków into the Nowy Sącz Ghetto. Erna survived outside the ghetto, with false papers, doing her best to support her family, but unable to see her then 11-month-old daughter, Irene Ruth, who stayed with her father.

In summer 1942 Erna heard the ghetto was to be 'liquidated', meaning the residents would be shot or sent to a death camp. Miraculously, she managed to have little Irene smuggled out by a Polish soldier. Her husband Ignaz, his brothers, Władek and my grandfather Elias, their mother, Ruchel and my grandmother Gretel, did not survive.

At Nowy Sącz's Museum, formerly the Great Synagogue, we had arranged to meet curator Elżbieta Długosz, who welcomed us warmly. Seeing the 'Exhibition of former Jewish life' in the entrance lobby, pleased and relieved me: I left an account of my family's fate there. Elżbieta, author of history booklet *Jews in Nowy Sącz*, had arranged for Jakub Müller to guide us. He had survived there in hiding. Like Bernard Offen, he returned to Poland each year, assisting visitors like me. Before the Second World War, Nowy Sącz's population was 30 per cent Jewish: over 10,000 people.

At the Jewish cemetery I was moved, seeing Barbara, the cemetery's keyholder, was clearly very fond of Jakub. Now, it seems strange I felt unable to cry for my disabled great-grandmother Ruchel and her son Ignaz. Erna had written that they died there 'of natural causes'. Ignaz was among those selected to 'clear' the ghetto, after most prisoners were deported to Bełżec. In the *ohel* [monumental tomb] of Rebbe Chaim Halberstam, a place of Hasidic pilgrimage, among many notes left by Hasidic Jews, I left mine, in memory of my relatives.

We then went to the street where my grandparents, Władek, Ignaz and little Irene had lived, in the 'workers ghetto' area. About 18,000 Jews, some from outside Nowy Sącz, lived in extremely crowded circumstances, only receiving 'starvation rations'. En route with Jakub and Sławka, I had a mixture of feelings, partly relief to be honouring the memory of family members I had never met and yet feeling connected by sending a message into the air, "I am here, you are remembered."

Later, Jakub led us along the path my grandmother and her son Władek were forced to walk to the place from which they were deported to Bełżec. I think I became emotionally numb. There was no indication of the events there in August 1942. It was very hard to imagine the horrific scene. I sensed that Jakub might be reliving his time of horror, so asked no questions. I now think I was unconsciously repressing my anger that such cruelty took place there, to so many. Local people walked by, enjoying a walk along the river Dunajec.

Back in Kraków, we attended a crowded Friday night service, my first with Elaine, in the Remuh synagogue. I was comforted to think many there would understand my feelings. We were afterwards invited to the communal Friday night meal, organized by the Lauder Foundation, then housed in the Izaac synagogue. I sat next to Bernard and opposite a Polish couple converting to Judaism, which I learned is not so rare, as more people discover their family history. I felt privileged to be there, my mind full of all my new experiences and sad that I could not tell my father about them. I was also angry and sad not to have known my murdered relatives. It was an extraordinary day: my mind and heart felt swollen with it all.

Tarnów

Tarnów, slightly larger than Nowy Sącz, was another emotional challenge. The population before the Second World War was about 40,000, about

50 per cent Jewish. My father's aunt Erna had written that my grandfather Elias had been arrested in Nowy Sącz and taken to the Gestapo prison in Tarnów. She had not said why. Perhaps it was due to his efforts to find food, thinking of his final letter to his American cousin. Erna had been bringing him food: on arriving one day, she was told, "It's not worth it", he was no longer alive.

Tarnów's Museum director Adam Bartosz, born in 1947, has shown immense kindness to countless people like me. His office was a wonder, with an Israeli flag and much else of great interest. As president and founder member of the Committee for the Care of Jewish Cultural Monuments in Tarnów, Adam has worked hard to get many places, including the former Gestapo building, recognized for their appalling wartime roles. When he mentioned his efforts to buy the building and convert it into a memorial site, I could not hold back my tears of relief and gratitude: hearing it was being used as accommodation was very distressing. Adam also founded the 'Celebration of The Days of Remembrance of Galician Jews', in Tarnów and surrounding villages.

After I gave him my account of my family history, Adam accompanied us to the former Gestapo building and the old Jewish cemetery, both places where the Nazis shot Jews. He also showed us the Ethnographic Museum, which commemorates the local Roma population: another side of his work. We watched him teaching youngsters there, including some Roma children. Adam has awards for 'actions to protect, preserve and develop the cultural identity of national and ethnic minorities, particularly Jews and Roma'.

He suggested we finally visit the Buczyna woods of Zbylitowska Góra, outside Tarnów, where Nazis shot about 8,000 people. About 6,000 were Jews, the others were Poles – some perhaps caught assisting Jews: the penalty was death, along with your family. My grandfather may have died there. Our taxi driver must have seen many people like us: he waited so patiently while we visited the memorial site. I lit a memorial candle and Sławka and Elaine said Kaddish, the prayer for the dead, at one of the memorials with plaques for Jewish victims; others were for Poles and the one with the most candles: children. The memory of this is always upsetting.

Bełżec

Erna assumed that in mid-August 1942, my grandmother Gretel and her brother-in-law Władek were deported from Nowy Sącz to Bełżec. We overnighted in Zamość, the nearest city, a UNESCO World Heritage site, and another important centre of Hasidic Judaism. We decided to pay our respects at the Rotunda Zamość, the region's Museum of Martyrdom.

The ashes of some 45,000 people are said to lie in the cemetery around the Rotunda. Plaques located in various alcoves and sections of the site are dedicated to different victim groups, such as Polish army soldiers killed during the 1939 invasion of Poland, Poles killed by the Nazis in the course of resettlement measures in the region, Jewish forced labour prisoners during Nazi occupation, as well as Red Army soldiers killed in battle.

Why did we visit the Rotunda the day before visiting a Nazi death camp? I was very aware that not only Jews had suffered from the brutality of that time: many others also had, in places formerly unknown to me, during and after the Second World War.

On the journey to Bełżec, we recognized the horrible irony of having return train tickets. Near the camp, a 500-metre walk from the station, are ordinary-looking houses, with the ubiquitous piles of logs outside for heating their homes in winter. Inside the entrance gate we read the information boards. We knew that in 1943 the Nazis tried to destroy evidence of their killings, so we could see only part of the original site, now partly wooded. There was a rather crude memorial Soviet-era sculpture of emaciated people and large symbolic urns – not much else. I walked alone up a path, through a wooded area, and heard a cuckoo. I felt numb, I didn't cry. I sent my "You are not forgotten" message into the air. There were no other visitors, but some candles indicated that others had visited recently.

We said Kaddish and I lit my candle, wondering if my grandmother and great-uncle had died there or on the train en route. We did not stay very long. I felt that we were walking on the ashes of those murdered there. We left when we felt we had shown our respect as best as we could. It was a relief that I had fulfilled my need to visit all these places. My family's deaths had been memorialized where they had died, as far as I knew. It helped, knowing we would soon be in Kraków with friends again.

In 2004 a modern memorial was built at Bełżec. I had wondered what the local people felt about living so close to a former Nazi extermination camp. Now with all the building work and the official ceremony for the opening of the new memorial, I cannot imagine why they would stay there – but I know nothing about them.

Expectations and responses to meeting people

Having received warnings, particularly from my Jewish Care colleagues, to expect hostility in Poland, meeting so many friendly, helpful people was a surprise and contributed to making my visits enjoyable – when not focusing on my relatives' terrible fates. Perhaps those warnings partly explain why I had not undertaken such visits earlier.

It is important to remember that my father's family was twice given shelter in the Leipzig Polish Consulate grounds by the Consul, Feliks Chiczewski: during the Nazi *Oktoberaktion* to expel Polish Jews from Germany in October and *Kristallnacht* in November 1938. Chiczewski also gave Polish passports to many Jews who hoped to emigrate. My father and Helga were always grateful for this.

It took a long time to fully address my responses, both while in Poland and after. I know I felt bewildered: much of what I saw and learned was unexpected, from the delightful to the appalling; sometimes within one day – or a few hours. Emotionally I had visualized Poland in black and white – like our family photos. Seeing internet cafés and hearing Kraków's lively night life had surprised me.

In Nowy Sącz I had also met a young teacher and her fellow members of the 'Nowy Sącz-Israel Friendship group': an unexpected contact from the IWM (Imperial War Museum) in London. She invited me to visit her; hence my second visit to Poland: more of a tourist trip, meeting Sławka's friends and Anna again, staying partly in Nowy Sącz. It felt very positive: I was not letting the past control my actions in the present.

Where I am now

The exploration of my Polish Jewish family history resulted in a positive, if belated, development of my self-identity. In 2003, for the final third of my career, I became the Association of Jewish Refugees' first qualified Northern Social Worker, visiting survivors and refugees – from Shropshire over to Northumberland: learning far more Holocaust-related history. This felt an appropriate combination of my new knowledge and professional skills. I have always been motivated to support those disadvantaged in life, for whatever reason. I think, due to my lack of grandparents, assisting older people was fulfilling. I have also 'found myself', enjoying music, dance and other aspects of Jewish culture.

In 2010, I helped organize a trip to Auschwitz-Birkenau for ten members of the AJR Northern second-generation group I facilitated. Bernard Offen 'walked with' us at Birkenau, which made a huge impression on all of us: being accompanied by a survivor of the darkest and most horrific of times. I was also able to commemorate my father's maternal uncle Friedrich and his daughter Ilse, whom Aunt Helga had told me were deported from Berlin to Auschwitz.

Currently I am writing up my family history, have contributed to Holocaust education groups, spoken at a Holocaust Memorial Day event and co-facilitated second and third generation discussion groups at Limmud Conference. Since retiring, I take part in interfaith groups, am actively involved in Manchester's Muslim Arts and Culture Festival and now, the Black Lives Matter movement. My family history impels me to address prejudice of all kinds.

Figure 15.3. Barbara, left, with two Bosnian volunteers for the Manchester Muslim Arts and Culture Festival (Photo courtesy of MACFEST, with permission to use the photo).

Finding Irene/Monica, my father's survivor cousin

In January 2018, Monica, formerly Irene Ruth the infant ghetto survivor and daughter of my great-uncle Ignaz who died in Nowy Sącz, suddenly made contact seeking to get in touch with my father, her first cousin. So, in June 2018, I went to Syracuse to meet Monica, then aged 80, lovable, fascinating and humorous. When she recounted her tragic experiences in the Nowy Sącz Ghetto, aged 4, having to leave her beloved father Ignaz behind, I had a visceral image of some of the horrors of the ghetto.

Monica and I felt very joyfully close, almost immediately – a relative, who shares my outlook. She loves reminiscing, hearing about cousins, my siblings: relatives whom she has never met. It has been life-changing for me to know I have a living ghetto survivor relative in Monica. Watching the video of her giving testimony to schoolchildren is a new and strange feeling: hearing a survivor describe her memory of my grandfather in the ghetto, talking in whispers with her father. The feeling is really hard to describe. It adds to my understanding of her mother Erna's written description in her letter to my father and his sister, dated 27 November 1947. As I speak and read German, I will help Monica with the historical papers and photos she has and so may discover more.

Bibliography

Offen, B. (2008). *My Hometown Concentration Camp: A Survivor's Account of Life in the Kraków Ghetto and Plaszow Concentration Camp.* London: Vallentine Mitchell.

PART III

Journeys undertaken for commemorative events

16 'Opening doors'

I never felt 'at home' in Durham, where I grew up. We moved there from Oxford when I was 2 or 3, after my father got a permanent university lectureship there. Durham was an especially rooted place: everybody knew everybody else since the time of their grandparents or before that. But there was more to my sense of being an outsider.

I left Durham as quickly as I could, never to look back and went to university (a return to Oxford); then I settled in London. London suited me: a fluctuating and diverse population, full of people who did not fit in easily elsewhere. Here, for decades, I was a left activist, made many friends and even got married. But if anybody had asked me where 'home' was, I would have been puzzled.

It took me till late middle age to finally dare to start to 'open the door' onto my past. My parents, Lotte and Siegi, both highly articulate people, became dumb when it came to answering questions about their lives in Germany. If I was told anything, I gradually realized, it was most probably a lie or, at best, an evasion. Having the doors to my own history shut tight against me, left me both ignorant of my roots but also lacking a sense of whom I was.

Long after my father's death, when my mother was in hospital, I finally raided their home. There I discovered piles of documents. I was in for a shock. I read the letters Lotte's parents had sent her – after they had been translated from the German. I found details of where my mother had lived when growing up in Berlin and of her parents, of whom I had known nothing. They had all lived at Gervinusstraße 20, in Charlottenburg, Berlin. I found – and this was a surprise – that my mother's parents had seen themselves as Jewish, increasingly so as the Nazi's anti-Semitic measures were introduced and brutally enforced. I found out that my father, Siegi, had not really had a home when growing up in Bavaria and that Hermann had not been his father.

Now armed with a little information, I confronted my mother, Lotte, who was by then, in an old people's home. As always, she made it very clear that she did not want to talk. "If you know so much, why are you asking me?" But maybe aware that she was not going to live much longer, maybe because the dementia she was developing was loosening her self-imposed restraints, she started to confess.

My mother, Lotte, was a wild child, the third daughter of a respectable Jewish bourgeois couple, Samuel and Luize Jacoby. Lotte left home (though 'ran away' might be more accurate) when very young because she could not bear the way her parents behaved towards their oldest daughter, Annamarie. They treated Annamarie, my mother said, as a skivvy. There was a 7-year age gap between the sisters and Lotte felt she was not able to protect her vulnerable sister and needed to get away. She moved as far away as possible from her parents' home to Berlin's eastern fringes, she told me.

Lotte met Siegi soon afterwards in one of the left-wing agit-prop troupes that were popular at the time. He was directing, she acting. Siegi was also active in the *KPD* [German Communist Party] and a number of KPD associated organizations, including the Red Front, an organization which tried to stop the provocation and street violence of local Nazi bullies, using force, if necessary, to defend themselves. Soon after Lotte and Siegi met, they started to live together in a variety of addresses, constantly moving as a precautionary measure.[1]

My mother with a terrible foresight predicted early on what was to come and insisted they would have to flee. On the night of the Reichstag fire, warned by the local milkman, my father crawled out of the window and was gone before the SA [*Sturmabteilung* the Nazi Party's original paramilitary wing, also known as the Brownshirts] came knocking on their door. Lotte and Siegi both left Germany early in 1933, though separately. Lotte did not realize that she was leaving her parents and Berlin forever.

It was time for me to find out more. I visited the research centre of the Berlin *Centrum Judaicum* [Jewish Community Centre], Oranienburgerstraße Synagogue. They were very helpful and told me that

---

1   An excellent account of German working-class resistance to the Nazis in the 1920s and 1930s can be found in Moos and Cushion (2020) (Editors' note).

Lotte's mother had died an ostensibly natural death in the Jewish Hospital in 1940, though as I was to discover, my mother had been and remained convinced the Nazis had murdered her. Hoping to comfort her, I tried unsuccessfully to convince her otherwise. Lotte's father 'died' in Theresienstadt.

I visited the beautiful apartment block where the family had lived. Gervinusstraße was heavily bombed, but my mother's block had survived and has indeed become a *Kulturdenkmal* [cultural heritage monument] for Berlin, on architectural grounds as well as for its local historical importance. Gervinusstraße curves along the railway line, along which trains rush eastwards towards Russia, westwards to Paris. As my mother told it, this encouraged in her an early awareness of the accessibility of faraway lands. The apartment block looks over the railway embankment, still thickly lined with linden trees. But the children's playground has gone, replaced by a large Lidl grocery store.

As I did not know anybody living in the block, I waited till a man happened along who was about to go in. I explained in English who I was and what I wanted. He was kind, opened the door for me and invited me in. The door is heavy carved wood, the hallway beyond, with its cupola, painted with a wonderful display of peacocks. The man offered to take me to his flat where he, his wife and three children lived. We walked up two flights of wooden stairs. There was a lift once, but it has not worked for many a year.

I did not then know which flat my mother had lived in and imagined it was his. Later I discovered that her flat was also on the second floor but on the other side of the stairwell. The flat is magnificent: a large front room with a balcony overlooking the linden trees and the railway line, three bedrooms down a long corridor and the small kitchen at the end, which had once been the province of the maid. So, I stood for the first time, imagining where the three sisters: Lotte, Kate and Annamarie, had done their schoolwork, where the table had been around which the family had eaten their meals together, with my young mother hiding underneath, and where they had slept. The man's flat was a glorious riot of colour, mess and bunk beds: all his children were still young; not, I knew, what my grandparents would have tolerated. This contrast was joyous but disconcerting. Nor, though I strained to do so, could I hear the sisters' voices. The man offered

Figure 16.1. Merilyn on the balcony of her mother's and grandparents' apartment in Berlin (Photo by Matthias Schirmer).

to open the door onto the balcony, and I stand and stare at the linden trees opposite, just as my mother had described it.

Then the man took me into the reception area near the front door where there was and is a brass plaque on the wall. The plaque includes the names of the many people who had lived in the block, been taken away during Nazism and never came back. The list includes my mother's parents. I thought I was going to pass out and sank onto the floor.

As soon as I got back home, I went to visit my mother, who was still alive. I showed her photos of the double front door she used to walk through whenever she went out, I showed her photos of the unforgettable peacocks on the walls of the hall, I showed her the view from the balcony. She said nothing and turned away.

The names on the plaque in the hall did not include Annamarie, Annamarie, my aunt who has been written out of history, whose memory has been all but forgotten. Annamarie had been put into a psychiatric clinic by her parents, probably before the Nazis took power in 1933 and was one of the first to be gassed in 1940 under the T4 Euthanasia Programme. It took me years to find out about her. Annamarie had been married, though to a man 25 years older than her. The relationship was not a success. Their daughter, Ruth, was brought up essentially by her grandparents. Ruth got out of Germany, aged 10, on the Kindertransport. But she has never really wanted to find out or talk about her mother.

I was to 'visit' the three places where Annamarie had been incarcerated, each worse than the next. The last is still a psychiatric prison, still surrounded by rolls of barbed wire, with bars on the small windows. From here, Annamarie was taken to Brandenburg and gassed. Her parents were informed that she had died naturally in Posner: of course, a lie. I stood where her body was burnt. I shall probably never know but suspect that her sin was that she did not fit in. And that warranted death.

One day in 2018, an unknown man, Matthias, contacted me. Would you like to come to speak, he asked? We are taking part in the *Denk Mal Am Ort* [Memorial on Site] celebrations. The initiative commemorates individuals or families persecuted during the Nazi era. The idea stemmed from a Dutch scheme started in 2012 and introduced to Berlin in 2016 as a way to remember people persecuted by the Nazis through the places where they once lived.

It will be in the courtyard of the block in twenty, Gervinusstraße, Matthias wrote. "How do you know of me?" I email back. Along the long descent into my family's history, I had informed the landlord of the Gervinusstraße block (the son of the original landlord, who never came back from Auschwitz) about my search. Matthias had got my details from him.

Terrified, I agreed. Matthias picked me up from the airport, we introduced ourselves and he took me to a nearby modern hotel on Gervinusstraße, which replaces the earlier bombed out apartment blocks. On the day of the event, the heavy front door was already open, and I walk hesitantly through to the inner courtyard. I sit down in the shade of the ancient arching chestnut tree, planted at the time the house was built in the early 1900s and which now reaches up to the top – fifth – floor of the building. I imagine my mother and her sisters playing around the fountain which, over a hundred years later, is still spouting its life force. It is protected by a low wall which also functions as a stone seat. It was around this fountain that my young mother had cycled her bike all those years ago, not a usual activity for little girls at that time.

I had about seven minutes to speak. Refusing to romanticize, I talked of how unhappy my mother had been living here when young, of the terrible fates of her sister Annamarie and their parents but how my mother, though deeply damaged by displacement and loss, had become a recognized poet and playwright in Britain. I said I had to speak on behalf of those who had been stopped from speaking. I said, while painful, I needed to return to Berlin, to open the door to my past and connect a broken circle.

There were about thirty people listening in the courtyard, many, though not all, who lived in one of the apartments around the courtyard. I have spoken often in the UK of my family and the long-term effects of Nazism, but this was different. The audience wanted to hear what I had to say and I could see that they cared and understood. Afterwards, there was a queue to speak to me. They wanted to tell me the stories of their parents and broader family under Nazism, of the relatives, some who had stood

Figure 16.2. Merilyn at Denk Mal am Ort event in the apartment courtyard in Berlin with her interpreter, Almut Rietzschel (Photo by Matthias Schirmer).

up to the Nazis and been killed, some who had fought and been killed, and how they now felt about the losses and contradictions of it all. It was as if I was healing their historic wounds. But what they did not know was that they were healing mine. It is almost the only time I have felt 'at home'.

But nothing is simple. Matthias had also arranged for me to see the flat where my mother and her parents had lived. Matthias knocks at the door to the flat and a woman answers and, stiffly, invites us in. So, here I am, entering into what I suddenly realized could have been 'my' flat, could have been where 'I' had lived. No, 'should have been my flat', is what I suddenly think. Two women live here, an elderly daughter and her even older mother. The flat has been largely decorated in the traditional style of the early twentieth century. I could see how uncomfortable they were with me there. I can only imagine but my guess is they too were thinking: 'This could have been her flat', or maybe: 'It's ours.' I got out as quickly as possible. How long had they lived here I wonder? Matthias later tells me that the block had become a *Judenhaus* so the mother could only have moved in after 1945. I think how different my life would have been if I had lived here and been a German *Mädchen* [young woman].

On another trip to Germany, I visited where my father had partly grown up. My father's family story is complicated; he does not appear to really have had a home when young. I will refer to Hermann as if he had really been my father's father. Hermann came from a rich sector of Bavarian society, specializing in wine and vinegar. He later died in especially dreadful circumstances in Theresienstadt. His large, detached house in Munich had once been magnificent. But when I visited, it had become a rundown multi-occupied wreck. The paint was peeling off the front door, the windows and everywhere else; inside, the electric cables hung loose along the walls. It smelt of damp and decay. The garden around the house which Hermann and my father when a boy had been photographed in together was an uncared-for mess of weeds and rubbish.

I also visited Augsburg, near Munich, where my father had gone to university. I was walking along the street leading to the university and there was my father, walking on the other side of the road, as real as could be. Later, as I was having coffee in an upstairs café, he appeared and upbraided me: "What are you doing here?" he asked. How could I, after he had protected me – or should I say banned me – from knowing of his history, how could I go against him and try to discover his past? Didn't I know how dangerous this was? I sat and wept.

My mother died twenty years after my father. She had placed the urn with his ashes next to her head where she slept. What was I to do with them? My mother had insisted, leaving multiple written 'directions' around her home in case I did not get the point, that her ashes should be strewn around a tree in Victoria Park, in London, opposite where she and Siegi had lived. Although never said, she wanted nothing to do with Germany, for was it not the Germans who had killed her sister, mother and beloved father.

But I had other plans. For my parents were shaped by their struggle against the rise of the Nazis and their need to flee. I was brought up in 'silence' because the 'deaths' of their families mattered so much, that they could not be spoken of. Their paranoia, at times acute, and their insatiable suspicions about me were rooted in their real experiences in Germany. As my mother wrote in one of her published poems, English would slither away from her as she reached out to speak or write it. As she wrote in another, she remained 'a stranger in a foreign land'. I had to take them back to Germany.

First, my dear friend Richard mixed my parents' ashes together in his kitchen. Then he halved them. With his usual fastidiousness, Richard tried to ensure that the ashes were divided equally, balancing the two identical bowls with the ashes in them on his scales. Then, he spooned one half little by little into the little boxes. The air filled with specks of ash and ash spilled over the kitchen floor. I started to laugh and cry. Then I, my son, Josh, and Lotte's friend and biographer, David Perman, scattered half of the ashes round the tree and we read out a few of Lotte's and Siegi's poems.

Strictly against the rules, I carried a number of face powder containers filled with my parents' conjoined ashes through German customs. All but one of the addresses my parents had lived in were in apartment blocks with little gardens or courtyards. I stood outside, knees shaking, till somebody appeared who opened the front door and then walked in as if I belonged there. At one place, the man must have been suspicious but when I explained what I was doing and why: that my father had fled Berlin because he was an active anti-Nazi and I had to bring him back to Berlin, the man embraced me and said how proud he was to meet me.

I scattered a small handful of the ashes in the different flower beds, flowerpots, around a bush ora tree. Finally, I stood high up on the balcony of the hotel my son and I were staying in and threw my parents' ashes into the winds over Berlin. Maybe I am the proverbial 'rootless cosmopolitan' but at least I had brought my parents back home.

Bibliography

Moos, M., and Cushion, S. (2020). *Anti-Nazi Germans:* Moos, M., *Enemies of the Nazi State from within the Working Class Movement*, and Cushion, S., *German Volunteers in the French Resistance*. London: Community Languages in association with the Socialist History Society.

17   I joined the dots and the dots joined me

The town of Gmünd is the place that I associate most closely with my paternal Austrian Jewish forebears. I first visited in 2018 but the journey towards it was a journey of understanding that started some years earlier, when a life event inspired me to join the historical dots and reconstruct my continental family's story.

I set out without a physical destination in mind and when the opportunity to visit Gmünd arose, I took it. Discoveries on the way had recast my views of close relatives, Austria and even my identity and it seemed a fitting terminus.

A consequential encounter in Gmünd persuaded me to claim Austrian citizenship. With that decision, I re-attached to my surname the umlaut that my father left behind when he fled the country (the other dots of the title) and began another journey with an unknown destination.

Gmünd is a prospering rural town surrounded by farmland and woods on the border with the Czech Republic, where my Jewish grandmother, Hedwig Löwy, was born in 1894. My father, Kurt Pöllinger, was born in Vienna in 1924 but Gmünd was his second home. He stayed in Gmünd frequently with his wider shopkeeping family as a child and many of the earliest pictures in Hedwig's now dog-eared black card photo album are of her friends and family in the town and nearby.

Visits to this much-loved place had to stop in 1938, when the town's Jewish population was evicted by the Nazis. In March 1939 my grandmother escaped to the UK after obtaining a British visa to work as a cook and my father followed her on a Kindertransport shortly before the war broke out. My grandparents had divorced by then and my 'Aryan' grandfather, who had ensured my father was brought up as a Catholic, remained in Vienna. Both my father and grandmother, who lived until 1967, made the UK their permanent home and said little about their ordeals to anybody outside of their closest surviving family. My father married my British-born mother, who did not have a Jewish background, in 1975 and died in 1990. I was born in 1976.

In 2012 the prospect of fatherhood caused me to think about the future at the same time as sparking an urge to look backwards. I gained the distinct sense of being a point in a continuum, but my understanding of what preceded me fell short: my father did not have the inclination to say and because he died early, I did not have the opportunity to ask. I set about researching my family tree, with the declared aim of filling in the gaps for the next generation.

During the course of my casual genealogical research in 2016 I made contact with Dr Friedrich Polleross at the University of Vienna after discovering his 1990s book, *Die Erinnerung tut zu Weh*, [The Memory is too Painful]. The book investigated the impact of Nazi persecution on the Jewish population of Lower Austria, the state in which Gmünd is located. It was out of print, so he kindly scanned and forwarded pages mentioning my family. In the 1980s he had coincidentally interviewed my grandmother's sister-in-law, Magda Löwy, for it in Vienna.

Later, he asked me for some photographic and documentary material for his next book, *Jüdische Familien im Waldviertel und ihr Schicksal* [Jewish Families in the Waldviertel and their Fate]. While searching through my mother's loft for my grandmother's photo album, I unexpectedly found a trove of letters that had belonged to my grandmother. They included forty letters from my father in Vienna to my grandmother in the UK in 1939, providing a dramatic account of his escape ordeal as it unfolded. One of the most upsetting things I learned from the letters was that my grandfather was in league with the anti-Semites. He wanted my father to have an 'Aryan' upbringing, tried in a threatening way to make him disassociate himself from his Jewish relatives and tried to prevent him leaving for the UK.

More than anything on my quest to investigate my Austrian family background to date, the letters were a direct encounter with aspects of my father's interior life. If in the past I may have put such a discovery away again 'for later' because I had avoided surfacing painful memories of his death, I found that I was able to cope. Questions arose for me, such as had he been affected by his ordeal, despite not appearing so on the surface and were there any consequences for my upbringing?

I was pleased when Friedrich invited me to speak at the launch of his book in May 2018, that happened to be in Gmünd. I was curious to see the 'hometown' that loomed large in the family story and thought that it might act as a kind of portal to the past to help me find answers to my multi-plying questions. I was also appreciative of Friedrich's efforts to cast a light on the fates of family members and their contemporaries, and I wanted to support his work, which defied Austria's reputation for burying shameful aspects of its history.

Before the visit, Friedrich introduced me by email to the Gmünd town archivist and publicist Harald, who had written the chapter on the town (each chapter is on a local town in the Waldviertel region of Lower Austria and is written by a different author). Harald kindly offered to guide me around Gmünd and the day after my Friday evening arrival, we arranged to meet in the town square.

I spotted the tall and solidly built blond figure smoking a cigarette before I really got my bearings. He was standing on one side of the elong-ated and well-kept square with a fountain and onion-domed building at its centre. In fact, he was standing outside of the nondescript and shuttered former family shop, founded by my great-grandfather Eduard Löwy in the late 1800s.

Figure 17.1. Nik standing in front of his family's old shop in Gmünd (From family collection).

After introductions we looked at a few photos that I had scanned from my grandmother's album together, to find how they corresponded to the surroundings. The town had been little touched by conflict, so it was easy enough to spot the locations. It was during this exercise that the connection between place and people, three of whom aside from my father I had met from the photos (Magda Löwy and my cousins Anita and Margit), became more concrete. I found myself playing short film-reels in my head to place the characters in this environment and envisage this lost world better and I became sorrowful at the thought of what would soon befall them.

Harald pointed out the large building across the square from the shop where my grandmother and her siblings went to school and the sites of formerly Jewish-owned businesses. We crossed paths with the mayor who said she would be at the launch that evening and thanked me earnestly and effusively for coming. I got the impression that the launch would be a larger affair than I had imagined. There were posters around town.

Figure 17.2. Poster in Gmünd announcing book launch (Photo taken by Nik Pollinger/ Pöllinger).

Harald and I went on to the town archive, with the bookish and bespec-
tacled Friedrich, who had just arrived in Gmünd by train. Harald showed
me various entries into municipal records such as the charitable contributions made by my great-grandfather and his listing in the town's male
choir. I took some photos.

Then I spotted a large home-made shop's banner proclaiming fealty
to Hitler propped against a wall. It could have been something that my
great-uncle Karl Löwy saw in a neighbouring shop's window, whilst his
was soiled by daubed-on swastikas after the Anschluss. I felt that it was
equally important to take a photo of the banner, because I was not sure of
how much I would learn about the conditions of life for my relatives before
and after the Nazi takeover: during the archive visit Harald had been keen
to emphasize how integrated the community had been before Nazi rule.
Friedrich was less sanguine about the climate for Jewish citizens, and they
agreed to disagree.

After lunch with Harald and Friedrich, I walked to the tranquil
Malerwinkel bathing spot that featured in many of my grandmother's
photos before heading to my nearby hotel to prepare for the launch event
at the Palmenhaus.

I met Friedrich at the entrance to the grand structure that once housed
a duke's botanical collection and is now used for social functions. He seemed
nervous at the sight of hundreds of empty chairs. With some help from his
publisher, he set up a pile of books for sale on a table, but he had no reason
to worry. The chairs soon filled, and people were even standing at the back.

After an introduction by Friedrich, Harald provided a measured, detailed and moving account of the fates of the fifty-eight strong pre-war
Jewish population of the town. Clearly, Harald had conducted a lot of
research, building on Friedrich's earlier work, to flesh out the characters
of the people the town lost. He also touched on acts of vandalism and intimidation perpetrated Nazi thugs, although we did not learn their iden-
tities. Harald finished by reading the names of the people from the town
who were later deported and murdered. He informed the audience that
I would be speaking after a musical interlude of traditional central European
violin pieces by Jewish composers and said that he was grateful that I had
come. Sat next to the mayor in the front row of the audience, I felt myself

becoming tearful for the first time since arriving in Gmünd but composed myself in time to take the stage.

I was greeted by a respectful silence from the audience, which had come from the area but also as far afield as Vienna. I have an idea of what they were half-expecting me to say from a telling comment in a local newspaper reporter's subsequent article. He noted that I spoke without *Groll* [resentment]. I imagine that this rather unsettling possibility would be front of mind for those who might not have heard testimony from victims or descendants. With only about 3 per cent of pre-war Jewish exiles returning to live in Austria and the culture of denial post-war, most of the audience would not have had the opportunity to hear directly from those impacted by historical persecution.

Instead of pointing fingers, I first spoke of my father's strong connection to the town (the little he did say about his childhood usually had to do with being out in nature there). Thereafter most of my talk focused on the experiences of Karl Löwy, my grandmother's brother and local shopkeeper. I relayed what I had learned from letters that he had written to my grandmother between 1939 and 1945, that I had found amongst the letters in my mother's loft.

His business was confiscated, and he was hounded out of Gmünd with the rest of the Jewish population in 1938. He escaped Austria for the UK at the last minute in 1939 and was moved around the world by the British authorities. In his final letter after the war's end, as he languished in Palestine, he wrote to my grandmother that he could not contemplate ever going back to Gmünd again. Necessity forced him to however, because he could not make a living abroad. He returned to Gmünd in the late 1940s, joined later by his brother Hermann, to reclaim the 'Aryanized' shop, which he ran until about 1970. The townspeople are unlikely to have heard from him after the war about his Nazi-era concerns for siblings Ella and Helene, who were murdered, and for his wife Magda, whose visa did not come in time. She had to hide for years in Budapest whilst exterminations and deportations ravaged the Jewish population around her.

I have often wondered how he coped with life in the town, surrounded by unhappy memories and inevitably some people who had looked on, benefitted from, or participated in his persecution. His experience accounts for my deeper interest in how Austria's denial and silence manifested beyond how it handled citizenship or restitution post-war and including how the survivors in its midst were treated.

The mayor wrapped up the book launch, stressing Gmünd's role as a bridge between communities: Czech and Austrian, east and west, different faith traditions, past and present. Her speech struck a chord: I felt like the audience regarded me warily at the outset as an envoy from the past, as much as I may have once regarded the town as an immutable portal to it. But the reciprocal curiosity and goodwill from the townspeople meant we had a basis for a future dialogue as contemporaries interested in reconciliation. Nevertheless, I felt it would be rare to encounter someone like Friedrich. At his exhibition tied to the book at the regional museum in the town of Neupölla nearby, he went as far as exploring publicly the participation of his own family in Nazi misdeeds.

Before departing Gmünd and going to Neupölla on my final day in the Waldviertel, I visited the old family shop deliberately early as the sun was just starting to warm the cobblestones in front of it. I was alone in the square apart from an itinerant lady who had stood out in the previous day's audience thanks to her colourful attire. She watched me curiously as I stood and surveyed the scene again.

Tears flowed freely. They were inevitably a result of having had to confront, all at once, upsetting historical and personal themes. It pained me to be reminded of the fates of the murdered and the experiences, in and outside of Austria, before and after the war, of those whom I had known. I also experienced a sense of accomplishment bordering on release. It felt like the end of a years-long quest, having learned almost all I could about my Austrian family and in particular, my father's early life. I was only saddened not to hear much of what I had learned from him directly.

The visit to Gmünd was not the end of my interest in understanding the past, but it provided me with a new focus on the future and on doing something with my knowledge. One of the most significant legacies of my visit to Gmünd was its role in my application for Austrian citizenship. For that I can thank the mayor, although her contribution was unintentional.

My desire for Austrian citizenship had waxed and waned over the six years proceeding my visit. I had first tried to claim it in 2012 but was rebuffed by Austria's London embassy. I had two primary motivations.

Firstly, I had begun surfacing suppressed memories of my Austrian-inflected upbringing and it felt like claiming a birth-right. I had been given German first and second names, we often ate central European cuisine and the soundtrack to my early life was classical music broadcasts from whatever shortwave German-language radio station my father could tune into. Even more significantly, I was brought up bilingual, my first word was *Schlüssel* [key], and I spent much of my first five years in Switzerland because of my father's work. Later, I went to the German School London for a while, which was only possible because my father pretended that he was an Austrian citizen. At home, he regularly press-ganged me into doing extra German grammar and vocab. homework.

Figure 17.3. Three-year-old Nik in Lederhosen in an Alpine setting (From family collection).

I am unable to explain fully the lengths he went to, to inculcate German language and culture in me: I have not yet come across a member of the 'second generation' with a similar upbringing. It was more akin to the experience of a child of a conventional expat who may return with his family, rather than that of a child of an exile with good reasons to despise his homeland.

It cannot be entirely explained by the fact that I grew up later than most in the second generation, when the integration of one's children was less of a burning priority and when speaking German in public was not frowned upon or not as frowned upon. I was still called a Nazi by an ignorant school bully in the 1980s. It may have simply felt more natural for him than for most refugees to hand on the baton of inherited belonging to me. It is possible that as a *Mischling* [The demeaning Nazi term for someone of mixed Jewish and 'Aryan' heritage] and a child of 13/14, his rejection by Austrian society post-Nazi takeover was not felt as absolutely as his fully Jewish peers. He was still allowed to go to school, for example, although the letters I found revealed he was also bullied there for his parentage. His ongoing ties to Austria had not been ruptured as completely either. He visited Austria post-war, his connection to place kept alive through Jewish family there (two uncles, three aunts and a cousin) and his father, though we have no evidence that they met again.

More speculatively, it is possible that, after the death of his mother in 1967, he found some solace in the effort to keep a connection to his roots through me. I brought up my children bilingual almost reflexively, which is where I get this idea. Being areligious, the option of continuity through religion or more broadly Jewish cultural tradition was not available to him, as it is not to me.

My father may also have wanted to arm me with the capability to survive in an emergency, as he had been forced to do. To prepare for his life in the UK he informed me that he had to memorize ten new words per day from the English dictionary. He used this as a yardstick for progress with my homework and yet his insistence that I learn to read Fraktur script, by then obsolete, suggests this was not the whole story. In any event, lacking the same urgent motivation, I made for an unwilling student. Whatever the reasons, my father's strenuous efforts to induct me and his disinclination to talk about the trauma of the past embedded in me the idea that I was part Austrian.

If the first motivation to claim citizenship concerned my own sense of connection to Austria, my second motivation was a keenly felt desire for historical justice for my father and his peers. He had to pretend to be an Austrian citizen because the refugees had been dispossessed of citizenship by the Nazis. Then, not long after the war, the large majority of refugees, who like my father in 1948 had naturalized in their destination countries out of practical necessity, were treated by Austria like anyone who had given up citizenship voluntarily. That is to say, it treated them like foreigners, because it did not recognize dual citizenship. The contemptible attitude of the Austrian state cemented the Nazis' objective of making Austria *Judenrein* [Free of Jews], stymying a minority of refugees who wanted to reclaim their citizenship, if not return (and who did so from 1993 when dual citizenship was finally allowed for them unconditionally, although it could not be inherited). My mother told me that my father had actually investigated Austrian citizenship and residency for his retirement in the 1980s and became angry at the barriers.

After 2012 however, my two motivations to claim citizenship were challenged through contemplation, events and encounters.

The exhumed, intact but to date largely unexamined Austrian aspect of my identity began to atrophy. After visiting Austria for the second ever time in 2012 (the first time had been as a child with my family in the 1980s), I was discomfited by feeling that I was in an environment freighted by meanings not shared by most inhabitants. In combination with the sense of being rebuffed by the embassy and a later unease with the success of the far right which gained almost 50 per cent of the Austrian presidential vote in 2016, I came to understand that if I belonged to anything beyond British society it was not to contemporary Austrian society per se. My attachment was largely to an offshoot: a parallel cultural community in exile in the person of my father.

After 2012 I also became more convinced that my father would have had a more ambivalent attitude to Austria than I had once assumed, causing me to doubt whether justice would be served meaningfully by the award of citizenship. Firstly, there were his letters to his mother with their evidence of persecution. I also met other refugees for the first time and appreciated more fully the nature of their experiences and the alienation from Austria that they felt as a result. An older relative reported that my father said Austrians were the cruellest people in the world, whilst my mother told me of times when she and my father were in Vienna together in the 1970s and he would disappear for a day at a time without explanation: my great aunt Magda told her that he needed to be alone. And on reflection, he was very agitated on our visit to Vienna in the 1980s. If moving back to Austria had been an objective of his once, it would surely have been accompanied by conflicts that a piece of official paper re-asserting belonging would not have resolved.

In the run-up to my visit to Gmünd citizenship had therefore become less appealing in principle. Nevertheless, my view changed afterwards.

In the background, citizenship became available. I learned just before my visit that the Austrian Government would soon be introducing a law to enable all descendants to claim citizenship. Shortly after my visit, I also discovered that the London embassy was mistaken in 2012: I had been eligible along with a certain group of descendants, under case law from the previous decade. My initial reaction was to welcome the law because it directly addressed my concern for historical justice, whilst acknowledging that I did not have to avail myself of it. Even a new reason, the prospect of continued EU citizenship for myself and my children post Brexit, was not quite enough to overcome the reservations that had accrued.

A comment by the mayor in Gmünd at the end of the evening of the book launch proved pivotal because it set in train thoughts about how I could derive something positive and future-orientated from citizenship.

I floated the possibility of placing *Stolpersteine* in Gmünd and she was not enthusiastic, batting the idea away hurriedly (although they are guerrilla installations, my preference was for consensus). She said they were not suitable for the town, and it would be more appropriate to commemorate the town's lost Jewish community with a monument which, to her credit, she was planning to erect. But I was not expecting my proposal to be summarily dismissed, because it seemed at odds with the mission of the book we were celebrating and the commitment – at the highest levels of Government at least – to face up to the past.

Taken aback at the time, I thought about what may lie behind the comment after I returned home. It is entirely possible that a sizeable part of the local electorate would find the *Stolpersteine* objectionable (the FPÖ, the far-right party whose first leader was a Nazi, had gained 25 per cent of the vote in the broader region at the 2017 general election although it was not the mayor's party). Being placed at many sites around town, they might also draw unwanted attention to the fact that something evil had occurred there, with reputational implications.

On the surface, this exchange could have put the nail in the coffin of any citizenship aspirations. It suggested forces intent on obscuring the prevalence of past misdeeds still had too much influence and cast doubt on whether the goodwill and curiosity I experienced during my visit extended to the kind of self-examination across society that can act as a bulwark against future recurrence. Moreover, some members of the Jewish community and representatives of organizations supporting Syrian refugees in Austria who I spoke to elsewhere felt beleaguered by rising intolerance. I could not ignore these concerns about the present and blithely accept a gesture, meant to rectify a past injustice.

But the exchange ultimately had the opposite effect. I thought back to a lengthy period I had spent in Germany as an adult. Many streets I walked down were strewn with *Stolpersteine*. Even though they commemorated terrible events, I was pleased to see them there and reassured by extensive efforts to breed vigilance from an acknowledgement that elements in one's country, town and even family were capable of acts and omissions that lead ultimately to the Shoah. I wanted to experience the same feelings in Austria, and it galvanized me to 'be the change' instead of throwing up my hands at a lost cause. After all, I had been encouraged by my visit to Gmünd too and there was definitely something to build on.

I resolved to contribute more to research such as Friedrich's, which has included helping an academic tracing the experiences of returnees such as Karl Löwy. I also committed to turn my occasional journalism to pertinent themes, which has included exposing my grandfather's role in persecution for the BBC and discussing justice in Austria's past and present for The Observer. I noted with satisfaction that the articles circulated in Austria. I also returned to Austria and Gmünd in 2019 with my mother and young daughter and put a visit to a primary school on the itinerary with Harald's help, to allow the children to meet and forge friendly relations. Lastly, I decided to take citizenship. It felt important to accept the invitation and become a living counterpart to the cobblestones installed to disrupt physical space, but in social space. As a 'human *Stolperstein*' I may be a similarly inconvenient fact for some but can bear more than silent witness to effect change, through the power to vote, for example.

As I conclude this chapter, I have two passports. My Austrian one has reinstated the umlaut over Pöllinger, something that my father left behind along with all his belongings when escaping to the UK. He threw himself into life here and saw himself as British but never lost his attachment to his homeland: Gmünd was his firmest anchor to the country as the tides of history swept him away. I went to Gmünd in part to understand his attachment and how it transmitted to me. I ended up auditioning the country to see if it could overcome my reservations about accepting an invitation that was a long time coming and that had particular resonance for me because of my sense, albeit attenuated, of inherited belonging. I do feel a responsibility to support the efforts of progressive forces in the country, something I realized in Gmünd. I am looking forward to forging closer ties with people there and hopeful that those forces will prevail but I am aware that my British citizenship gives me the luxury of options if they do not.

Bibliography

Polleross, F. (ed.) (1996). *Die Erinnerung tut zu Weh, Jüdisches Leben und Antisemitismus im Waldviertel*; [The Memory is too Painful: Jewish Life and Anti-Semitism in the Waldviertel]. Waldviertel, Austria: Waldviertler Heimatbund Publications.

Polleross, F. (ed.) (2018). *Jüdische Familien im Waldviertel und ihr Schicksal*; [Jewish Families in the Waldviertel and their Fate]. Waldviertel, Austria: Waldviertler Heimatbund Publications.

18 Haunted, or at home?

I grew up only knowing the bare facts: that my mother had come from Germany on a Kindertransport aged 9 and her parents and brother had been 'killed in a concentration camp'. She had been fostered by an elderly Christian English couple and swiftly turned into a little Christian English girl. The past was a very closed book and a terrifying abyss of mystery that fuelled my nightmares. I only finally began to find out the truth eleven years ago, by an increasingly absorbing and compulsive process of research, mourning and commemoration which has taken over much of my life. Since then, I have visited Germany ten times and been involved in the laying of nineteen (soon to be twenty) *Stolpersteine* and organizing two exhibitions (one in Laisa, my mother's home village, the other in Battenberg, the nearest town where her grandfather was born and grew up). At some point in the process my mother's parents and brother became my grandparents and uncle.

Treading on the same ground

Visiting Laisa, a place that for decades had been a barely mentioned name, akin to a place of myth, was to begin the process of concretising the truth. My mother's integration had been so thorough, her RP [received pronunciation] accent so flawless, the expunging of her first identity so complete, I had never been able to equate the facts of her past with what I saw before me and experienced as 'Mum'. This disjunction was demonstrated when I found an old exercise book from my last year at primary school – I had drawn a family tree in which my mother descended from an entirely

English sounding family with very un-Jewish names. As I walked around Laisa in a daze I began to feel, sense and understand at a deep level that she really had been a German Jewish girl originally. When I saw its pastoral setting, surrounded by green sloping valleys, I suddenly understood why she had said to me in the hospice that she wanted to be buried in a little village outside Cambridge – an approximation of Laisa.

Thanks to a kind tenant I was able to look round the only house owned by a relative that had not been demolished. My grandfather's maiden aunt Settchen Freudenthal had lived here. Stepping into the half-timbered little house, where my grandfather had no doubt visited his aunt, where my great-grandparents might have started their married life, I tried to see beyond the twenty-first century trappings – computer, mugs, telephone – noting the low ceiling height, rough wooden staircase – 'axe hewn', the tenant told me. The bathroom used to be a stable. He agreed I could go up the little staircase – at the top, a landing with a sloping floor, a view for miles across the valley beyond. I went down the steps to the cellar, where potatoes were once kept on the earthen floor. Here time had stood still. I inhaled and connected. The long garden at the back sloped up the hillside, still containing the fruit trees Settchen would have relied upon. A whole way of life glimpsed.

Visiting the cemetery in Battenfeld where my Freudenthal ancestors were buried, standing by their graves, their bones below, touching the old stone, placing a pebble from my own garden upon each one, lighting a candle, saying Kaddish, all were profoundly meaningful, a tangible way to connect, a pathway to the past, incontrovertible proof that these people had existed, this was where my mother's first life had begun. I was standing where my grandparents, great-grandparents had once stood, feeling the peace and tranquillity of the trees above, sharing the view over the valley below. Later, in letters found in my late second cousin, Steve's study in Tampa, unopened and unread for at least sixty years, I would learn of a final family group visit in 1938 to the cemetery by my uncle, grandfather, great-grandmother, great-aunt and great-uncle. Layers of history.

I soon became preoccupied by the absence of my great-grandfather's gravestone. As he had died in Laisa, the only Jewish cemetery in which he could have been buried was in Battenfeld. I scoured the cemetery; near my great-great-grandparents' grave I came across a fragment of gravestone with a scrap of inscription – ... *x F* ... I worked out it must relate to my grandfather's brother Max Freudenthal who had died in infancy. A remnant and reminder of the destructive havoc wreaked on and after *Kristallnacht*. I arranged for a new gravestone for my great-grandfather Joseph and his son Max, incorporating the fragment, using the same font and type of stone. Finding a suitable inscription in Hebrew (ensuring it was correctly inscribed) and coming up with a form of words, in German, to cover the circumstances in which the new gravestone was being created were complex challenges. Steve and his family came from Tampa for the installation of the new gravestone for our great-grandfather. My husband, the stonemason, the granddaughter of the man who had acquired my grandfather's house and store, a historian and the owner of the local *Heimatmuseum* [Local History Museum] were with us. I was told no one else (e.g. the local paper, radio) had been informed, just in case. The past – the fear and dread, the need for secrecy – came very close.

Another cemetery, Hatzbach, for many decades a centre for Jewish burials, including my grandmother's Buchheim and Katz relatives. Now cramped and curtailed, a pinched relic, hemmed in by buildings and a garden, strawberries growing upon the formerly hallowed ground. My great-great-grandmother's gravestone is here, her name all that remains on the eroded surface. Her bones could be anywhere, possibly beneath the strawberries or twee summer house. The cemetery had been Aryanized; then, as the American army approached, the gravestones that had not been used as building materials were dotted randomly around the small remaining patch of cemetery land, to hide the multiple desecrations. I wanted to take the gravestone in my arms, to cradle, comfort and connect with Elen's long departed spirit. I lit a candle, placed my pebble, recited Kaddish through tears of rage and disgust. How could people sit so close, in plain view, and enjoy such a garden, only separated from this ravaged cemetery by a hip-high chain-link fence?

Looking for the site of the book burning in Battenberg, which my relatives would have known about, my husband and I saw an open area, opposite the house of a distant relative. As I realized this is where it happened,

I heard a sudden noise – a group of young lads were shouting, laughing, kicking something – almost on the site of the conflagration. As I pointed out this eerie echo to my husband the youths ran off and silence returned, almost as if they had been conjured up from the past.

Encounters

Germany has proved to be a treasure trove, a repository of memories, memorabilia and oral history. On my first visit to Laisa an elderly gentleman came up to me and grasped my hands with tears in his eyes, "Lorechen!" He thought I was my mother who had finally returned. Through my own tears I had to break the news to him that she had died many years earlier. He was one of several people I met there who had been at school with my mother and uncle, who knew my grandparents, great-grandmother and great-aunt. A class photo showed my mother, the only Jewish child in the school. These people reinforced the idea that indeed my mother's first life had existed.

Herr M., the son-in-law of the man who had acquired my grandfather's house and business premises after *Kristallnacht*, was still living in a house he had had built on the site of the Freudenthal family home; his daughters had grown up in the original house and were able to describe it to me in such detail that in my mind's eye I could look round the kitchen, step into my grandparents' bedroom, see the staircase with its ornamental banisters. Their aunt told me my grandmother had shown her mother where they had hidden on *Kristallnacht* – in the cupboard under the stairs. She gave me a slim skein of fine blue, green and red wool which had been exchanged by my grandparents for food. I then had to come to terms with the idea that they had been short of food before the camps.

When my brother and I attended the *Stolpersteine* ceremony in Laisa, Herr M. observed on first seeing my brother "Da ist der Willy", we realized for the first time that he looked like our grandfather. The elderly people explained that Willy was tall, whereas his wife Berta was short, my height. Finally, an explanation for the discrepancy in our heights. A lady explained that my grandmother had sewn a back brace for her mother. It had solved her back problem. They had always kept it in case anyone else in the family needed it. She gave it to me. I could hold and touch something my grandmother had created, see her fine stitches, appreciate her kindness and skill, learn something of her character.

At the opening of an exhibition in Battenberg about local Jewish families, including my own, Herr M. showed me a letter my grandfather had written, found that afternoon by Herr M.'s daughter while cleaning her windows. I asked to keep the letter, rather than the photocopy. To own something my grandfather had written, to touch what he had touched, was breath-taking. That I couldn't decipher or understand it was a bitter reminder of how dislocated I was from the immediate past. Several years later I would teach myself to read *Sütterlin* [Historical form of German handwriting] script and learn sufficient German to read such letters unaided.

A former neighbour told me her mother would meet my grandmother in secret in Marburg, my grandmother covering her yellow star with a shawl. The neighbour would give her food and they would talk. She mentioned casually in passing that she still had my grandmother's *Kochtopf* [cooking pot]. My grandmother had told her mother to take it from the things they had had to leave in the house after *Kristallnacht*. Sobbing into it, I overheard her saying, "It's only an old cooking pot. I used it for doughnuts." I carried the heavy black cast iron pot back to London on the train, in my arms; inhaling deeply, hoping for some lingering scent of all those meals my grandmother had prepared in it for the family. At home I cooked one vegetable soup in it, seasoned with tears. It felt too sacred to use again.

In Berlin a lady who had stayed in Marburg while my grandparents were working there as a servant couple was able to tell me they had sought sanctuary with her uncle after *Kristallnacht*; that my grandfather was tall, good-looking, had a dry sense of humour, was a very interesting man; her mother adored my grandmother's soups, especially her chicken soup.

Back in England, while going through the contents of the family home, following the death of my father, I found over 100 photographs of the relatives in Germany and, late one evening, at the very bottom of the bottom drawer in a filing cabinet, a dark leather rectangle. I opened the two press studs and saw a collection of pencils and the words 'Ernst Freudenthal' handwritten on the leather. My uncle's pencil case. Two swastikas had been drawn on the leather, and someone had tried to ink over them. I still don't know how this pencil case came into my mother's possession, whether she brought it with her on the Kindertransport (it is not on the mandatory list of items in her suitcase). I wonder still that it lay there in my parents' combined study for all those decades. Evidence of the bullying and persecution Ernst must have experienced at school, a precursor of the deadly fate he would later meet.

As I arrived in Coburg, where my uncle Ernst had been sent to a Jewish boarding school, after he could no longer attend the village school, walking towards the station exit I became intensely conscious I was walking where once he walked, my footsteps in his. I managed to reach the exterior and, hiding against a wall, wept uncontrollably. With a helpful local historian, I walked up the hill to the building that had been the school. We went around the exterior as I tried to gain a sense of what it had been like when Ernst and the other teenagers were there. The interior was being refurbished. Builders were walking in and out, the front door was wide open. I went in and looked around. As if I were invisible, no one stopped me or seemed to notice. The dark wooden staircase I'd seen in photographs was still there. I could connect, in the only way left to me, with my posthumous uncle.

Commemoration and memorialization

On a German study tour to Poland with a mixed group of students and professionals none of whom had lost relatives in the Holocaust, I visited the camps where my closest relatives were murdered: Majdanek, Sobibor, Treblinka. It felt important to do this at some point in my life, to face the unknown, to give shape to the faceless horror, to be where they had met their deaths, to connect with their experience, to say Kaddish, to honour their memories, ensure they are not forgotten. In retrospect it may have been as much for them as for myself, even for my mother, to face what she could not bring herself to do in the short life she had had.

It felt surreal on arriving to see something as mundane as a road sign to Lublin – the juxtaposition of the quotidian with something so redolent of horror. To have seen the gas chambers, ovens, dissection-table at first hand was important if eviscerating. The groups of Polish teenagers slouching round, chewing gum, seemingly oblivious of their surroundings, was distressing, as were the blocks of flats built on top of parts of the camp. Likewise, when later, we were greeted by three youths shouting, *"Heil Hitler!"* with straight arm salutes as our group returned to the coach after visiting a Jewish cemetery, itself vandalized and used as a picnic spot. In Poland I became very conscious, particularly beside the mass graves, of the psychic residue of so much slaughter, and, in the empty countryside, of the gaps where the murdered people should have been. I was ill for months after this trip.

My trips to Germany have given me another perspective – I soon learned the burden of the past had not left the Germans unscathed. At the end of my visit to the death camps in Poland, a German lady asked me how I felt, "Better." I had said Kaddish where they had died. I asked how she felt, "Worse, much worse." She knew so much more about the horrors her country had perpetrated.

Twenty *Stolpersteine* – Each stone is the chance to encapsulate a person's life, their laying an opportunity to connect with previously unknown relatives from Israel, Canada and the USA; to share information, stories and photographs; to create links with local residents and researchers; to hold the equivalent of a funeral for those who in many cases had none.

In Laisa the ceremony for five members of the Freudenthal family, whose fates had been unknown to the villagers they left behind, became the occasion for group mourning as I addressed a gathering of some ninety people, followed by readings by local school children, we were all in tears. They mayor of Battenberg welcomed my brother and me as *Laisaer* – members of the community. I had a fleeting sense of what it might feel like to be rooted somewhere.

Figure 18.1. *Stolpersteine* commemorating the Freudenthal family in Laisa (Photo by
Gina Burgess Winning).

I contributed a chapter in German to a book commemorating the seventy
fifth anniversary of the deportations from Marburg, detailing the lives of
my grandparents and uncle who were deported from Marburg on 31 May
1942 to Majdanek and Sobibor. Writing it in German seemed essential,
to tell their story in their language, even if my own mastery of German
was incomplete. Drawing all the threads together, choosing photographs,
providing an account of their lives and fates was ultimately immensely
satisfying, albeit the process of liaising, haggling, arguing and negoti-
ating (hard) with the German editor was at times stressful, upsetting and

difficult. As with the tributes I read out at the *Stolpersteine* ceremony, I felt like a tigress defending her cubs.

Conclusions

As I prepare for a twentieth *Stolpersteinverlegung* [Laying of *Stolpersteine* ceremony] there is the usual mix of dread and excitement, an undertow of anxiety, yet I am definitely drawn to Germany. Almost always there is a sense of too much history, the overlay of the past too close, too omnipresent.

The emotional impact has been immense, often gruelling and excruciatingly painful, yet also enriching and satisfying. I have far fewer persecution nightmares. For my nephews and niece our Holocaust heritage is now something that feels natural, accessible and can be discussed openly. We have all, including my brother, acquired restitution of German citizenship.

I have peopled the void; given my ghosts faces; rescued my relatives from oblivion, so they are at peace; having served as a conduit for accumulated ancestral grief (my own, that of my mother and other relatives), the rawness of my grief and depth of pain has lessened. I have answers, but countless questions. My encounters in and with Germany and Germans have been rewarding, heart-warming, enriching, healing; painful, difficult; at times frustrating and stressful; occasionally disturbing, chilling. As I have pursued my research, many Germans have been very generous with their time and energy, patiently answering my innumerable questions, offering help and advice tirelessly. My understanding of my mother and her experiences has deepened and sharpened my regret at my teenager's lack of sympathy and tolerance – if only we had had longer and could have visited Laisa together.

Over a decade into a tapestry of experiences, parallel journeys of research and mourning, I am less haunted, more at home within myself; in Germany, with so much more detailed knowledge of what happened there, the haunting comes from without, as do faint beginnings of feeling at home. I cannot say at this stage if these feelings will ever come to outweigh the haunting.

Like my mother before me, I wonder if I will ever feel entirely at home anywhere.

Epilogue

The laying of that twentieth *Stolpersteine* on a freezing February morning (my mother's 90th birthday) marked the end of an era for me, and indeed the world as the Covid-19 virus began to seed and spread. My drive to commemorate and honour the memory of some of my relatives who had been persecuted and or killed during the Holocaust was spent. I allowed myself to decide that number twenty would mark the end of the stones I would initiate. If I were to be approached in relation to one of the many remaining relatives I would of course participate, but otherwise it was time to call a halt. The years of research, struggles, pain and grief, exhaustion and illness, had born their fruit, across Germany – these hitherto unknown and forgotten people had now been remembered, in their communities, their names and dates and places of death, where known, were engraved, set in the pavement, discrete but distinct. The *Stolpersteine* had provided a focus for my pain, an outlet for my grief, a challenge to my research and linguistic skills, a way to connect with the places where my relatives had lived, their mother tongue and even, to my astonished delight, with a precious handful of their former friends and neighbours. The *Stolpersteine* enabled me to move beyond the negativity and loss, towards positive action: to do something concrete for my unknown, unknowable family members. To give a future to the past.

19 Three unexpected ceremonies

The first journey that I made with a Holocaust connection was at the age of 10 in 1962. I had no idea then of its relevance to what has become a dominant factor in my life. My parents took my elder brother David and me on our first foreign holiday. I didn't really understand that this was also a return to my mother Ruth's birthplace, twenty-three years after she had said goodbye to her parents at the age of 19, never to see them again.

Our first stop was Dortmund in Westphalia, Germany, where my mother was born in 1920 and where she spent her childhood. We were visiting her Uncle Siegfried and his second wife, Irene. Siegfried was the brother of my late grandfather Max Löwendorff, who was a successful businessman and proud holder of the Iron Cross. He was confident that the Nazis would not harm such a person but was murdered at Auschwitz-Birkenau together with his wife Gertrude.

Siegfried had been sent to Theresienstadt. He lost his wife and children, but he survived and returned to live in Dortmund. Of course, I never knew or understood any of this at the time. My main recollection is that he and his second wife didn't speak any English and my parents conversed with them in German, so it all seemed very strange, although I was reasonably used to hearing older people speaking German. I remember that one day my parents went off somewhere. On their return, we learned that they had been to visit the site of the house where my mother grew up, which had been bombed during the war. Everything was spoken about in whispers so as not to interrupt our idyllic childhood holiday.

Our next stop was Amsterdam. My Uncle Norbert lived in a flat on the Keizersgracht with his wife Kay. He survived the Holocaust despite spending time in the Westerbork transit camp, for many a precursor to a one-way trip to Auschwitz. After the war, he met Kay, an Auschwitz survivor who was born in Rotterdam. She became a special aunt to me. I was fascinated by the numbers tattooed on her arm. Much later, I came to understand what they meant. I also learned that, when she was in Auschwitz, 'Dr' Josef Mengele had carried out experiments on her. So now I understand why she never had children. I shudder to think about it as I write this. *"Ja Ja"*, she would often say phlegmatically, "That's how it is." Little did I know the terror that this comment concealed. Indeed, our times with Norbert and Kay were always filled with fun and laughter.

Unsurprisingly, I only gradually became aware of the horror of my family history as I grew older and put together some of the jigsaw surrounding the fate of my grandparents and wider family. I never realized the void created by not having any grandparents, and for that matter far fewer relations than would have been the case if it hadn't been for the Nazis, but I now think that this was actually hugely significant for my brother and me.

I felt something about me was different, but I wasn't able to identify what it was. I remember travelling to Holland in 1971, this time with a friend, and I recall saying something to him about my background being different to his. His slightly frightening, English grandmother lived next door to us in Salford. I was already eight when I met her and remember not understanding what a grandma was.

In retrospect, there weren't many elderly people in our lives. There was one older, slightly exotic, couple whom we saw from time to time. They were my dad's only relations living in England, known to me as Auntie Frances and Uncle Charles. I couldn't understand why my father called them Fanny and Karl. They were very kind and warm to my brother and me, had thick accents and my parents spoke mostly in German to them. I didn't think about it at the time, but I now realize that they were the nearest I had to grandparents. Now that I am a grandparent, I have a better understanding of what I missed.

Many of my parents' friends were also refugees with German accents. When my brother and I had our respective Bar Mitzvahs, relatives came from various parts of the world, many being German speaking. I thought this was very exciting and had no real idea why they were scattered around the world. That realization grew as the years went on.

All in all, looking back, I suppose that the contrasts between the non-Jews at school with thick Lancashire accents, the local Jewish community predominantly from an eastern European background and my own, Germanic background were quite confusing. As a child you tend to take things at face value. I have spent the rest of my life putting all this together. Overall, I look back with fondness at the melange of influences that surrounded me. I feel that my German background in many ways played a positive role in my upbringing, especially culturally, and I am proud of my roots.

In 1975, after I graduated from Cambridge, I met my darling wife to be, Monica. She was introduced to me by a good friend of German Jewish parentage who rightly thought we were made for each other. Was it chance, choice or fate that brought me together with her? I ask this because one wonders what effect our common background had on our relationship. Monica's father grew up in Berlin. Like my maternal grandparents, her paternal grandparents were murdered in Auschwitz-Birkenau. Her mother grew up in Hamburg and came to the UK with her parents in 1938.

Through Monica and her parents, I discovered another side of my background. I knew that, whereas my father had come from a traditional more orthodox/Eastern European background, my mother had come from a liberal German background. Monica and her family belonged to Belsize Square Synagogue. I had never come across this synagogue, which had been established by refugees from Germany and elsewhere in 1939. Its form of worship was totally unfamiliar to me. With its organ and beautiful choral music, much composed by Lewandowski and Sulzer, I imagine it would have been more familiar to my mother, but we never got to discuss this. Gradually, I came to know more about this community and the hard core of German refugees who still belonged there, maybe not religious in the traditional sense but amazingly close and supportive and very proud of their origins. I can see that growing up there gave Monica a feeling of belonging that perhaps I lacked, as I don't think my parents ever truly felt part of their synagogue community.

Another small but influential link between Belsize Square Synagogue, Monica and I, is that as well as Monica having always retained her links with Belsize Square, she and I have for many years been members of the

New North London Synagogue under the inspirational spiritual guidance of Rabbi Jonathan Wittenberg. Jonathan's grandfather, Rabbi Dr Georg Salzberger became the first Rabbi of the Belsize Square Synagogue in 1939. We hugely value this link because of the importance of Belsize Square to us and because Rabbi Jonathan shares a German Jewish background. It therefore felt very fitting that in 2001, we were fortunate to accompany Rabbi Jonathan on a pilgrimage to the Auschwitz-Birkenau concentration/extermination camps. This was a defining moment for us. Standing at the very place where Monica's paternal grandparents and my maternal grandparents were gassed – this was almost too much to assimilate. Rabbi Jonathan's words regularly inspire deep emotions, and his carefully chosen prayers and readings did not so much assuage the grief that engulfed us but allowed us to glimpse into the void that this hell on earth had created in the lives of our dear parents, and perhaps for the first time come to terms with what it meant.

It is through the story of Monica's father that this chapter begins to unfold. In 2014, Monica and I were due to go for a second time to Berlin, where I was attending a legal conference. Our previous visit had been in 2002, as part of a group led by Rabbi Rodney Mariner from Belsize Square (just one year after our Auschwitz trip) and we had seen the outside of the house in Zehlendorf, where her father and uncle had grown up. Ever since then, Monica had dreamed about what her father's life there must have been like. She longed to see inside and understand more about her father's childhood. A week before our second trip, Monica googled the address of the house at Forststraße 31 and imagine her surprise when a picture came up showing a pair of *Stolpersteine* in commemoration of her paternal grandparents, Georg and Margarete Lövy. She immediately wrote a letter to the address and received a reply by return. A week later, we were standing inside the house. The owners allowed us to wander round the house and garden and Monica was able to fulfil her dream. It transpired that responsibility for the *Stolpersteine* lay with the family next door. Their 17-year-old son's teacher had set his class a research project about Holocaust victims in the area and the boy had discovered that the couple next door, Monica's grandparents, had been two such victims. Briefly, having managed to send their sons to England in 1937, the parents had fled to Rotterdam and illusory safety. In

1943, they were deported via Westerbork to Auschwitz, where they were murdered. Having discovered these facts, the young non-Jewish schoolboy next door persuaded his parents to pay for a permanent memorial, so that whoever walked past the house should be reminded of the dreadful fate suffered by its occupants. A ceremony was organized, a leaflet produced with brief biographies and a psalm recited, all without our knowledge, because they were unable to trace the children or grandchildren, probably because they had changed their name. Monica and I knelt and lit candles by the memorial stones on the pavement one damp and dark November evening and then stood silently, with the aid of a couple of faded photographs, trying to picture the grandparents she never knew, together with her father and his brother, innocent and carefree, riding their bikes in that beautiful road.

Galvanized by the discovery of *Stolpersteine* outside Monica's grandparents' home in Berlin, I turned my attention to my own family history. My father had grown up in Vienna, in Birgittenau, Vienna's twentieth district and I wanted to investigate the possibility of laying *Stolpersteine* outside the apartment block at Klosterneubergerstraße 60, where his parents, Gitl and Manele Böhm, had lived. My father had grown up in that apartment.

For many years, my dad had been adamant that he wouldn't go back to Vienna. It would clearly have been too upsetting for him. He relented in the early 1980s when he was contacted by an old friend called Hermann Tell, who was living in Vienna. My parents made two visits to Hermann, but sadly he then passed away. However, having broken the taboo, my father fortunately decided that he wanted to take my brother and me to Vienna to show us where he grew up and we joined him for a memorable visit there in 1990.

We saw his old haunts and the places that he remembered from his childhood and youth, including the famous Prater. My father vividly recalled events from that time, both personal and political. These ranged from his visits to the local football stadium to watch not only football, but also opera, to the events of July 1934 when Chancellor Dollfuss was assassinated and there was fighting in the streets as Nazi sympathizers tried and failed to seize power. My father described the chants of "Rot, Weiss, Rot" from the supporters of Schuschnigg who took power and managed to keep the Nazis at bay until the Anschluss in 1938. Soon after that, on *Kristallnacht*, 9 November 1938, my grandfather was seized and taken to Dachau concentration camp where he spent several weeks, and my father was arrested and held in a large hall with many others. He told me that Adolf Eichmann made an appearance while he was held there. He was released after a couple of nights through the intervention of a senior official from the Zionist organization to which he belonged, who explained that he would be emigrating to Palestine. My father returned home to his distraught mother, and he told me that as he told her about his experience, his hair came out in clumps in his hand from the shock of what had happened.

My father did manage to leave Vienna in early 1939 through the good fortune of obtaining a permit to come to David Eder Farm in Kent. This was a Zionist training farm, where people prepared for agricultural life on a kibbutz in Palestine, although for various reasons my father did not ultimately emigrate. He remained in England and spent several years during the war working on a farm near Oldham in Lancashire, leading to his meeting my mother. My grandfather was murdered in Buchenwald and my grandmother at Mały Trostinec (Mały Trascianiec), a death camp near Minsk.

Before we completed our trip to Vienna, my father took us to Klosterneubergstraße 60, which stood unchanged from when he had lived there with his parents. We persuaded him to knock on the door and ask to see inside. A startled woman answered, and he explained that he used to live there and would like to show his children where he grew up. She immediately slammed the door and we never got to see inside. We can only speculate as to how long she had lived there and the reason for her refusal.

I have been to Vienna on several occasions since that visit. Each time, I venture to Klosterneubergerstraße, stand opposite the apartment block, gaze at the upper floors and try to imagine the childhood in the 1920s and 1930s of the man who became my father. I had toyed with the idea of laying *Stolpersteine* outside number 60 in the early 2000s, but I had the impression they might not have been welcome. However, on a subsequent visit, I noticed a few and, in April 2015, I contacted an organization called *Steine der Erinnerung* [Stones of Memory] in Vienna to find out whether we could arrange for stones to be laid. To my amazement, I was informed that, by a remarkable coincidence, a non-Jewish German resident of the block was in the advanced stages of organizing a commemorative plaque in memory of

Figure 19.1. Plaques in Vienna commemorating Peter's grandparents (Photo taken by Peter Bohm).

the residents of number 60 who were murdered in the Holocaust. He was about to give final instructions for their production, but for some unknown reason he had been unaware of my grandparents, and I was able to provide him with their details just in time for them to be included.

Subsequently, in October 2016, my brother and I, accompanied by our wives and seven other family members, travelled to Vienna to participate in a memorable ceremony, organized by *Steine der Erinnerung*, taking in five separate locations, and attended by local dignitaries and family members from as far away as Australia. Life stories were told, and we recited Kaddish outside our grandparents' apartment block. As the reader can imagine, this was an incredibly moving experience and we would not have been able to participate, were it not for the remarkable turn of events the previous year. We were also invited to go inside the apartment next door to that of my grandparents and were able to form a picture of the interior of the home where my father spent his formative years.

This was not the end of a series of surprises regarding memorials to members of my family. I find these events particularly touching because they all involve third parties who had no apparent need to take the steps they did, to memorialize victims who were unconnected with and unknown to them.

In March 2019, my first cousin Michael, on my mother's side, received, out of the blue, an email from a lady in Amersfoort in Holland informing him that a ceremony was scheduled to take place the following week in Amersfoort, memorializing, amongst others, five members of our family, including our aunt, Doris Löwendorff, who was murdered in Auschwitz – Birkenau, aged 19, in 1944. This had come about through the research of a group of local non-Jewish residents who were determined to commemorate every victim of the Holocaust who had lived in Amersfoort. For some reason, they had only just managed to trace my cousin. As a result, he, my brother and I and two other family members, travelled to Amersfoort at short notice to attend another exceptional ceremony, taking in eleven houses in a beautiful district and attended by a large number of locals and relatives.

Figure 19.2. Plaques in Amersfoort on the day of the commemoration (Photo taken by Peter Bohm).

There were printed biographies of each victim and Kaddish was recited outside each house by the family, or otherwise by a local survivor. Doris had latterly lived there with her uncle and aunt and their children, having fled from Germany, but tragically was unable to escape the Nazis. Her elder sister, my mother Ruth, came to Oldham in Lancashire in 1939 as a domestic and ended up meeting my father who delivered milk from a nearby farm, but that's another story. Auntie Doris was from time to time the subject of hushed mentions by my parents, but we had never really been able to acknowledge her as a real person. Now, after all these years, there is a tangible memorial to her and, at long last, we were able to pay our respects.

While we were standing outside the house in Amersfoort waiting to begin the dedication ceremony, a neighbour emerged from his house holding a single crystal wine glass wrapped in tissue paper. He said that it had come from his late parents, who had lived there before him. The night before they were to be deported by the Nazis, my mother's uncle and aunt had given a set of these glasses to the neighbour's parents for safekeeping and eventual return. Now, after so many years, he wanted to return the sole remaining glass to its rightful owners! To hold that glass in my hands and feel the connection to my family sent an enormous shiver down my spine.

Sadly, none of our parents lived to see any of the memorials to their family members. In some ways maybe that was not such a bad thing. The pain they suffered in losing their parents and other relatives was beyond our understanding. They dealt with it in different ways. Some spoke about it, some did not. Monica's father only talked about the subject if asked. We never saw him shed a tear, but he did occasionally have a faraway look in his eyes that said it all. My father couldn't speak about these events without crying and, if anything, he became more emotional about them as he grew older. My mother generally kept her feelings bottled up, but they did escape from time to time. She passed away before I had a real opportunity to discuss the subject with her. How I wish I could have done!

For me, it is difficult to encapsulate the thoughts and feelings that are generated by the memorials I have described. I think that attending the ceremonies and knowing that the memorials are there provides some comfort and a degree of closure, primarily because I believe that our parents would be pleased to know of their existence.

It is gratifying to me that, in recent years, there has clearly been a desire amongst second and third generation descendants of non-Jews in Germany to try to recognize the calamitous wrongs that took place and in which perhaps even their own family members may in some ways have been actively or passively complicit. The descendants cannot in any way be held responsible or vilified for what happened, but many try to demonstrate that they feel shame on behalf of their parents' and grandparents' generation and would like to acknowledge this to remaining survivors and their descendants. A non-Jewish German lawyer called Nikolaus, whom I came to know through my work, has lived in two apartment blocks in Berlin where he has been responsible for arranging *Stolpersteine* in memory of victims of the Nazis who lived there. He did the research, arranged and ensured payment for the plaques and endeavoured to trace and invite relatives from all over the world, including Israel, to attend ceremonies unveiling the stones. He has written to me that he is dedicated to ensuring that people do not forget and should learn from history.

As exemplified by Nikolaus, what is most amazing about the above stories is not that the memorial stones were placed and that the ceremonies took place, but that, in each case, this was the result, not of actions by our family, but of those of the respectful and dedicated efforts of non-Jewish people who had no connection whatsoever with the victims concerned. These marvellous people were determined that the individuals who were murdered, should be remembered, not just as statistics, but as individuals, each with their own story, each being a light that was tragically extinguished. In Berlin at least, the people who placed the *Stolpersteine* clean and polish the stones and light memorial candles on the anniversary of *Kristallnacht* every November. In each case, my family and I remain truly humbled by their efforts and dedication, and all this gives me hope for the future.

Figure 19.3. Children cleaning *Stolpersteine* (Photo taken by Janet Eisenstein).

Spurred on by these remarkable and admirable examples, I seized on an opportunity to make my own contribution to interfaith and intercommunal dialogue and understanding, through my involvement in the schools' programme at Belsize Square Synagogue that is presented by volunteers in February each year as an adjunct to Holocaust Memorial Day. Every year, about one thousand year 9 and 10 pupils from local schools visit the Synagogue to learn a little about Judaism. They are also taught about the Holocaust and why it is important for them to know about and learn lessons from it. Most of them are not Jewish and a significant number are Black or Asian. I consider that it is incumbent on Jews to teach about this and the importance of combatting anti-Semitism, racism, intolerance and discrimination of all kinds. I am pleased to have had the opportunity to do this.

In my case, the story of family memorials continues. I have been in touch with the *Stadtarchiv* [City Archives] in Dortmund and through them the *Jugendring*, a non-Jewish youth organization that is involved in laying

Stolpersteine there. Young people from *Jugendring* organizations all over Germany learn about the Holocaust and visit death camps in ongoing educational projects. As a result of my enquiries, I have obtained further information about my maternal grandparents, Max and Gertrud, and subject to delays caused by the coronavirus pandemic, I am hopeful that *Stolpersteine* in their memory will be laid in 2022.

20 Compass points in a nomadic life

My family was nomadic and seemingly without a compass to guide them, though I did grow up with a map of Europe in my mind, with certain fixed points.

London has always been like the North point in the compass of my life, the place where I was born and could always return to. Berlin, to some extent, was a South point, a place of departure. Not my own, but definitively for my parents, both born in Berlin and leaving as refugees before reaching adulthood.

But I knew little of that in my early years. London was where I was born and where my paternal grandparents lived; Berlin, where my maternal grandparents lived and Rome, where we lived, from 1952, as a family of four. My sister and I went to the French Lycée, my father worked and my mother painted. I grew up having to manage several languages. English at home, French at school, Italian playing with the neighbourhood kids and German with my grandparents in Berlin. That is, until 1959, when my parents split up and I went to Vienna with my mother and sister until 1962, when I was uprooted again.

Early visits to Berlin

I did not take to Berlin upon our first acquaintance, aged about 7. My grandfather, Siegmund Weltlinger, a tall and stern man, was rather forbidding; my grandmother, shorter and plump, was more welcoming. Conversations were awkward at first, as I could not speak German and

Figure 20.1. David with his sister, parents and grandfather by a lake in Berlin (Photo taken by Grete Weltlinger).

my grandmother spoke but a few words of English. To make matters worse, my mother, in an attempt to please her parents, had dressed us up in traditional garb. I was wearing *Lederhosen*, with a Bavarian style jacket and my younger sister was wearing a traditional *Dirndl* dress. In the only photo I have of that visit, I was looking rather glum, my body stiff and I felt rather uncomfortable.

As I got to spend occasional holidays there and my German improved, my grandparents and the city grew on me. I was shown around the city. When still young the zoo became a familiar place. Later, the museums held more attraction, as I was keen on ancient artefacts and the Egyptian collection. My grandmother enjoyed taking me shopping and eating out. One winter I remember her buying me a pair of ice skates so that I could skate on a small nearby lake. I must have already been in my early teens by then.

On rare moments, my grandfather would show a more tender side to his nature, as happened when he sang me a lullaby he had composed when I was born. I was probably eight or nine at the time and failed to realize the full import of the song, but I can still hear his voice, singing the lullaby, ever so close to me, in a deep baritone.

Figure 20.2. David with grandfather, Siegmund (Photo taken by Grete Weltlinger).

Jewish lullaby by my grandfather, Siegmund Weltlinger

As the day wanes, my heart grows heavy, my thoughts pull me over the sea,
my longing sails with the evening wind towards little David, my grandson.

You dear little David, listen closely to the winds,
that bring you my greetings and sing to you their song in your sweet sleep.
Sleep, overseen by the love of your grandfather, little David, sleep well!
Your dear Mother I sent from home,

to protect her from the certainty of being snatched.
We have been separated for many anxious years.
She was only part child then and now cradles her own child!

When the day darkens, my tears tremble.
I only know my son-in-law and grandchild from letter and picture.
My hair is white and the years travel.
Oh, when will I see you, loved ones, at last!

You dear little David, listen carefully to the winds,
that bring you my greetings and sing to you in your sweet sleep.
Sleep, little David, sleep well![1]

As I grew a bit older, my grandfather, already prominently involved in politics as a member of Berlin's House of Representatives, would make some reference to international affairs. On one of our walks, he pointed to a landmark in the distance, a radio or television mast, saying "Over there, see that, that is the German Democratic Republic, which is neither German, nor democratic, nor a republic." Although strongly identifying himself as a German Jew and proud of it, he belonged to the Christian Democratic Union and held quite conservative views. At that stage I do not remember having political discussions with him. It is only much later that I became aware of the complexities in his decision to stay put in Berlin through good times and bad times. He had made Berlin his city, even though he was brought up in Kassel.

My parents: Continually displaced

By contrast, my parents were never able to put down roots. It was something that completely eluded them. The shadow of the Holocaust followed them everywhere but so did the shadow of the cold war.

My mother, Resi Weltlinger, born in 1921 in Berlin came to Britain on the Kindertransport as a teenager in January 1939. She was taken in by

---

1   Translated from the German by my sister, Deirdre Gordon.

relatives, treated as a domestic and physically abused. As soon as she could, she ran away. She was brave as it was war time and she was alone. Due to her artistic talents, she found a job as a draftsman's apprentice and mixed largely in refugee circles, meeting artists and writers. But she soon came to the attention of the security services; she had joined an anarchist group because as she put it, they organized the best dances in town. At one point she had a Trotskyite boyfriend, which also counted against her.

My father, Ralph Clark had a different background. His mother, Bertha Braunthal, born in Vienna, spent the First World War in Berlin campaigning against the war and in the 1920s was prominent in the German Communist Party. She met William Clark in 1913 in London, when she was visiting and exhorting women workers in the East End to join trade unions.

William had been spell-bound by Bertha's fiery speeches. Imprisoned in England as a conscientious objector, he left for Berlin after the war, seeking to woo Bertha. They married and my father was born in 1923. Ten years later, when the Nazis took over, Bertha was arrested and given twenty-four hours to leave the country with her British husband and child.

My father led a charmed life in England at first. He did well at school and obtained a scholarship to study economics at Cambridge. He graduated in 1943 and enlisted in the army. Towards the war's end, he met my mother at one of those dances she so loved and they got married in June 1945.

But the British Special Branch, in charge of political surveillance, decided my father was a security risk. His parents had remained active in the British Communist Party; he also had married a refugee linked to an anarchist group. To my father's consternation, he was debarred from the British civil service and could no longer obtain the only kind of job his degree in Keynesian economics had prepared him for.

So, in 1948, the four of us, including my sister, were uprooted. We left for India at first and from there to Australia, where my father found work as an economist, working for the Wool Marketing Board.

We might well have stayed in Australia for the rest of our lives. But this was not to be. My mother was keen to return to Europe. Her parents' health had suffered as a result of their wartime ordeal in hiding and she now wished to visit them. There was another reason she wished to leave Australia. Without hiding her Jewish background, she had joined an Austrian folk dancing group in Melbourne, as she loved dancing. After a while she was horrified to discover that most of the group were convinced Nazis. She had gone to the ends of the world, only to be confronted by the very people from whom she had fled!

Rome in the 1950s

So, in 1951 we returned to England, but my father still could not find employment in Britain. He did get a job as an economist, working for the United Nations Food and Agriculture Organization in Rome. So, we all went off to Rome, where I quickly learnt Italian playing with the other kids in the street and on my 6th birthday was sent to the French lycée.

The street where we lived was only partially tar-sealed, ending in a mud path descending all the way to Trastevere, on the south bank of the river. I used to love clambering up and down that path; on either side lay abandoned orchards and fields. After school I could often be found there, playing with the other kids. It gave me a sense of adventure which stayed with me for the rest of my life.

Looking back on it, my years in Italy were the happiest times of my childhood. I could roam about the city, taking the bus to school, a bus that crossed the Tiber near the Castle of Sant Angelo (scene of Tosca's undoing, in Verdi's opera), then through the city centre and ending up at Porta Pia, a short walk from the Lycée. On the way back from school I would occasionally hop off the bus half-way and visit my father in his office. Then I would walk back across the Circo Massimo, the old Roman racecourse, strewn with broken columns lying on the ground. Rome, in the 1950s, was still being rebuilt after the devastation of war and bits of columns could also be found strewn strategically along the embankment of the Tiber, serving as makeshift benches.

Anti-Semitism and my Jewish identity

My first experience of anti-Semitism, aged 9, came as a shock. There was only one other English boy in my class and we had got on really well. But one day, during break, he suddenly called me a "bloody Jew". I had no idea what he meant and when I got home, I immediately told my mother, who burst into tears. She then told me that when she was sent to school in Berlin in 1938, immediately after anti-Semitic riots all over Germany, her schoolmates set upon her, beat her up and threw her out of school. It was the first time I had any idea that anyone in my family had been affected by the Holocaust.

My father immediately phoned up the boy's father to complain. Even more significantly, it propelled my parents into making sure we had more contact with the Jewish community. My father joined the Jewish community in Rome, paying his dues. This then entitled us children to join the Zionist youth movement, with outings to the pine forests of Rome and attendance at Purim and Hanukkah parties. But we did not join the *Cheder* [Sunday classes], so did not learn to read Hebrew or any Jewish practice. Upon reaching the age of 13, I had a Bar Mitzvah in the main Orthodox synagogue in Rome. I was given an *Aliyah* [called up for the Torah reading] and learnt by heart the blessing before and after the Torah reading but was not taught to read from the scroll.

Misery in Vienna

My world changed abruptly once again. My parents' marriage had been rocky and in 1959 they separated. My mother had been accepted to study at the Vienna Academy of Applied Arts, thus fulfilling her life's ambition of going to Art College.

Prior to that, my sister and I had managed to pick up sufficient German to get by, at holiday camps in Austria, while my mother studied painting and lithography at a summer school in Salzburg. We settled into some kind of routine, though my mother struggled as a single parent, studying and working at the same time and in truth, we were under much reduced circumstances.

We lived in a tiny flat. My mother had the only bedroom, just enough space for a single bed and a cupboard, while my sister and I shared the living room, which contained the sole heating for the flat, a coal stove. You reached the living room by crossing a narrow corridor, on the left a kitchen area consisting of a gas cooker and the only sink in the house, to the right a shower cubicle and a separate toilet.

I do not know how we would have survived in Vienna, were it not for our wonderful school lunches during the week, with *Wiener Schnitzel* [Thin slice of meat dipped in flour, egg and breadcrumbs and fried] or roast chicken on our Sunday outings to the Viennese woods in good weather. For my mother was no cook, we had no fridge and there was precious little food to be had at home.

Holidays provided much welcomed relief. Sometimes, in the summer, we stayed with my great aunt Liese on the Italian Riviera, where she had been hidden during the war, sometimes with my grandparents, in Berlin. When I reached 16, my mother chose to take me on a short trip to Prague during the Easter break.

It was something very special to look forward to. My sister was to stay in Vienna, in the care of a former landlady, while we were to stay in a hotel in the centre of Prague. I was quite excited by the prospect and wondered what it would be like to be on the other side of the Iron Curtain.

Prague 1962

We obtained a week's tourist visa for our visit. The border crossing proved uneventful and we reached Prague late on a Wednesday afternoon. The following day, after a good breakfast, we began our sightseeing, finding our way to Saint Wenceslas Square. What caught my mother's attention was the row of small shops selling books and records, some new, some second-hand. The prices on display were incredibly cheap compared to what we were used to and my mother eagerly bought some art books. As we walked further towards the river and the Charles Bridge, what struck me above all was the sense of dullness and grey everywhere. The buildings had an air of neglect, the pedestrians were all sombre, nobody smiled, everyone went quietly along their way, in glum silence, as if weighed down by a sense of doom.

By contrast, lunch in the canteen-style bar was much livelier, frequented by a youthful crowd, talking animatedly amongst themselves. I took them to be students, though I had no way of entering conversation with them, as only the older generation were likely to speak some German and no one spoke any English at the time.

The next day we tried to get into the Jewish Museum. It was closed, but one of the caretakers showed us a few exhibits. It did not mean much to me at the time; I had only minimal knowledge of Jewish ritual. On our last afternoon together, we visited the main Jewish cemetery, where Kafka was buried.

In the evening, we ate in a wonderful restaurant, a darkened rustic atmosphere, with traditional Czech food. I chose a beef-stew with red and white cabbage, followed by fruit dumplings as dessert.

That night my mother died, breathing in carbon monoxide fumes from a faulty stove. I did not find out what had happened to her for some days, contacted the British consulate and was put on a train back to Vienna. They also alerted my father, then on a year's contract in Pakistan, who then came to pick up my younger sister and me and whisked us off to Pakistan.

Several weeks later, after a post-mortem, my mother was buried in the very same cemetery in which Kafka was lying. Nobody came to the funeral, there was no seven-day *Shiva* [the bereaved stay at home for seven days, receiving well-wishers] no stone setting ceremony after a year, nothing at all to mark the mourning process. I was completely bereft, without any guidance or support; merely grieving silently inside me, not able to shed a tear or voice my feelings, even to myself. I was numb.

Searching for home and community

My father's contract in Pakistan soon came to an end and we relocated back to London, an enlarged family, with my stepmother and my half-sister Deborah, then just 7 months old.

London was a culture shock to me, in so many ways. Parachuted into suburbia, Hampstead Garden Suburb, I went to an English school for the first time, where a third of the pupils were Jewish. I fitted neither into the English nor the Jewish world and found it difficult to adjust. Three years later, my exam grades were disappointing and I failed to get into a British university. This time, I displaced myself and with my father's blessing and financial support, went to Canada to study anthropology in Montreal.

By the time I reached Canada, my father was on a two-year secondment in Kenya, where I visited him the following summer. This led to an interest in African studies, and upon graduating from McGill University I embarked on an MA programme in East Africa (by then my father had moved to Swaziland). In Nairobi, I found a warm welcome in a third-generation Muslim minority group from Southern Sudan, but it was not my community. So, upon completing my MA, I returned to London and after several false starts, including a spell studying in the USA, began to settle down and gradually adjust to what London had to offer.

Prague 1992

Thirty years after my first trip to Prague, I was able to visit my mother's grave. I had much to tell her. Most importantly, in 1976, I married a young woman from a German Jewish refugee background. We had twin sons a year later and in 1982 joined our nearest synagogue, a reform synagogue in Wimbledon, so that our children could go to Sunday classes and come to appreciate their Jewish heritage. But at the same time, I too was to gain a Jewish education, learn to read Hebrew and follow the prayer book, take an active role in the congregation and become one of the wardens. I took a variety of Jewish courses and I began to feel much more at ease within the Jewish community.

This time when I visited the Jewish Museum in Prague, I recognized many of the ritual objects there, for I was now using such objects on a regular basis both at home and in the synagogue. I had come to love these objects and the ritual associated with them. I felt part of the Jewish community in a way that I had never felt while growing up.

I was able to say all this at my mother's grave, even though I knew she could not hear me and I was able to recite the Kaddish. This was the moment that I realized I was able to mourn, a process that had been closed off to me until then. And now, the grieving continues and evolves.

Berlin 2001

I had visited Berlin many times from the 1950s onwards, but my journey in September 2001 proved quite a turning point for me.

I had been full of anticipation before the visit. I had been invited to the press opening of the new Jewish Museum in Berlin, as a press representative for *Jewish Renaissance*, a London based Arts and Culture magazine. I was just completing my own doctoral dissertation on Jewish museums in Italy and it felt particularly apt.

But once I touched down and emerged from the U-Bahn in search of my modest bed and breakfast accommodation, my heart sank. As I looked around in the street, it suddenly hit me like a thunderbolt, I was alone in this city and felt bereft.

All the relatives I used to visit in the past, my grandparents, who had patiently shown me around town, taking me on outings and looking after me, my favourite great aunt Liese, who used to tell me endless stories about what mischief my mother used to get up to as a child, my mother's cousin, were all gone.

I knew they would not be there; what I had not anticipated was the sense of desolation and loss I would feel once I arrived on the scene.

Fortunately, fate had been kind to me. I realized that I did know someone in Berlin after all, very much alive and with a big heart. I had met Rabbi Walter Rothschild at a Jewish conference back in England. I contacted him and he kindly agreed to host me for Shabbat meals. As it turns out, he did much more.

He took me along with him to Shabbat evening and morning service. On the Friday evening, at an Orthodox synagogue, a young girl of 12, from a Russian background, was having her Bat Mitzvah. Afterwards, I was introduced to her family; they were beaming with pride.

The next morning, at the Oranienburgerstraße synagogue, at a reform service, the daughter of Daniel Libeskind, the architect of the Jewish Museum building, was having her Bat Mitzvah. And here too, the whole family was overjoyed. For both these families, this was their first Bar or Bat Mitzvah.

A complete revelation to me. There I was, mourning the death of my German Jewish family and right there and then, I was witnessing a rebirth of a new and vital Jewish community, where East meets West, where a new Jewish Museum is launched with great fanfare, with renewed hope for the future.

Searching for where I belong, once again

That trip in 2001 to Berlin pushed me into finding a new point on the compass. The world around me was changing and so was I. Visiting Berlin had forced me to face up to the loss of an older generation. Faced with a void, there was still hope for the future, for me and for others.

Similarly, back in 1992, when I went back to Prague and stood for the first time by my mother's grave, I could mourn her early death and realize that despite my loss, I had overcome my despair. I had met my soulmate and together we had built a thriving home for our twin sons, surrounded by a supportive Jewish community.

But by 2001, it was clear that another new direction was presenting itself. Our marriage was tottering. In 2002, with heavy heart, I left my marriage of twenty-six years. I spent the next twelve months grieving.

I needed to venture out and find new points on my compass. I volunteered for a month to help at a recently renovated and re-dedicated synagogue in Crete. The pre-war community had been wiped out during the Shoah, with only one survivor. The synagogue was kept open largely with the help of a small band of local volunteers, Jewish and non-Jewish. As I am still a member of that synagogue, I visit as often as I can, so Crete has been added to my internal compass.

I moved to a new neighbourhood in South London, Colliers Wood and began establishing new connections. I joined the local community choir, the ball room dancing class, the Sunday walkers' group.

I met my new wife at one of our choir concerts, a piano teacher who had come to listen to an evening of international music. She comes from Gdańsk, Poland and we now frequently travel to Poland, where her family and friends live. I have also been regularly attending the annual Jewish Culture Festival in Kraków; another place where I now feel quite 'at home'. So, Gdańsk and Kraków are new points on my compass.

Rome 2019

I had revisited Rome in 2010 on a guided tour of Jewish Rome. On my return to London, I wrote a number of poems describing my feelings on revisiting my childhood haunts. Writing poetry is another way I could made sense of my life and create a new persona for myself.

In 2019, my sons approached me, saying they would like to take me for a long weekend as a birthday treat. It was a splendid idea and I chose Rome as our destination, where I could show them all the places that were special to me.

We stayed in an Airbnb in Trastevere, not far from the apartment block where I had lived as a child. On our first morning, a Friday, we made our way to the synagogue, our only opportunity that weekend to view the Jewish museum, located in the synagogue basement. We were given a guided tour of the synagogue itself and there I was able to show my sons exactly where I sat for my Bar Mitzvah. On leaving the synagogue we walked into the ghetto area, now alive with cafés and restaurants.

We strolled around before choosing one of the restaurants specialising in Judeo-Roman cuisine. We had deep fried artichokes and *Melanzane alla Giuda* [Stuffed Aubergine]. After lunch we made our way to the Circo Massimo, now a large well-maintained area occasionally used as a concert venue. It was here that I took out one of my poems and read it out:

Walking on Roman ruins

The joy and awe of walking back home,
after visiting father's office,
walking across the Circo Massimo,
the old Roman racecourse,
strewn with broken columns lying on the ground,
paving stones in wild disarray.

I imagined myself a Roman soldier, maybe a trader,
a householder on his way home,
never a slave or a chariot driver,
I felt I was walking across time,
a boy dreaming of the past,
imagining a glorious future.

Now, fifty years later, strolling on the same ground,
gone is the romance of broken columns,
childish dreams, but awe remains,
nostalgia for childhood rather than Roman times.

From there it was a short walk to the offices of the United Nations building where my father had worked. Outside the building, an armoured car kept guard and as we had no official reason for being there, we were not allowed to enter the building.

In the evening we made our way to the synagogue for the Friday evening service. We had notified them before leaving London and so after showing our passports, we were let in. This was no mere bureaucratic formality as there had been a terror attack in the synagogue in 1982. The service was in Hebrew and I felt much more at home than I had at my Bar Mitzvah. After the service we crossed the river on an old Roman bridge and found ourselves on the Isola Tiberina, and there, tucked away in a corner, an inviting restaurant. We sat down, ordered our meal and waited; the service was very slow indeed, but that, together with a good bottle of wine, gave us ample time to talk and memories flowed freely.

Next day, after seeing some of the tourist sites, we climbed up a steep road leading from Trastevere to the apartment block I had known as a child. There we were met by a locked gate in front of the building and we were lucky to be let into the lobby, now quite imposing, with mirrors, plants and scenic prints on the walls. Unfortunately, no one was at home in the top floor flat where we had lived, so our visit ended. Before leaving, I took out another one of my poems from my folder and read it out aloud.

Retracing steps in Rome

Where are the meadows and fields in which I played?
All gone, the rubble amidst the fruit trees,
tarmac abruptly ending, thorny paths.

Instead, rows of neat flats, gated driveways,
blocked off streets, no through road,
only a few well-cared cats roaming the streets.

No loud shouts from windows, calling children back,
sound of radios blaring the latest jingles,
or display of laundry.

Yet the old apartment block still stands there,
a new coat of paint, still the grand old building,
surveying the changes.

I was left with a sense of nostalgia for Rome of the 1950s. I also came away with a tremendous sense of achievement. Here I was, with my sons as companions, I knew I could always count on them for support. I had parented two amazing sons and had a sense of continuity and stability in an otherwise uncertain world. I also know that they were as enchanted by the trip as I had been.

Post-script

London will always remain a key reference point in my life, but my life has revolved round many different points of the compass. Berlin, Rome, Vienna and Prague featured much in my childhood. In my adult life, there have been other places that have loomed large. Montreal and Nairobi, as a student; Bologna, the focus for my PhD research on Italian Jewish

Figure 20.3. David's sons, Michael and Malcolm, in front of ruins and synagogue cupola in Rome (Photo taken by David Clark).

museums; Chania, in Crete; Gdańsk and Kraków which I frequently visit these days (when regulations concerning Covid-19 allow it).

I came back to London to seek a sense of rootedness and belonging that I lacked as I grew up, and yet at the same time, I was drawn to other places as well. My longing for adventure and 'otherness' never quite left me. As a result, my life has been one of constant movement and constant re-enactment of the inherited trauma and existential question: should I leave, or should I stay?

Over the last fifty years or so, I have stayed put in London, while keeping open the possibility of flight, of movement, maintaining links to other points on my compass with regular visits.

It appears that my sons have more of a sense of rootedness that I had as a child. They feel much more at home in London and in Britain than I ever will. I am glad of that. But that sense of rootedness has eluded me, just as it eluded my parents.

TERESA VON SOMMARUGA HOWARD

Epilogue

It's no metaphor to feel the influence of the dead in the world, just as it's no metaphor to hear the radiocarbon chronometer, the Geiger counter amplifying the faint breathing of rock, fifty thousand years old ... Human memory is encoded in air currents and river sediment. Eskers of ash wait to be scooped up, lives reconstituted.

Grief requires time. If a chip of stone radiates its self, its breath, so long, how stubborn might be the soul. If sound waves carry on to infinity, where are their screams now? I imagine them somewhere in the galaxy, moving forever towards the Psalms.
— Michaels, 1998 53

The legacy of suffering

In this epilogue the experience of twenty descendants of Holocaust victims and survivors are brought together and placed within a wider socio-political context with some further thoughts about how these experiences can be applied to all such catastrophes.

Although not generally recognized, it is now well-established that such catastrophic events as the Holocaust, leave their mark on future generations. In 1968, a ground-breaking series of workshops was organized at Wayne State University in Detroit, to study the lasting effects of massive psychic trauma. In the proceedings, Henry Krystal (1968: 3), a psychoanalyst and psychiatrist, explains that survivors are left with life-long problems, a very common one being "suppression of all affect" and the turning of aggression against the self, increasing the already prevalent tendency to depression resulting from survivor guilt. In another chapter, William Niederland (1968 8) records that the suffering of Holocaust victims did not end in 1945 with the liberation of the camps. This group of mental health professionals recognized early on that when comparing various survivor groups, the emotional repercussions of all genocides, wars and disasters follow a similar emotional pattern, noting, for instance, that those who survived the Hiroshima and Nagasaki bombing, were similarly suffering.

Since this early recognition, there have been countless such catastrophes that are still escalating. The UNHCR reported at the end of 2019, that about eighty million people around the world had been forced to flee their homes and of these, nearly twenty-six million were refugees and around half under the age of 18. There are also millions of stateless people, who have been denied a nationality and lack access to basic rights such as education, health care, employment and freedom of movement (UNHCR, 2020). Despite the huge numbers involved, there is relatively little social or political recognition that takes account of what displaced people themselves endure and what is then passed on to their children.

Social catastrophes, such as the Holocaust, are a form of social trauma resulting in the destruction of whole communities, cultures and ways of life and yet, according to Patrick Bracken (1998: 38) a British psychiatrist with years of experience working with victims of torture, it is this social aspect that is systematically ignored, leaving many individuals to cope alone. What happened to them was a public collective experience, accompanied by memories that are social as much as personal. Together these carry "views of history and identity, of past crises and tests, and paradigms of struggle, heroism and wisdom", thus offering "time-honoured modes of coping, adaptation and problem solving on a collective basis" (1998: 22).

Adrift from their former social surroundings, survivors are mostly left without the comforting support of understandable structures and without the certainties that previously prevailed and governed social norms. In many countries, such individuals were left alone to cope with a world that seemed to have been turned upside down.

As Henry Krystal (1968: 3) noted, there was a growing awareness that an expanding population of Holocaust survivors were presenting themselves for psychiatric examination, as required by the German Restitution laws. Apart from this one concrete acknowledgement from the German government that so much had been lost, survivors and refugees had to fight to have their long-term suffering recognized, and for decades in the immediate post-war period, few structures were set up to provide adequate help and support.

With the inevitable break in community-based support and meaning-making, it is difficult for the survivor to mourn what has been lost. Trauma tends to be seen as something that happens inside individual minds, ignoring the community-based experience of being forced into exile. It leads to what Bracken (1998: 38) refers to as the ubiquitous and inappropriate diagnosis of Post-Traumatic Stress Disorder, (PTSD). Rupture occurs not only in the narrative thread running through a refugee's life, but also in their familiar, social networks. So, with few perceived alternatives many individuals present medically with somatic expressions of their distress (Bracken: 21). They are then given a diagnosis and treated individually without attention being paid to the fact that whole social structures have been destroyed around them. This somatic conversion often makes itself felt in subsequent generations.

Consequently, most of these experiences are shrouded in silence. With little socio-political recognition, most people try to forget what is too painful to remember. For some of the first generation it may be possible to engage in a process of 'rethinking' and 'reframing' their former experiences over time, but the written experience of people like Elie Wiesel and Primo Levi suggest that this is not always the case. Wiesel (2006: ix) writes in the second edition of his book *Night*,

> Deep down, the witness knew then, as he does now, that his testimony would not be received. After all, it deals with an event that sprang from the darkest zone of man. Only those who experienced Auschwitz know what it was. Others will never know.
>
> But would they at least understand?

Like Wiesel many felt silenced by those around them. No one really wanted to hear about such atrocities. Some societies actively dissuade individuals from talking about what happened there and then further reinforcing the often, self-inflicted silence. In, *The Eichmann Show: The Nazi Trial of the Century* (Bowen and Marshall, 2015), one of the camera operators, a survivor of Auschwitz, collapsed during the filming. It was the first time he had heard anybody describe an experience like his.

Although shaming, it was a watershed that enabled him some relief for the first time.

Many first generation were unable to tell their story to their children and unable to answer questions. Many second generation knew little until they made the journeys described in this book. They grew up in a veil of silence accompanied by volatile behaviour that communicated suffering that could not be named. A confusing standoff often persisted between the generations. How was a traumatized parent who wanted to protect their children from knowing about the worst excesses of humanity to proceed? Many just decided to say nothing in what we now know was not a very successful attempt to shield their children from what had happened. Others apparently said a lot, but usually in a form that could not be heard, words shooting out like bullets or as a prepared and repetitive mantra, inhibiting further discussion. Often bare facts, lest it might awaken what they most wanted to forget, many second generation learnt to cope with emotional outbursts, contradictory behaviour by quietly watching and listening all the while trying to make sense of the confusion around them. They often had no other choice except to silently contain the emotional overload. The remnants of all this unspoken trauma are often passed on along with the injunction that no one wants to hear: a ubiquitous experience for the next generation. As Gabriele Schwab (2010: 1 and 43), who grew up in the aftermath of the Second World War in Germany in the "wake of one of the most atrocious genocides in history" describes her role as a child. She was

> the silent witness to those war stories, the one not allowed to ask questions or interrupt the flow of word …. It took me almost half a century to understand that the purpose of these stories was not to remember but to forget.

Schlant (1999: 7), in her review of German literature after the Second World War, suggests that "silence is not a semantic void; like any language, it is infused with narrative strategies that carry ideologies and reveal unstated assumptions". There is a naïve tendency to believe that if only the first generation could speak about their experiences, there would be no transmission of trauma. It is more complicated than that as our authors illustrate.

The next generation

In 1967, the International Psychoanalytical Association held their first symposium, "Psychic Traumatization through Social Catastrophe" where common features were described in survivor families. After that, Kestenberg (1972) investigated the effects of the Holocaust on the second generation and highlighted the idea that survivor parents could transmit conflict and psychopathology to their offspring as a result of their own trauma. Along with Epstein (1979), Kestenberg initiated scholarship on the transgenerational transmission of Holocaust-related traumas to subsequent generations who grew up with parents who were silently and secretly suffering as a consequence of the destructiveness of what they both witnessed and experienced.

The question often is, "What is the mechanism that transmits the trauma of the first generation on to the next?" Jill Salberg (2015: 23) a New York-based psychoanalyst, believes that it is the result of 'the texture of traumatic attachment'. She refers to a vast body of literature and writes,

> Children are constantly observing their parents' gestures and affects, absorbing their parents' conscious and unconscious minds. In the shifting registers of attunement and misattunement, children adjust and adapt to the emotional presence and absence of their caregivers/parents, always searching for attachment. These searches begin at birth and occur before there are words, when there are gazes, stares, sounds, and touch – as well as the absence of these. This is how stories are told, even when not spoken, in the nonverbal and preverbal affective realms – silent and vocal, yet played out in subtexts, often on the implicit level.

In this way, Salberg (2015: 24) believes it is important to,

> conceptualize transgenerational transmissions in multiply determined and non-linear ways: transmissions are always multigenerational and richly influenced by context, both historical and personal, and are carried in the mind and in the body. No one theory can begin to explain this, and for that reason we must draw from many sources and interweave various points of view to understand the complexity of experience.

> In moving to an attachment-based theory focusing on mutual affect regulation
> between mother and child, we can more easily recognize the constant interchange
> between parent and child around mood, affects, and their intensities.

In the same way as Schlant (1999: 3) was able to use literature as a "seismograph" to reveal what is implicit in both the content and process of
writing, we discovered just how embedded the patterns of the first generation were in the second generation. As she explains, this seismograph

> lays bare a people's dreams and nightmares, its hopes and apprehensions, its moral
> positions and failures. It reveals even where it is silent, its blind spots and absences
> speak a language stripped of conscious agendas.

Schlant (1999: 14) quotes Eric Santner, a scholar of German film and literature, who suggests that "the second generation inherited not only the
unmourned traumas of the parents but also the psychic structures that
impeded mourning in the older generation in the first place".

This anthology tells us what it is like growing up in an atmosphere
of denial that is accompanied by a life-long search for what many often
describe as 'normal', often attempting to hide their very different origins,
desperately attempting to fit in with the prevailing cultural norms of the
new country.

Searching for identity

Second generation children of refugees often say, "They got out in time",
referring to parents who left in the 1930s as if nothing traumatizing had
occurred. This is the mythology they were often served by their elders and
which is so confusing to a growing child. Anne Schutzenberger (1998), a
French psychoanalyst and psychodramatist, who developed an innova-
tive approach to working with transgenerational transmission of trauma,
describes how survivors of the trenches in the First World War had to
live with having heard and felt "the wind of the passing bullet". She used
this phrase metaphorically to describe the often-misunderstood trauma

of survival. Her particular contribution was linking physical and emotional illness in descendent generations to the impact of catastrophic history such as war through what she called hidden obligations or 'psychosomatic bookkeeping'. This is the result of unconscious processes related to trauma-induced disruptive attachment patterns. In order to find some level of attachment and soothing, the next generation learn to read their parents' emotional states very carefully. Often the most intense bond could only be generated from the traumatized and deeply buried yet emotionally alive part of the parent. As Salberg (2015: 36) explains.

> As a consequence, the child – in order to attach to this parent and get this parent attached to her/him – will need to enter and become enmeshed in the trauma scene. Through empathic mirroring and what Hopenwasser (2008) called dissociative attunement, the parents' trauma story enters the child's cellular makeup before there are words, and thus before a narrative can be told.

And so, the child is often left with loyalties to those extreme experiences that could not be understood and so often led to somatic symptoms that persist for life.

Even those first generation, who got out in time, suffered. At a very simple level, many were separated from their parents, alone with no one who could understand what they had endured or would continue to endure. Although taken to physical safety, the need for emotional understanding was not usually recognized. The longed-for reconnection, if it finally happened, often brought no longed-for reunion or acknowledgement. Their parents when and if they did arrive from the camps or hiding, were not in any position to comfort their children. Instead, there was usually a reversal; the child was expected to comfort the parent.

For the next generation, history often repeated itself. The second generation also found themselves having to comfort their parents; an impossible role for a child requiring a denial of their own need for love and support. Many write of not upsetting their parents. Although they had usually worked out that something terrible had happened in the past, they only had fragments of the story to piece together. Within the confines of the home, there was often an unspoken injunction that restricted the open expression of thoughts and emotions. It protected parents from an emotional overload their children sensed they could not take. As many of our twenty authors tell us, to fulfil a long-held wish to find a new 'home' where they might feel less constrained and better understood, they left the family as soon as they could. For Tina Kennedy, boarding school provided a way out, for Marilyn Moos going away to study at university proved a welcome relief. Leaving the country altogether was another solution for Rosemary Schonfeld and David Clark.

Oliver Hoffmann left New Zealand after completing his university studies and ended up spending seventeen years in Berlin. At first, he sought to connect with his non-Jewish father's relatives, but found them unresponsive. After several false starts, he managed to find a group of like-minded people, who wished to confront Germany's dark past and research the topography of terror within that city. At the same time, he was able to find a surrogate family, a former close friend of his father's, who in a way became the father he always wished for.

Finding a spiritual home such as a second-generation group or a second-generation workshop also provided relief and new learning. These become important 'homes' where it is possible to talk, often for the first time, about the struggles of growing up and discovering that everyone else present had been silently dealing with almost exactly the same dilemmas. They feel understood and supported, which often leads to taking on a more proactive role in finding out more about their family history.

Making sense of silence

The stories in our book display the long-term implications of socio-political trauma as experienced by twenty descendants of Holocaust victims and survivors. By writing about their journeys home, including the emotional journey that accompanied their travels, the process of making sense of puzzles that many had struggled with for most of their lives could begin.

Although the injunction that no one wants to hear is often passed on to descendant generations along with the remnants of the unspoken trauma, what our book demonstrates is that it is possible for the second generation to piece together various fragments and seek to place them not only in a narrative that bears retelling, but also one that connects their family's past to their own present-day lived experiences. But such a task is by no means an easy one.

The process of writing these chapters as well as the editorial process of encouraging authors to think more deeply and more emotionally about their experience as children of their parents, illustrated the consequences of catastrophe and subsequent forced physical displacement, tightly held secrets and silences as well as the emotional confusion that almost all had to live with. Despite the fact that I had previous experiences of convening workshops for descendent generations of many socio-political catastrophes including the Armenian genocide, the Great Irish Hunger as well as the Holocaust, in Germany for thirteen years, neither editor was initially sufficiently aware of how deeply the editorial task would take each of us and our authors into the many dark places that emotionally replicated their lives as second generation.

Although many people offered to contribute, excited by the prospect of recording their experiences, when it came to writing them down several gave up despite a lot of encouragement and one-to-one support. It proved to be a difficult task that took many of our writers to places they hardly expected. The meaning of the word 'journey' was often misunderstood and to start with we received beautiful travelogues but not much about the emotional impact of these trips. Only after many drafts and much prompting did the full meaning and emotional impact of such journeys emerge. The embargo on feelings passed on from the first generation was difficult to break.

Very few of our authors, even those who recognized themselves as writers, found it easy to take on this task of describing their experience of growing up second generation and visiting the places their families originated from, except in well-known generalities relying on an observer-position-style, all a likely outcome of growing up with traumatized parents who could not express their emotions directly.

Interestingly many thought it an act of betrayal of their parents' suffering to actually write about what they themselves felt. Others gave up. Some got furious with us for challenging words they had also used and often employed to sanitize horrific events. Facing the intentionality of the

Nazis is unbearable. It is difficult to acknowledge that what happened to our parents was an escape from a regime that was trying to wipe them out so we of the next generation would never be born.

Most were in touch with their parent's difficulties but not their own. Some described feeling empty inside and had turned to self-help books to find a way of coping. Unfortunately, reading that trauma of such depth can be resolved or left behind, only served to reinforce much confusion and distress. When social beliefs such as these fail to recognize the profundity of trauma that exists in families that have faced such catastrophes, this only serves to reinforce the life-long habit of having to hide what one feels even from oneself. We found ourselves as editors explaining over and over, that what we had found most helpful was to realize that this pain and suffering is a needed response to unthinkably painful events and that there would always be moments when it would catch up with us. The skill is to begin to recognize it more quickly. When the tears finally do flow and yes, in convulsions, it is such a relief. We found a helpful metaphor, "The tears water the desert".

It's not easy to overcome a life-long pattern of taking care of one's parents and not having your own feelings acknowledged. We discovered that our job as editors was to facilitate the possibility of breaking through the suffocation of a pain that could only be glimpsed at in the writing. To write these chapters, many of our authors found themselves having to overcome a life-long tendency, learnt from their parents, of silencing their own thoughts and emotions. It took time and a lot of soul-searching to relieve the silences. These accounts speak powerfully for themselves.

Implications of mixed backgrounds

Those born into mixed marriages describe suffering confusing, mixed messages. Often growing up not feeling at home either in their family or in wider society, they were often surprised that 'going back' brought some approximation of feeling at home as they began to understand the origins and depth of the secrets they had always lived with. In this context, Nazi language and definitions such as "I am a Mischling or half Jewish" often crept into the narratives almost unnoticed. It perhaps foretold the discomfort they often found themselves having to deal with when they met new relatives from a non-Jewish background.

Oliver Hoffmann was confused by his father who had always claimed the importance of family yet when he went back to Berlin, his relatives did not welcome him with open arms. He puzzled about family connections that turned out to be 'meaningless' while discovering old friends of his father's to be more sensitive, consistent and loving surrogate parents and siblings of choice. Having faced the disappointment and confusion, Oliver adjusted to living in Berlin and enjoyed it for nearly two decades.

For Monica Lowenberg, the confusion was particularly acute when making close bonds with the non-Jewish side of her family in Germany, as she discovered that her grandfather had been a card-carrying member of the Nazi party. The resulting inner turmoil was partly resolved by reference to a fictional play by an eighteenth-century German ancestor in the same Lessing family. It gave her hope as she saw that the trials and tribulations of mixed Jewish-Muslim-Christian marriages could end happily. Monica concludes her chapter with a visit to the German embassy to receive her German citizenship enabling her to come full circle by embracing both her Jewish and German heritage.

Social and political activism

Many passionately engaged in political or social activism, such as Oliver Hoffmann chronicling the resistance in Berlin, Tina Kennedy working with refugees, Barbara Dresner supporting elderly Jews, or Monica Lowenberg demonstrating against neo-fascist marches. Others, including Marian Liebmann were involved in mediation, peace and conflict resolution and coordinating a Victim Support group. Still others, including Barbara Dresner were involved in interfaith work, as a means of healing old wounds and making use of a deep sensitivity that came from their background.

Educational initiatives

Following the exploration of their family histories and subsequent journeys, many of our authors describe their involvement in educational initiatives. Although one might expect that the outcome of these journeys
into their family's past might naturally lead to an urge to reach out to a
wider audience, these stories could only be told when there was a receptive willingness to listen. It also needs institutional support at both local
and national level. As touched upon in our introductory chapter, these
testimonial events would not be taking place without the sanction of a
whole raft of other agencies and institutions at the neighbourhood, city,
regional, national and international level.

Many of our authors including Vivienne Cato, Barbara Dresner and
Rosemary Schonfeld regularly visited schools and educational establish-
ments, either as part of Holocaust Memorial Day events or taught as part
of the regular school history curriculum as Zuzana Crouch did. Peter
Bohm was involved in hosting school visits to Belsize Square synagogue.
Even within the Jewish community, specialist organizations, such as the
Holocaust Education Trust and Generation 2 Generation (G2G), make
use of family histories as a means of talking about the impact of persecution and genocide. As the number of first-generation speakers dwindles,
many second generation are increasingly being called upon to give testimony on their behalf.

Reclaiming heritage

Brexit was a watershed for many second generation who had felt themselves
to be Europeans living in Britain. The referendum in June 2016 brought
us face to face with our heritage and difference. Not feeling English,
Scottish or Welsh lots of us decided to take advantage of the possibility
of becoming citizens of our parents' 'home' country. Monica Lowenberg
asked her father if he minded her applying for 'dual citizenship'. "One can

never have enough passports!" he told her. Nik Pöllinger wrestled with ambivalence but finally decided to become an Austrian like his father and reinstated the umlaut in his family name that his father had left behind. Rosemary Schonfeld applied for and received her Czech citizenship.

Implications for the future

The trauma first-generation survivors of the Holocaust lived through, and descendent generations are still grappling with, is the result of a series of socio-political events that extended over many years. It occurred in a political frame that sought to make Jews scapegoats for all society's ills and to exterminate or exclude them to solve this pseudo-problem. While the Nazis were planning mass murder, many countries around the world sought to keep them out and others having let a comparatively small number in, such as Britain, interned them as Enemy Aliens. This is a form of political humiliation that is not easy to recover from unless there is political acknowledgement and or compensation. The current situation in Britain with the Windrush Generation has resonances with this experience as has the plight of indigenous populations all over the world.[1] These are all people who have been mistreated and humiliated by the state and it is the state that needs to make amends. No amount of personal emotional working through can do that. Later, after proper political recognition, maybe.

As Göran Rosenberg (2017: 279), Swedish journalist addressing his survivor father writes,

> You can look forward only if the world looks backward and remembers where you come from, and sees the paths you pursue, and understands why you're still living.

---

[1] The Windrush Generation refers to people who were invited to Britain from the Caribbean to staff the public transport system and the National Health Service and other services. They were later joined by their relatives, many of whom were suddenly informed decades later that they were undocumented illegal immigrants.

The aftermath of the Holocaust is well-documented, providing a much-needed template for what can be expected from all disasters, wars, genocides, colonialism, natural upheavals and cataclysms. No other group has a comparable history of assault, duration of persecution, or degree of destructiveness, apart from indigenous populations who suffered and still suffer at the hands of colonizers and are largely unacknowledged.

Conclusion

These chapters were written during the Covid-19 pandemic from 2020 to 2021. It is a time of existential fear fuelled by fear of death and disease that is terrifying in the present and resonates with many anxieties from the past, bringing us face to face not only with the interconnectedness of our world, but also with a trauma that persists. We are all living with it. Some are forced to carry on working in unsafe conditions and do not have the privilege to isolate themselves from being exposed to greater risk of death and disease. The likely mental health problems that will emanate from the pandemic occupies many articles and a lot of airspace but there appears little understanding about what surviving such trauma might mean for all of us and particularly those families most affected. Perhaps these twenty stories will give some clues.

Bibliography

Bowen, L., and Marshall, K. (2015). *The Eichmann Show: The Nazi Trial of the Century*. TV Movie BBC Two. <https://www.imdb.com/title/tt4163668/>.
Bracken, P., and Petty, C., with Save the Children (1998). 'Hidden Agendas: Deconstructing Post Traumatic Stress Disorder'. In *Rethinking the Trauma of War*. London: Free Association.
Epstein, H. (1979). *Children of the Holocaust: Conversations with Sons and Daughters of Survivors*. New York: Putnam.

Kestenberg, J. (1972). 'Psychoanalytic Contributions to the Problem of Children of Survivors from Nazi Persecutions', *Israel Annals of Psychiatry & Related Disciplines*, 10, 311–325.

Krystal, H. (ed.) (1968). 'Patterns of Psychological Damage', *Massive Psychic Trauma*. New York: UJP Paperback.

Michaels, A. (1998). *Fugitive Pieces*. London: Bloomsbury.

Niederland, W. (1968). 'The Psychiatric Evaluation of Emotional Disorders in Survivors of Nazi Persecution'. In H. Krystal (ed.), *Massive Psychic Trauma*. New York: UJP Paperback.

Rosenberg, G. (2017). *A Brief Stop on the Road from Auschwitz*. S. Death, (trans.), J. Cullen, (ed.). New York: Other Press.

Salberg, J. (2015). 'The Texture of Traumatic Attachment: Presence and Ghostly Absence in Transgenerational Transmission', *The Psychoanalytic Quarterly*, LXXXIV (1), 21–46.

Schlant, E. (1999). *The Language of Silence: West German Literature and the Holocaust*. New York and London: Routledge.

Schutzenberger, A. A. (1998). *The Ancestor Syndrome: Transgenerational Psychotherapy and the Hidden Links in the Family Tree*. A. Trager, (trans.). London and New York: Routledge.

Schwab, G. (2010). *Haunting Legacies: Violent Histories and Transgenerational Trauma*. New York: Columbia University Press.

UNHCR (2020). <https://www.unhcr.org/uk/figures-at-a-glance.html>.

Wiesel, E. (2006). *Night*. M. Wiesel, (trans.). New York: Hill and Wang.

Notes on contributors

JUDITH TYDOR BAUMEL-SCHWARTZ was born in New York in 1959 and immigrated to Israel with her Holocaust survivor father and American-born mother in 1974. She completed her undergraduate and graduate degrees at Bar-Ilan University and specializes in Holocaust Studies and Israel Studies with emphasis on rescue, religion, gender, commemoration, and descendants of Holocaust Survivors. She has written and edited numerous books and articles about these subjects. Today she directs the Arnold and Leona Finkler Institute of Holocaust Research at Bar-Ilan University where she is a Professor of Modern Jewish History. She is married to Prof. Joshua Schwartz and together they have a blended family of children and grandchildren.

PETER BOHM is the son of refugees from Vienna and Dortmund; his grandparents and many other family members were murdered in the Holocaust. Peter is a practising solicitor, and as he believes passionately in the need for the lessons of the Holocaust to be learned, he is involved in Holocaust education for schools. He has written articles for the monthly journal of the Association of Jewish Refugees and is the editor of a business law book, *Business Law – A Guide for Entrepreneurs* (2007).

GINA BURGESS WINNING worked in legal and educational publishing prior to qualifying as a solicitor. She is a member of the Association of Jewish Refugees, the Jewish Genealogical Society of Great Britain and actively involved on the Committee of Second Generation Network. Gina has researched her family history with articles appearing in *Shemot*, the *AJR Journal* and *Second Generation Voices*. She contributed a chapter in German detailing the fate of the Freudenthal family to *Von der Ausgrenzung zur Deportation in Marburg und im Landkreis Marburg* (2017) and a three-part history *Die Familie Buchheim in Schwarzenau*, which appeared in the *Wittgensteiner Heimatverein e. V.* (2018 and 2019). Her own book on her family history will be published shortly.

VIVIENNE CATO is a teacher, researcher, facilitator and writer. She holds a BA (Hons) in English (Cambridge), a PGCE (the Institute of Education, University of London) and an MA in Conservation Policy (Middlesex University). Vivienne has published in educational research, Judaism and spiritual environmentalism, including *Sacred Texts: The Torah and Judaism* (2003), *Religion in Focus: Judaism in Today's World* (2001), 'Judaism and the Natural World' in R. Vint, (ed.) *Faiths for a Future – A Resource for Teaching Environmental Themes in Religious Education* (1998), 'Down to Earth Religious Education' in H. Ucko, (ed.) *The Jubilee Challenge: Utopia or Possibility?* (1997), *Green Means Business: The Contradictions of Commerce and Environmentalism* (1993), *The Teaching of Initial Literacy: How Do Teachers Do It?* (1992).

DAVID CLARK was born in London, studied Anthropology (BA, McGill), (MA Makerere, Uganda) and Tourism (MA, Surrey University), completing his PhD on Jewish museums in Italy (London Metropolitan University). He co-edited, together with Maria Kousis and Tom Selwyn, *Contested Mediterranean Spaces* (2011) and contributed a chapter on his life story to the volume edited by J. Baumel-Schwartz and S. Rafael-Vivante, (2021). David is a long-standing committee member of Second Generation Network. He was on the editorial committee of *Jewish Renaissance* and currently of *Exiled Ink*, a magazine devoted to works by exiled and refugee writers. A retired lecturer, David is currently an honorary research associate, Uzhhorod National University, Ukraine.

ZUZANA CROUCH was born in Czechoslovakia in 1948. She entered Charles University of Prague in 1966 to study journalism, worked for *Prace* [a daily newspaper] and during the Prague Spring of 1968 for *Literarni Noviny* [a weekly journal]. After the Soviet invasion, Zuzana left for Britain and studied for a BA in history, politics and Russian at Bristol University. After graduation she worked for *Keesings publishers* and co-edited a book focusing on the political 'thaw' during the Cold War. Thereafter, she took a teachers' training course and taught history at different schools until retirement in 2009. Zuzana also published a teaching booklet entitled *Rights and Responsibilities*.

BARBARA DRESNER CQSW, BA (Hons) in social policy and welfare, is a retired adults social worker, who contributed a chapter to *Jewish Issues in Social Work and Social Care* (2000). Her career is linked to her heritage, a German Catholic mother and Polish Jewish refugee father. Barbara is a founder member of the Second Generation Network and member of its editorial team for *Second Generation Voices*, contributing articles and editing.

JANET EISENSTEIN works as a writer. Her first short film, *Kinder*, won awards and qualified for several international film festivals. Her first play, *Marrano*, set in fifteenth-century Spain, was performed at Upstairs at the Gatehouse, a famous fringe theatre in London. Subsequently, Janet was awarded a place on the 'Feature Development Workshop' at the NFTS (National Film and Television School, UK). Currently, she is writing a novel and developing a feature film called *Citizen of Nowhere* about a daughter of a German Jewish refugee who applies for German citizenship.

VIVIAN HASSAN-LAMBERT, born in New York City and raised in Los Angeles, has spent her adult life in London. With a BA in literature, a Diploma in drama therapy and an MA in creative writing, Vivian has worked in community theatre, employee development and as a writing coach and facilitator. Her novel, *Big Basin Yellow Sky*, won first prize with London Magazine, and other short stories have won first prize with Cinnamon Press or been shortlisted for the Bridport and Serpent's Tail awards. Vivian is a recipient of an Arts Council *Grant to Write*.

OLIVER HOFFMANN was born in 1944 in Auckland, New Zealand, to refugee parents from Berlin, Germany. His background is in mathematics, computer software and education. He has been involved in various Holocaust projects, including local research into terror and resistance in one of Berlin's main boroughs, writing and editing texts for Auckland's Jewish Online Museum and for the Holocaust-related website, *World Upside Down*. Oliver has assisted in compiling the archives for a local oral history group and in translating Freya Klier's book, *Promised New Zealand* (2009).

TINA KENNEDY is the daughter of Jewish refugees who fled from Vienna to London to escape Nazi persecution. She spent much of her life feeling like a fish out of water, most at home when hanging out with other waifs and strays. Tina graduated from Bristol University with a degree in Spanish and art history and has lived in Berlin and Madrid. Tina has worked in the cultural travel industry, as a human rights researcher and as an English teacher. She currently lives in Devon with her husband and son.

NAOMI LEVY has a BA (Hons) in economics, professional legal qualifications, a diploma in psychodynamic marital and couple counselling and an MA in attachment psychoanalysis and the couple relationship. She was a family law partner and subsequently worked at Tavistock Centre for Couple Relationships as Couple Therapist. Currently Naomi is doing family research and writing, producing a book about her father's 1941 Australian Diary. She is now working on a book about her mother's war story. She has written articles for *Second Generation Voices*, The Association of Jewish Refugees and contributed a chapter to the volume edited by J. Baumel-Schwartz and S. Rafael-Vivante, (2021).

MARIAN LIEBMANN was born in the UK to Jewish refugee parents from Berlin. She has completed her BA (Oxon), PGCE (Leicester), MA (University of Central England), CQSW (Bristol) and PhD (Bristol). She has worked in teaching, educational writing, probation, victim support, mental health and work with refugees. Marian worked as an art therapist for nineteen years in inner city Bristol, specializing in work on anger. She currently supervises art therapists, is a mediation and restorative justice practitioner and travels internationally to contribute to conferences. Marian has written or edited fourteen books on art therapy, mediation and restorative justice, and numerous articles and chapters.

MONICA LOWENBERG holds a first-class degree from Sunderland University in Modern Foreign Languages, a PGCE, an MA in German twentieth-century history from Sussex University and trained as an interpreter in France and the UK. Monica has numerous publications, including *Linguistic Proficiency in Young Immigrants* (1997), *The Science of Acting* (2009), *German Speaking Exiles* (2000). Monica has translated and narrated a German film about the Riga Ghetto and written numerous articles regarding Holocaust obfuscation in the Baltics today. Monica's next project is to write up the testimonies of sixty interviews she previously conducted with Holocaust refugees.

MERILYN MOOS was born to German refugees who opposed the Nazis and fled in 1933. They both lost many of their families but did not want to talk about the past; so, she had to discover it for herself. Upon graduating from Oxford and obtaining an MA from Birmingham University, Centre for Contemporary Cultural Studies, Merilyn became a lecturer, writing on education policy, the experience of being second generation and on resistance in Nazi Germany – in particular, *The Language of Silence* (2010), a semi-autobiographical novel, *Beaten but not Defeated* (2014), a biography of her father, *Breaking the Silence* (2015), an ethnographic study of the second generation and *Anti-Nazi Germans from the working-class movement* (with Steve Cushion, 2020). Presently Merilyn is completing a book on 'anti-Nazi Germans who fled to the UK'.

NIK POLLINGER/PÖLLINGER, MA (Oxon), MSc (University College London), currently works for the British government, in communications. He began writing for the national media as a creative outlet in 2004. Nik has written long form and news journalism for *The Daily Telegraph*, *BBC News Online* and *The Observer*. Latterly, his journalism has focused on the experiences and legacy of Nazi persecution in Austria. Nik's degrees were in philosophy and anthropology.

DITI RONEN is a poet, an editor and a translator of poetry. She has published nine full-length poetry books, mainly in Hebrew as well as in translation in German, Spanish, French, Georgian and Romanian. Ronen's poetry was awarded national and international awards and numerous prizes. Her poems are published in anthologies, magazines and literary websites worldwide. Besides her literary work, Dr Diti Ronen is a researcher, lecturer and advisor of Arts and Cultural Policy. She is a former lecturer at the Hebrew University in Jerusalem and former head of the Cultural Policy, Literature and Theatre departments in the Israeli Ministry of Culture.

ROSEMARY SCHONFELD, BMus (Hons), is a professional musician and composer now based in Devon. She toured internationally with her band OVA, recorded and produced/co-produced six albums, co-ran a recording studio and devised a teaching package called *Drumātrix* for percussionists. Rosemary published an illustrated book of Nonsense Poetry *Standing on Your Head* and has had short stories published in collections. She has co-authored an e-book *Words on the Street* documenting the street stall campaigning in Devon to stop Brexit. Rosemary has written a book about her family history *Finding Relly – My family, the Holocaust and Me* (2018) and gives talks on the subject with the aim of giving the Holocaust contemporary relevance.

ELAINE SINCLAIR is a chartered occupational psychologist and has worked with children in a variety of education and play settings, in the engineering industry focusing on the selection and training of apprentices, as a university lecturer and as a consultant and researcher mainly in education settings. Most of her publications have been reports on research and development work carried out for government and local authority clients.

TERESA VON SOMMARUGA HOWARD, Dip Arch (Hons), Member of the Institute of Group Analysis (London) is the daughter of a German Jewish refugee father and non-Jewish British mother. Born in England, she grew up in Aotearoa New Zealand but now lives in the UK and works internationally. Teresa's professional background mirrors her diverse personal background. She is an architect, systemic family therapist and group analyst, mainly focusing on the long-term effects of socio-political trauma. She has written and published extensively about all aspects of her work and co-authored a book, *Design through Dialogue: A Guide for Clients and Architects* (2010), which integrates her background as both an architect and group analyst. Teresa is currently writing a biographical book based on her father's internment diaries.

DIANA WICHTEL is an award-winning journalist, becoming the joint recipient in 2016 of the Grimshaw Sargeson Fellowship, which enabled her to write the memoir, *Driving to Treblinka: A Long Search for a Lost Father* (2017). The book won the Royal Society Te Apārangi Award for General Non-fiction and the E. H. McCormick Best First Book Award for General Non-fiction at the 2018 Ockham New Zealand Book Awards. The North American edition was shortlisted for the 2020 Vine Awards for Canadian Jewish Literature. Diana has an MA in English from Auckland University and wrote for the *New Zealand Listener* magazine for thirty-six years. Born in Vancouver, Canada, she lives in Auckland with her family.

Index

Lightning Source UK Ltd.
Milton Keynes UK
UKHW051441180122
397345UK00020B/152